AND WE GO ON

WILL R. BIRD

AND WE GO ON

Introduction and Afterword
by
David Williams

Carleton Library Series 229

McGill-Queen's University Press
Montreal & Kingston · London · Chicago

© McGill-Queen's University Press 2014
First published in 1930 by Hunter-Rose Co., Limited, Toronto

For ease of reading, minor changes to the original text to use contemporary
Canadian spelling, punctuation, and to correct misspellings in the original
publication have been made in this edition without being indicated.

ISBN 978-0-7735-4395-9 (cloth)
ISBN 978-0-7735-4396-6 (paper)
ISBN 978-0-7735-9618-4 (ePDF)
ISBN 978-0-7735-9619-1 (ePUB)

Legal deposit third quarter 2014
Bibliothèque nationale du Québec

Reprinted 2017

Printed in Canada on acid-free paper that is 100% ancient forest free (100%
post-consumer recycled), processed chlorine free

McGill-Queen's University Press acknowledges the support of the Canada Council for the Arts for our publishing program. We also acknowledge the financial
support of the Government of Canada through the Canada Book Fund for our
publishing activities.

Library and Archives Canada Cataloguing in Publication

Bird, Will R. (Will Richard), 1891–1984, author
     And we go on / Will R. Bird ; introduction and afterword by
David Williams.

(Carleton library series ; 229)
Includes bibliographical references.
Issued in print and electronic formats.
ISBN 978-0-7735-4395-9 (bound). – ISBN 978-0-7735-4396-6 (pbk.)
ISBN 978-0-7735-9618-4 (ePDF). – ISBN 978-0-7735-9619-1 (ePUB)

     1. Bird, Will R. (Will Richard), 1891–1984. 2. World War,
1914–1918 – Personal narratives, Canadian. 3. Soldiers – Canada –
Biography. 4. Canada. Canadian Army. Battalion, 42nd – Biography.
I. Williams, David, 1945–, writer of introduction, writer of afterword
II. Title. III. Series: Carleton library series ; 229.

D640.A2357 2014   940.4'8171   C2014-904204-3
                                             C2014-904205-1

This book was typeset by True to Type in 11/14 Minion

Contents

Will R. Bird in uniform, 1917. (Courtesy of Betty Murray)

And We Go On, a Lost Classic of the Great War

DAVID WILLIAMS

"*Ghosts Have Warm Hands*," the grey-bearded librarian said, scanning the laminated cover of the book I had just handed him. "I read this myself a few years ago. I don't ever recall a more compelling book about the First World War."

"It's powerful," I agreed. "But I prefer the original version from 1930, which was called *And We Go On*. It reads like a richly textured novel, while the other, published almost forty years later, is more like a blog. It's neither as raw nor as fresh, more like an afterthought of the original."

His next remark caught me off guard.

"I admired it because of how the ghost of the author's brother returned to the battlefield to save his life." He hesitated, glancing at me over the top of his gold-rimmed spectacles. Then, with astonishing candour, he confessed, "His book convinced me there's an afterlife."

It was the sort of admission you rarely hear in a university setting. Normally, we academics don't talk about things we can't explain or theorize. And I hardly knew this academic librarian; he'd only been assigned to the college from our main library in the autumn.

"Then you'll love *And We Go On*," I exclaimed. "Steve's apparition doesn't appear just twice to save Bird's life, as he does in *Ghosts*. He's there most of the time, tapping Will's shoulder in the dark to warn him to avoid a German patrol out in No Man's Land, or to move before a machine gun starts to rattle, or to leave a cellar an instant before a bomb goes off. The ghost saves Will's life a dozen times, at least."

"*And We Go On*, you said it was called?"

"*And We Go On*," I repeated, watching this quiet, dignified man jot down the title like an enthusiast of Oprah's Book Club. "It's been out of print for seventy-five years. And it's hard to say why. The book is a gem, a genuine lost classic."

"A war story fused with a ghost story," the bespectacled man said. "You don't find a blend like that very often. How is it classified?"

"That's a bird of a different feather," I said, regretting the unintended pun even before I wondered if I might be casting aspersions on his profession. "The university library where I tracked it down couldn't even find it for a while. Someone had catalogued it by the title *And On We Go!*"

The librarian scowled. "That wouldn't happen here," he said sternly.

"I'm sure it wouldn't," I offered apologetically. "If I ever do find a copy for sale, I'll bring it to you for cataloguing. But no bookseller has it listed. It doesn't exist even on the World Wide Web. I had to hunt it down in the Fisher Rare Book Library at the University of Toronto before I was able to read it."

Later, I was sorry that I had not told this well-read man the whole story, about how I'd experienced a strange sense of déjà vu on reading *Ghosts* for the first time, before I'd heard of *And We Go On*. Now I tell all my students in CanLit how "the abomination of desolation" that Bird survived at Passchendaele is the likely model for Dunstan Ramsay's miraculous deliverance by an apparition in Robertson Davies' *Fifth Business* (1970). Whether Davies had read *And We Go On* in the 1930s or *Ghosts Have Warm Hands* when it appeared in 1968 – about the time that he was starting work on the Deptford Trilogy – the "Magus of the North," as the *New York Times* called him, seems to me to be deeply indebted to a self-taught writer and veteran of the Great War, William Richard Bird.

And who can forget that scene in Timothy Findley's *The Wars* (1977) where Robert Ross and his Canadian platoon are caught in a deep mine crater by a lone enemy scout? "The German shifted his gaze – saw that Bates had moved and then looked back at Robert. He nodded. It was astounding. He nodded!" The roles and the outcome are reversed, but the sentiments are exactly the same as those you find in *And We Go On* where Bird, out on patrol near Vimy, spots a German officer in No Man's Land:

I'll never forget the look that was on his face. He was so surprised that he seemed paralyzed. A long minute passed, and then another. Neither of us moved. I had my finger crooked, ready, and he saw that I had. He whitened, turned red, paled again, his eyes watching mine, and then he smiled!

I had fully intended taking him prisoner, or shooting him, and yet, as he backed away, smiling at me, I did not do a thing. Back he went, foot by foot, watching me closely, and smiling ... If he had picked up a bomb, or hurried, or did anything but what he did, the spell would have been broken, but he backed and smiled his way down the sap until he reached a bend, and there he stopped – and saluted me! (56–7)

Even the impulsive wave that Robert Ross gives the first German soldier he sees appears to come from Bird, who describes in similar terms the first "uncaptured German" he sees in the line:

He was only a boy, as young-looking as Mickey, and he was standing waist-high above his trench wall as one of our flares burst directly above him and placed him in dazzling light.

He did not move at first, but his face looked very white and ghost-like, and then I knew that he had seen me for I was standing as high as he on our side. Some wild impulse caused me to wave to him – later I would not have done it – and he waved back. The light flicked out and I jumped down as MacMillan cursed me soundly. (21–2)

One is reminded as well of Xavier Bird, the Cree-Anishinaabe soldier from Joseph Boyden's *Three Day Road* (2005), whose surname renders homage to Bird while his uncanny experiences are recognized in a chain of events that Xavier experiences on the Somme, at Vimy, and in the Ypres Salient.

And We Go On not only ought to be recognized as a progenitor of three important works in our literary canon but can be regarded as the equal of several Great War classics that appeared a few months apart in 1929–30: books like Erich Maria Remarque's *All Quiet on the Western Front* and Siegfried Sassoon's *Memoirs of an Infantry Officer*. And yet Bird is mostly forgotten today – hardly read, let alone acknowledged – when he should be required reading for all students of Canadian history and literature. How did we lose sight of this seminal work? Do books have their own fates, as Bird, in his recurring meditation on destiny, seems to think individuals do? Or was such Calvinist fatalism the problem, leading to rejection of the book because it supported irrationality and superstition, which our post-Christian, high-tech culture left behind long ago. Apparently not, if one recalls the recent reception of Boyden's work.

Bird's contemporaries were largely untroubled by his "mysticism." After the publication of *And We Go On* in 1930, he was invited by the Royal Canadian Legion to address overflow crowds at more than one hundred branches across Canada. In the words of historian Jonathan Vance, Bird became "the unofficial bard" of the Canadian Expeditionary Force by virtue of his speaking engagements, his memoir, his war stories, and his war novel *Private Timothy Fergus Clancy* (1930). He received thousands of letters after publication of *And We Go On* as taciturn veterans wrote to tell him their stories.

His fame and his literary stature were so great, in fact, that in 1931 *Maclean's* took the unprecedented step of sending him to Europe for five months to write nineteen articles about the "Old Front," which appeared in successive issues of the twice-monthly magazine (1 January–1 October 1932). In the issue of 15 August, a boxed announcement on a page unrelated to Bird "canonized" him as the epic voice of the Canadian Corps. The caption, "Canon Scott to Mr. Bird," referred to the beloved Senior Padre of the 1st Division, Frederick G. Scott, whose own memoir, *The Great War as I Saw It* (1922), was widely read and admired. Scott, who had stayed with the men in the Line until he was wounded out of the war in the attack on Cambrai, wrote:

> As one who had the privilege of being in every battle that the 1st Division was in from 1915 to September 29, 1918, may I express my congratulations to you and Mr. Bird for the splendid and vivid series of articles you have published about the battlefields? Not the least part of the pleasure in reading them was the thought of the thousands of old comrades all over Canada, and beyond Canada, who have been linked up once again in the sacred memories of the past by the spiritual revisiting of the war zone, which these articles have made possible. (24)

With the canon's blessing, an expanded version of the articles was published as a book by Maclean's Publishing Co. later that year under the title used for the series, *Thirteen Years After*. And Bird kept up his work of link-ing "old comrades" through a self-published volume of trivia, *The Communication Trench* (1933), revisiting the war zone in a more statistical and anecdotal fashion. Two of Bird's nine historical novels (*Here Stays Good Yorkshire* and *Judgment Glen*) received the Ryerson Fiction Award in 1945 and 1947 respectively, propelling him to the presidency of the Canadian Authors Association in 1949–50.

These were extraordinary achievements for a son of rural Nova Scotia, born in May 1891 and forced to leave school after grade eight at the Amherst Academy in Amherst, Nova Scotia, in order to help support the family. His father had died of pneumonia in December 1895, barely five months short of Will's fifth birthday, while his mother, Augusta, was pregnant with Stephen. Perhaps the birth of his beloved little brother in April 1896 was some compensation for the loss of his father, since the infant, who bore his father's name, was virtually the last trace of his father's passage on earth. Having worked for a dairy farmer and a grocer in Amherst, in 1914 Will headed west on a harvest train – one of those special trains run to transport Maritimers to the prairies where labour was in short supply – out of a sense of adventure, remarks his daughter Betty Murray, née Bird, as much as any need for work.

From Betty, we learn that her father liked to read adventure stories about the Canadian wilderness. On an October day in 1915, Bird had a great adventure of his own that was as compelling as any adventure story. He was "pitching sheaves on a wagon" in Saskatchewan when he saw an apparition of his brother Steve, who was fighting in Belgium, having enlisted in November 1914. (His attestation papers give his age as twenty-one when, in fact, he was just eighteen.) Steve "walked around the cart and confronted me. He said not a word but I knew all as if he had spoken, for he had on his equipment and was carrying his rifle" (8). Unlike Hamlet, who procrastinates after he sees the ghost of his dead father, Will's response was to immediately return home to enlist, even though he had already been rejected twice for medical reasons. So began Will Bird's journey into the devouring maw of the Great War and his experiences with the ultimate mystery of death, his mysterious brush with the world of the dead leading, beyond all expectation or reason, to an eventual career as a distinguished and popular writer.

Of course, none of this was apparent in 1915 when Steve's ghost stepped around the corner of a hayrack, causing Will to drop his pitchfork, along with the bundle of grain he was about to pitch onto the load. This scene is eerily familiar to me, having pitched sheaves in the 1950s for a farmer in Saskatchewan. But Steve's opening scene had been cut from *Ghosts*, the version I read first, and so my sense of déjà vu was purely literary, although my training as a reservist in the North Saskatchewan Regiment added further layers of familiarity.

Certainly, Bird could not have foreseen on that autumn day in Saskatchewan that a summons from the beyond would lead him to experiences on the Western Front that would serve as his school and college. The war even prepared him for a career in provincial tourism. On the battlefield he became a reliable guide, first in 1917–18 for his men, crawling out on patrol behind him into No Man's Land or listening to the stories he found in his "little French guide book," then, in the 1930s, for the army of tourists who crisscrossed those torn and anguished battlefields with *Thirteen Years After*, his plangent book of retrospect, in hand. Unlike the author of *All Quiet on the Western Front*, who never names a town or geographical site, the author of *And We Go On* resisted the tendency to generalize, let alone to universalize, and so his war books offered guidance to writers like Davies and Findley, as well as to new generations of readers wanting to know more about the Great War. To my knowledge, his influence was never acknowledged, and Bird was too humble to take credit for the success of others. The war shaped his innovations in the field of tourism, where he campaigned to make local history part of the advertised attractions. Accepting a position with the Nova Scotia Tourist Board in 1933, Bird joined the provincial Historic Sites and Monuments Advisory Council in 1938, serving as chair until his retirement in 1966.

•••

Once I had read *And We Go On*, I knew I had to make a pilgrimage like Bird's in *Thirteen Years After*. I had no illusions whatever about war: my Cold War training as an infantryman had cured me of all that. And Bird's era seemed to me to be the convulsions of a dying Empire, perhaps of the imperial idea itself. Yet here I was seventy years later, like the thousands of Canadians who had been drawn to France for the unveiling of the Vimy Monument in 1936, feeling that I needed to absorb in person and in situ the memory of all that agony.

I have no illusions about what Bird's title meant to my wife as we drove the length and breadth of Picardy and Flanders, visiting the major battlefields and more than fifty Commonwealth cemeteries. *And We Go On* indeed! Still, I am pleased to say that we found Stephen Bird's name in Ypres on the Menin Gate Memorial, not far from the panel of the 1st Battalion where my own great-uncle's name appeared.

It had not been the call of a bugle that had sounded for me in Bird's work. It was more as if I'd been introduced to a long-lost family member. And I needed to go where he had been, to breathe the air he had breathed – air now mercifully free of the "fearful stench of death" still "hovering, clinging" to the soil on which Bird had once stood. Above all else, I had to visit Parvillers, that fox-warren of criss-crossing trenches where the 42nd battalion had gotten terribly lost, and where death lurked around every corner. I felt as well the pull of the Ypres Salient, that "cesspool of human desolation, shaking into abominable rottenness, a succession of stagnant, discoloured, water-logged shell holes, cankering the dead crust of a vast unhallowed graveyard," where, returning at war's end, Bird had heard the "shuddering sighs, saw broken forms twisting in agony, visioned once more hell's hurricane over that most-tortured scene that man has trod" (225).

Even today, I can't fathom what "life" was like in that bottom circle of hell, lower than anything in Dante's Inferno. How had we let Bird's depiction of that tortured scene slip into oblivion? Was it because the Second World War had come along and pushed the First War into the shadows? Was it because the generation after Lester B. Pearson accepted holus-bolus the myth of the Canadian peacemaker? Or was it because Bird, hoping to interest Clarke, Irwin, the publisher who brought Bird back into the public eye in the 1960s, had focused on his own heroic exploits, with regrettable results, as the new memoir now passed for the original, despite the fact that forty percent of the text was new? The sixty per cent that survives is a flattened version of the original with a narrow range of voices: none of the soldiers in *Ghosts* gives the vitriolic anti-war rants that echo in a variety of voices throughout *And We Go On*. The usual complaints about military stupidity do survive; that goes without saying, especially for a reservist. But in the year of the Tet Offensive, *Ghosts* shows just enough of the class inequality between the ranks to appeal to readers sympathetic to the flowering of Haight-Ashbury's hippie culture and anti-war protests.

In 1930, however, readers were increasingly exposed to portrayals of the horror of modern, industrialized warfare. On that score, *And We Go On* is just as evocative of the terrible futility of war as Erich Maria Remarque's *All Quiet on the Western Front* (1929) or Charles Yale Harrison's *Generals Die in Bed* (1930) – books that most readers know today. Here is the naked truth, we assume, about the desperation, dehumanization, and disillusion of soldiers of all nations in that conflict. And yet Bird disdains such books for being "putrid with so-called 'realism.'" As he writes in his original preface, "Vulgar language and indelicacy of incident are often their substitute for lack of knowledge, and their distorted pictures of battle action are especially repugnant. On the whole, such literature, offered to our avid youth, is an irrevocable insult to those gallant men who lie in French or Belgian graves" (4–5).

While sharing none of Remarque's ignorance of warfare or Harrison's vulgarity, Bird rivals their scorn for the "platform patriots" back home. He dismisses all those who "ranted about the Germans, and their 'hate,'" remarking "how different it was in the battalion ... [O]utside of ... jesting at old 'Heinie,'" he adds, "the German was seldom mentioned in billets" (43). This description resembles that by the unnamed narrator in Harrison's *Generals*: "We have learned who our enemies are – the lice, some of our officers, and Death ... Strangely, we never refer to the Germans as our enemy." True, in *All Quiet* Remarque's Paul Baümer visibly widens the gulf between Home and Front by characterizing it as a generation gap: "We often made fun of [our elders] and played jokes on them, but in our hearts we trusted them. The idea of authority, which they represented, was associated in our minds with a greater insight and a more humane wisdom. But the first death we saw shattered this belief. We had to recognize that our generation was more to be trusted than theirs." But Remarque's account reads like an essay; Bird, more bitterly and dramatically, relates a conversation with a Canadian from the 7th Battalion in which, "We talked of patriotism. He said it was not a password in his company, that loyalty was a word they sneered at; discipline, with the death penalty behind it, a canker we could not cure. Then he derided the caste of the nation and cursed the propaganda passed out by preachers, editors, staff officers and platform patriots of both sexes" (43). The 7th Battalion man sounds like a mouthpiece for Bird himself, who was sceptical of the prayers of ignorant believers in a Church of England service he attended on leave: "They were asking God to make England and her Allies victorious, pleading that right should conquer, that the German and the devil be defeated. And in my haversack was a belt buckle I had taken off a dead German. Its inscription was 'Gott Mitt [sic] Uns'" (99) [God With Us]. It is an incongruity that recalls the high irony that the literary scholar Paul Fussell (35) regards as a trademark of British writings about the Great War by Siegfried Sassoon, Wilfred Owen, Edmund Blunden, and Robert Graves.

In *The Great War and Modern Memory* (1975), Fussell is openly contemptuous of Remarque's descent into German "gothic" by dwelling on the grotesquery of war; for Fussell, Remarque lacked the stiff upper lip and ironic sensibility of upper-caste Britons. One wonders what Fussell would say of the unschooled Bird's account of a section of men rocking a burned-out tank until "a head squeezed out in the muck, a face without eyes, the skin peeled as though from lard, a corpse long dead and frightful" (77). Such horrors darken nearly every other page of *And We Go On*. What would he say about Bird's description of the battalion taking refuge in a graveyard from an artillery barrage? "A shell came as I looked up and erupted almost under the body, and the dead man stood straight up a moment, as if saluting, then tumbled down on the other side" (82). Later, "near us," appears the shocking sight of "a man with a long black beard and with some decoration on his black frock coat. He looked as if he had not been buried more than a week and was in a sitting-up position, thrown that way by a shell explosion" (179). Each of these events is more "gothic" (and therefore, for Fussell, more "Germanic") than Remarque's character Baümer's account of taking refuge from "shelling" which "is stronger than everything. It wipes out the sensibilities. I merely crawl still farther under the coffin, it shall protect me, though Death himself lies in it." After the barrage lets up, Baümer emerges from the casket to find the graveyard "a mass of wreckage. Coffins and corpses lie strewn about. They have been killed once again; but each of them that was flung up saved one of us."

Bird's depiction of "gothic horror" is unrivalled by any other writer, except, perhaps, the American-Canadian Harrison. The most harrowing scene in *Generals Die in Bed* may well be the one in which the narrator's bayonet gets caught in the ribs of an enemy soldier during a trench raid. He insists that he "will go insane" unless he frees himself from the shrieks of the dying man, and yet, should he leave his rifle sticking in his foe, he will be left unarmed. With his anguished opposite looking up plaintively into his face, he pulls his "breech-lock back" and squeezes the trigger. "In this flickering light," he concludes laconically, "this German and I enact our tragedy." Safely back in his own dugout, the narrator learns that he has not freed himself at all: "The image of Karl [the dead German] seemed to stand before my eyes." Bird's description of his "first and only kill with cold steel" is similar: "I felt my bayonet steady as if guided, and was jolted as it brought up on solid bone. My grip tightened as my rifle was twisted by a sudden squirming, as if I had speared a huge fish" (90). Later, out on rest, he finds himself unable to sleep: "I was bathed in perspiration, though the night was cold, for I had been feeling again live flesh sliding over my bayonet, seeing again Mickey's white face close to mine, while his blood seeped from him and warmed my knees" (92–3).

The death of his friend Mickey in the mud of Passchendaele is the true nadir of Bird's experience of the futility of war; his very title echoes Mickey's dying words:

He had been hit in several places and could not possibly live.

"Mickey – Mickey!" I called his name and raised him up and he nestled to me like a child, his white face upturned to mine.

"At last," he murmured, "I'm through." Then his whisper was shrill and harsh. "I never had a white tunic or a red one," he said. "I didn't want – to kill people. I hate war – and everything. Why did they do it – why – did – they?"

He seemed delirious and I tried to soothe him, but he would not listen. He talked about what we had read in my little guide book, the way boys trained for fighting, the soldiers killed in France and Belgium, the other wars that had been fought, the futility of the endless repetition. "And we just go on and on," he finished. "Doing things because – because –"

His voice sank so low I could not hear but his lips still moved. Little white-faced Mickey! I held him there, held him tight, and tried to comfort him as he grew weaker and weaker. Then he twisted, strained in my arms, "… and we go on – on – on – on," he shrilled, and stiffened. (91–2)

In a scene marked by similar pathos, Baümer, in *All Quiet*, describes his attempts to comfort "a recruit in utter terror. He has buried his face in his hands, his helmet has fallen off. I fish hold of it and try to put it back on his head. He looks up, pushes the helmet off and like a child creeps under my arm, his head close to my breast. The little shoulders heave." For Remarque his "fatherly" attempt to care for a "child-soldier" is another sign of the total bankruptcy of the older generation, who have sent boys to die in circumstances they themselves could not imagine, let alone endure.

Like Baümer, Bird is keenly aware of the multiple ways he has been changed by war. While on leave, Remarque's narrator had tried repeatedly to tell himself: "'You are at home, you are at home.' But a sense of strangeness will not leave me, I cannot feel at home amongst these things. There is my mother, there is my sister, there my case of butterflies, and there the mahogany piano – but I am not myself there. There is a distance, a veil between us." Yet Remarque had been at the Front for only three weeks and his description of home leave, available to Germans, French, and Britons, was always out of reach for Canadians and Australians. Bird had just one leave – to England – in the two years he spent at the Front. He first entered the line in the Vimy sector on 5 January 1917 and was there at Passchendaele in November 1917 and through the Last Hundred Days, stretching from the fiercely fought battle of Amiens (8–11 August 1918) to Arras and the breaking of the Drocourt-Quéant line (26 August–2 Sept), to the crossing of the Canal du Nord (27 September) and the capture of Cambrai (8–9 October), before pursuing the fleeing German army all the way to Mons in Belgium, the site of the initial British defeat in 1914, where the Canadian Corps ended hostilities on the eleventh hour of the eleventh day of the eleventh month. Bird, a battle-hardened veteran, knew far better than Remarque what it meant to have once "marched to Mount St. Eloi [near Vimy] ... with a cheeky retort for every comment ... not knowing what it is to scrape a hasty grave at night and there bury a man who has worked with you and slept with you since you enlisted" (47).

Out of the horror and mud at Passchendaele, Bird recalls meeting "remnants of relieved battalions, men who looked like grisly discards of the battlefield, long unburied, who had risen and were in search of graves in which to rest" (76). After November 1917, he recalled in his very nerve-endings how "every man who had endured Passchendale [sic] would never be the same again, was more or less a stranger to himself" (93). His daughter Betty has informed me that he never talked about the war in her childhood, except for what he recalled of his tour of the Front in *Thirteen Years After*. Betty remembers, however, that he sometimes shouted in his sleep; presumably, it was the horrors of Passchendaele returning to haunt him as he slept.

Nearing the end of the Last Hundred Days, after two years of incessant battle, Bird concluded that it was "a desolation that seemed increased, that seemed peopled with grisly spectres when the Very lights became fewer just before dawn. War – I hated it, despised it, loathed it – and yet felt I was a part of it" (220). More than Remarque and Harrison, Bird, like Wilfred Owen and Siegfried Sassoon, had earned the right to despise war. Yet few have described it better; others rival, but none exceeds him.

Like Sassoon in *The Memoirs of George Sherston* (1928–36) or Owen in the *Poems* (1920), Bird, in *And We Go On,* writes with a painterly eye. His account of tramping over duckboards floating on a bottomless pit of mud at Passchendaele recalls nothing so much as Owen's "Dulce et Decorum Est." In Bird, one glimpses the "flashes and glows of fire, the great Salient's maw, a huge death-trap," before hearing the "shells whining and rushing through the air. There were red and yellow flashes, and streaking sparks of fire, and flares, ghostly, looping, falling, unreal, now and then silhouetting a straggling line of steel helmets and hunched shoulders; bewildered men in the dark, bone-weary, shell-dazed, treading on old dead and new dead, and slipping in the foulness of slimy ditches" (92).

Bird's description brings to mind Owen's similar portrait of men leaving the Front line: "Bent double, like old beggars under sacks, / Knock-kneed, coughing like hags, we cursed through sludge, / Till on the haunting flares we turned our backs." It recalls as well *Memoirs of an Infantry Officer* (1930) where Sassoon describes a "grinding jolting column lumber[ing] back ... Thus, with an almost spectral appearance, the lurching brown figures flitted past with slung rifles and heads bent forward under basin-helmets" (117).

And yet, in the midst of the horror, Bird paints scenes of a terrible beauty: "The red glows made some small pools of water look like big blots of blood, and the green lights gave everything a ghastly, corpse-like sheen" (66). At Vimy, we experience from the outset his paradoxical use of all the senses to engage us in an elemental conflict: "At nights the Very lights soared like great soap bubbles and often there were salvos of shells near us. There would be a screaming, whistling sound, a clanging, crashing explosion, and clods of earth and chalk would come flying about, then smoke and fume would drift across the trench and sting our nostrils" (18).

There is a paradox in this "terrible beauty" that Bird translates into moral terms. An older man who detested war and all its accoutrements "talked about the sunset and asked, rather curiously, how I could be interested in such things, and at the same time intent on killing my fellowmen." This man, whom Bird calls the Professor, "spoke of the beauty that belongs to sunsets and dawns and high mountains and still waters and moonlight, and pointed out the incongruity of a star gleam in a stagnant pool beside us. Everything about us, he said, should be horrible, distorted, repulsive" (66–7). In contrast to the Professor's dismay, the entry in Sassoon's *Diary* for 5 February 1916 describes his return from a visit to a neighbouring battalion: "The mare brought me home straight as a die across the four miles of plough and mud – gloom all around and stars, stars, overhead, and hanging low above the hills – the rockets going up behind, along the line – brief lights soon burnt out – the stars wheeling changeless and untroubled, life and deathless beauty, always the same contrast" (38).

Bird shares Sassoon's breadth of vision and his writing encompasses far more than those books he labels as "putrid with so-called 'realism'" (4). And this breadth, which encompasses everything in those works except Remarque's passivity, should have been enough to make his book endure, save that he did not, like Sassoon, unequivocally denounce the war, even though he came to hate it with equal passion. Bird, however, never doubted that it was necessary; unlike Sassoon, whose words were pacifist, though his actions were bloody, Bird never questioned the war aims of the nation. And yet it would be a mistake to lump him with "warmongers" like the German Ernst Jünger, recipient of the Iron Cross 1st Class, who never wavered from the view, stated in his preface to the English edition of his memoir in 1929, that "Time only strengthens my conviction that it was a good and strenuous life, and that the war, for all its destructiveness, was an incomparable schooling of the heart."

In *The Communication Trench*, Bird noted that, of the seven translations he had read of German war books, he found Jünger's *The Storm of Steel* to be "the best," while the "poorest of all, I think, [is] *All Quiet on the Western Front*." What Bird liked most about Jünger's work was its emphasis on soldierly agency; what he found so very dishonest in *All Quiet* and

Generals Die in Bed was the utter passivity of the soldiers. As the historian Modris Eksteins comments in an essay entitled "*All Quiet on the Western Front* and the Fate of a War," the characters of Remarque's brutalized generation "do not act, they are merely victims." By contrast, Bird writes, "Action helped me in the Salient. It was the deadly waiting, helpless waiting, that was unnerving, for always it seemed as if swooping Death were just above us, hovering, or reaching tentacles from dark corners" (79). He even admits that "I liked patrol work, loved crawling near the Hun wire … In the dark of no man's land you had all the elements of surprise in your favour, it was your wits against the other fellow's, your cunning against his" (114–15). His recognition of the contrasting aspects of war makes it easier for armchair moralists – who know little of the inescapable paradoxes of warfare, or who fail to think about the moral complexity of doing a job for which you signed up, as Sassoon is often reminded by Dr. W.H.R. Rivers in Pat Barker's novel *Regeneration* (1991) – to carp and moan.

In taking responsibility for his own life and those of his men, in pitting his wits against those who would take his life, in fighting to the death and describing it poetically, Bird is closer to Siegfried Sassoon than to any other writer in the English tradition. In a Hobbesean world of war where life reverts to its primordial state – "nasty, brutish and short" – Bird, like Sassoon, is obliged to lead two lives simultaneously. Sassoon, at the end of *Sherston's Progress* (1936), comes to realize that the soldier-writer "really needs two lives; one for experiencing and another for thinking it over. Knowing that I *need* two lives and am only allowed one, I do my best to *lead* two lives" (104). In fact, "Siegfried had always coped," as Pat Barker remarks in her Great War novel *The Eye in the Door* (1993), "by being two people: the anti-war poet and pacifist; the bloodthirsty, efficient company commander" (233). Bird's work, like Sassoon's, is made from the same dichotomies: a keen eye for beauty, whether in a sunset or a reflecting pool reeking of death, and a sharp eye, focused on the instinct for survival, on night patrol through enemy territory. These give Bird's writing a psychological and ideological complexity mostly lacking in *All Quiet* and in *Generals,* which are both founded on pretence – Remarque's private pretence of having been a true veteran of combat, and Harrison's outright lie that Canadians had committed a war crime at Amiens to revenge a hospital ship that had been sunk by Germans for carrying munitions. The "judgment" meted out by Canadian troops was not without cause – the hospital ship had not carried munitions and the "surrendering" foe at Amiens had in fact led the 14th Battalion, in which Harrison served, into a deadly ambush in which they responded by annihilating the "surrendering" Germans to a man (Williams, "Film," 182).

Contrary to Bird and Sassoon, Remarque and Harrison made the dehumanization and the bestializing of men at war central to their work. In *Generals,* to take a single example: "We fight among ourselves" when the rations arrive: "Cleary is sharing it out. Broadbent suspects that his piece is smaller than the rest. An oath is spat out ... In a moment they are at each other's throats like hungry, snarling animals ... Cleary wipes the blood from his face. He scowls and holds this hunk of bread in his hands like an animal" (49–50). By contrast, Bird sees an inherent dignity in men who, as if by some sixth sense, glimpse their deaths, and yet respond not as victims but as seers and visionaries, even when, "White-faced, unsmiling, filled with a strange courage, they greeted that which waited them" (4). A man named Freddy is the first of Bird's comrades to dream of "a woman in white" passing through the wall of their tent and pointing, he said, "'at you, and you, and you.' He jerked a thumb toward six of the men who were in their blankets. 'And I know,' he went on, 'that I'm going to get mine – I'll never see Canada again'" (6). The truth of Freddy's premonition is soon confirmed at the Battle of Vimy Ridge. In the moment, Bird is enough of a rationalist to say, "Long after all the others were snoring I lay there in the dark and thought about Freddy's dream. Was there anything in dreams? Why had he seemed so certain?" (6). Later on, a man named Gordon, who "was quiet, thoughtful, kind in manner" insisted that he was "going to his death ... and would meet it like a soldier, and there was that in his voice that told me any argument of mine would be futile. My skin was pricked with goose flesh as he talked" (74).

At least eight times in *And We Go On*, privates and officers approach Bird to take their leave of him before they die. Perhaps the most interesting of these is the atheist Christensen who has always refused to go on church parade and is "crimed" for it. All the same, he tells Will of his premonitions of death just before the Battle of Amiens:

"Good-bye, Bird," he said. "I'm going to find out to-day which of us is right."

He and I had argued about the hereafter, and I had tried hard to convince him everything, even to a blade of grass, cried out that there was a God who governed creation. But ... "What's got into you," I said. "You'll not get hit."

"I'll be killed," he said, smiling in a way that startled me. He didn't seem the least frightened, but was as matter-of-fact as if his leave had come through. "An hour ago," he said, "something came to me. It was as if every sound in the world was stilled at once, as if there was nothing more for me to hear, and I knew what it meant. I'm not the least bit afraid, and I'll be satisfied if it comes quick." It was useless to try to console him, he didn't want sympathy. Not one man who had mentioned the same thing to me had acted the same as he did. He almost seemed glad, and when I pointed out that, if he were right, there was some power beyond the visible that imparted information, he partially admitted it. (143)

Even in the face of death, the atheist remains open to other possibilities. But the outcome is both unsettling and ennobling. When Bird sees Christensen "hit in the arm by a piece of shrapnel," he tells him "you were wrong ... You're away for Blighty" (a word derived from Urdu, and long used by British soldiers in India to refer to home). To which Christensen replies, "By night I'll be a corpse. Remember what I tell you" (148). The next day, their Sergeant-major comes to inquire of Bird, "Wasn't it funny about Christensen?" Well back of the line, "a shell came and he was killed by shrapnel. He was away back there and one would have thought him safe for Blighty" (150).

While this is the most uncanny of the eight stories of premonitory deaths, each works to undermine the position of the "passivists," or so-called "realists," who claim, as even Owen had done in "Anthem for Doomed Youth," that "these die as cattle." For Bird, the truth is quite different: the war "drew from even dulled and uncouth natures a perception that was attributed to the mystic and supernal" (4). And it prompts him to one of his most fierce expressions of egalitarianism among the men: "the private in the trenches had other thoughts than of the flesh, had often finer vision and strength of soul than those who would fit him to their sordid, sensation-seeking fiction" (5).

Bird sees himself and his fellows as actors in a great tragedy, one similar to that of the ancient Greeks: "Men glimpsed, or thought they glimpsed, that grim cross roads we all must pass. It was as if for them a voice had spoken, a hand beckoned them on. And at once there fell from them all frenzy and confusion" (4). Whether he realized it or not, such recognition is Aristotelian, describing a moment of *anagnorisis*, realization and acceptance of one's fate, that ennobles dying heroes, whether in myth, on the stage, or at the Front. Bird's vision is essentially tragic: both the worst and the best of which human life is capable is written on his pages in blood. Hence Bird's anger, often palpable, at the "irrevocable insult" given by "passivists" to "those gallant men who lie in French or Belgian graves" (5). This sentiment is expressed far less aggressively at the end of another scene: "Privates in a dirty, wind-blown, rain-soaked tent, unshaven, strangers to each other … discussing topics that cause any man to sober. I think of Spike and that 7th man every time I read of the 'sodden cattle' of the dugouts" (44). Bird has an unwavering respect for the courage and dignity of men facing what they see as certain death.

This respect explains why his work is so often filled with what Owen, in his famous "Preface," had called "the pity of War": "It was the Professor, riddled with bullets, dead," whose body Bird came upon at Passchendaele: "He was covered with mud, had lost his steel helmet, had evidently got lost in the darkness, and there he lay, after years of study and culture, with glassy eyes and face upturned to the sky, a smashed cog of the war machine, with not a hope of burial excepting by a chance shell" (81–2). At war's end, Bird's friend Tommy, dying of the Spanish Flu and wanting only to "join the Boys" beneath the sod, will pity the poor survivor: "As long as I have memory I'll not forget Tommy's look as he watched me go from his ward. It was almost as if he pitied me, were sorry that I could not share his joy" (228).

Just as often, fraternal pity extends beyond Bird's band of brothers, for instance when he expresses empathy for the German officer he had let go at Vimy, or a German youth still in uniform and hiding in the closet of Bird's billet at Mons: "'Kamerad?' he whimpered. I shook my head, motioned him to be still. No use to put him out on the street for that crazed bunch of celebrators. Even the Belgians would kill him" (221). So he scrounges civilian clothing to disguise the defeated "enemy" and lets him escape: "The change was effective. He appeared a young Belgian and would never draw a second glance" (221). At the same time, Bird can't forget what the invaders have done to ordinary French folk: "We saw refugees with great, sweat-dried Percherons drawing farm carts heaped with mattresses and furniture, with lean cows tethered to the rear, and old men following with barrows and push carts piled with other possessions, nearly everyone dressed in his or her Sunday best, usually black, and very tired, foot sore and pathetic" (198). These are a type of victim rarely seen in *All Quiet* or in *Generals Die in Bed*. For good or ill, Bird acknowledges, if he does not condone, the thirst of non-combatants for reprisal: "The Frenchman stamped on the battered face [of a German officer] with his boots until we spoke sharply to him and walked away" (198). In Mons, he watches a German soldier trying to escape: "He had to pass a big gate to get outside the yard and as he did a burly Belgian rose from where he had been waiting and struck with a sledge, crashing [sic] the German's head like an eggshell. No one rebuked him or went near the body" (218).

Turnabout is also fair play. When the pursuing Canadians came upon a German soldier in grey-green field dress resting from flight in Raismes Forest, one of Bird's men, Giger, crept "up behind the unsuspecting Hun like a great, blood-thirsty tiger," showing no mercy to the surrendering prisoner as he stood up with raised arms. Giger, who had always been disappointed in his failure "to kill a Hun," viciously drove his bayonet into his prisoner's belly:

> It was a ghastly, merciless thing, and I shuddered. Tommy stood, white-faced, and looked around for an officer. Giger grinned back at us. "How's that?" he called. "I …"
>
> A second German shot up from some hiding place at the far end of the logs. He had not his bayonet but the woodman's axe that had been left there, and before Giger could jump from danger or withdraw his bayonet he was cut down by a fearful blow on the neck and shoulder. Then the German ran like a deer – and no one fired a shot at him. (206–7)

This representation of war seems less one-sided, less ideological, and more honest than those other narratives of passivity. It is also a vision of war that is less blinkered and far more complicated in terms of the moral dilemmas that individuals face in the field. And yet one cannot doubt the moral decency of the memoirist himself. Here is a man whose senses might have been dulled but were certainly not erased by war, and whose canvas thus holds a much broader picture than the one too often mistaken for a "true" portrait of war. Even Bird's title, *And We Go On*, reveals more than the bare futility of war, since it valorizes the courage and doggedness of infantrymen who have no choice but to "go on." It also hints at the idea of continuity of the self, in spite of all the depredations of war and the lasting changes wrought in the psyche. With equal force, it evokes a sense of historical continuity. On occasion, Bird's fellows appear to be astonished and even annoyed at what he tells them about the various villages and towns and battlefields where they are deployed:

> As we passed Mount St. Eloi and its twin towers I dug up a little more history for Tommy. ...
> He looked at me. "Where did you get all that dope?" he asked.
> "In a little French guide book I bought in London," I said. "I've got it with me. What's the use of coming over here on a trip if you don't know what you're looking at?" (13)

It is a telling comment about the desire of common soldiers to go on the Grand Tour, that cultural phenomenon familiar to readers tracking young English aristocrats on their yearlong excursions to the Continent. To Bird, the outbreak of war permits men from the lower classes to share in the "finishing school" tradition of their social "betters." On occasion something of the dilettante's optimism even shines from the pages of his memoir. During one of the Professor's rants about the war as "a ghastly paroxysm of civilization," Bird tries "to ease the condemnation" for the sake of young Mickey, who "stared at him, wide-eyed." Since Mickey's courage has begun to flicker like a guttering candle, Bird points out "that war was not new, had always been. I got out my little guide book and tried to divert Mickey's thoughts as I read about the history of the country. Arras, Boulogne, Cambrai, Verdun, had all been towns under the reign of Julius Caesar, and a German invasion was nothing new. Attila and his heathen Huns had poured into France when it was Gaul, burning and plundering and had lost 160,000 men before they were driven away" (72).

Bird next tells about "King Edward at Crecy with his expeditionary force," recounting how "Thirty thousand men of France fell in that battle, twelve hundred knights and eight princes, so why should we consider we were entangled in an original catastrophe." At which Tommy sneers, "How many knights and princes are going to be killed up in Passchendale?" and begins to rave once again "about the officers, the gilded staff in fine chateaus and billets, waited on hand and foot, living like lords, travelling in cushioned cars, stroking away – with careless pens – thousands of lives. The Professor and Mickey did not speak" (73).

Although the long view is often beyond Tommy's comprehension – his very name suggests the working-class British infantryman, resentful of class injustice and social inequality – it is the soul of Bird's method, forming part of the mental equipment by which he is able to keep his balance, rarely descending into self-pity or a "sodden" obsession with his own sufferings. While Harrison and Remarque speak fairly and truly in the first-person plural for the "we" in ranks, the plural first person of *And We Go On* speaks the "we" of all sides of the conflict, not just those in uniforms of grey or blue or khaki but mothers and fathers and other civilians who have to endure the catastrophe. For example, there is the French mother who introduces Will and Tommy to her white-haired, twenty-three-year-old son. He fought, she says, "at Verdun. His mind is what you call at the halt – it cannot get past Verdun. He was wounded there, with dead men on him, and could not move. A day and a night he was like that and now, in his mind, he is still there." Bird admits that, "We expected to hear her breathe maledictions on the Boche, as some of the French did, but she did not utter a word of hate … He would never, his mother said, go out into the fields or gardens, and his face was the waxen colour of death. For days after I could visualize his ghastly features and those awful staring eyes" (125). Contrary to Remarque and Harrison, Bird's awareness transcends the temporal and spatial horizons of his own, and even the enemy's, trenches. He never forgets the humanity of those around him, and what it will mean for this poor woman to care for her "only living son" for the rest of her life. And yet "we go on," both she and her wreck of a son, and everyone living, if only because "we" must.

Above all else, what distinguishes *And We Go On* from other Great War writings is the support it gives to the idea of personal continuity. Throughout the years 1914–18, a sense of the uncanny was widespread among the combatants and citizens of every nation. Setting this phenomenon in the context of the Spiritualist movement of late Victorian times, the cultural historian Jay Winter remarks in *Sites of Memory, Sites of Mourning* (1995) on how the loss of so many millions in the Great War had led to a revival of Victorian and Edwardian spiritualism that supplemented where it did not rival orthodox religion. Given the grief of so many millions in Britain and its dominions, as well as in France and other countries, it would be surprising if mourners had not tried to contact their lost loved ones, or at the very least had not yearned for proof of life after death. Winter remarks how "Sir Oliver Lodge, Professor of Physics at Liverpool and later Principal of Birmingham University," had already served as president of the Society for Psychical Research in 1901–03; the loss of his son Raymond in the Ypres Salient would lead him to publish a book which was "both a personal memorial and a scientific exposition" of the evidence for his son's survival after death.

If Lodge put the stamp of scientific credibility on spiritualism, Sir Arthur Conan Doyle gave it emotional and imaginative force. "Conan Doyle's fame as the creator of the ultimate rationalist, Sherlock Holmes, as well as his writings" and his overseas tours promoting the spiritualist movement, "ensured that other parents in mourning would consult him" (Winter 58). Conan Doyle had lost a son, a brother, and a brother-in-law in the Great War, and his grief overcame his innate scepticism to make him an evangelist of the spiritualist movement on his world tour in 1919. In 1923, he visited the legendary Dr. T.G. Hamilton, Canada's leading researcher in parapsychology, to attend séances held in his Winnipeg home and examine his spirit photography. At the time, Hamilton was immediate past-president of the Manitoba Medical Association (1921–22), and member of the Dominion Council of the Canadian Medical Association. His scientific prestige provided Conan Doyle with further support for his attempt "to create a new synthesis between Darwinian evolution and humanistic Christianity" (Winter 59). In *The History of Spiritualism* (1926), the detective novelist, speaking in the third person, says about the ultimate mystery: "Evidence of the presence of the dead appeared in his own household, and the relief afforded by posthumous messages taught him how great a solace it would be to a tortured world if it could share in the knowledge which had become clear to himself" (vol. 1:226).

Will Bird had no contact with men of letters like Sir Arthur Conan Doyle or with scientists like T.G. Hamilton or Sir Oliver Lodge. His occult experience, unlike theirs, was a product of uncanny events on the battle-field, of unsought and unmediated exposure to the paranormal. But he was not alone in his experience of supernatural phenomena: "The sense of the uncanny, of the overdetermined nature of survival in combat can be found in many memoirs and letters written by serving men" (Winter 65). What Bird shared with scientific researchers, imaginative writers, and sol-diers alike was a secular, rather than a religious, view of occult phenome-na. While he would continue for the rest of his life, with his wife Ethel (née Sutton), to attend the Methodist Church in which he was raised, his daughter Betty insists that, "Religion did not play a major role in his life." Nor did he dabble in the spiritualist movement after the war; his outlook was phenomenological to the extent that it was directly based on his expe-rience of battle (Williams, "Spectres," 115–19).

Among the occult events he and other soldiers experienced were the startling admissions of those "not visibly in immediate danger" who had "premonitions of death." Much like Bird's story of Christensen's premoni-tion, Winter tells of a certain "Captain V., who approached a chaplain, said his time had come, turned to walk in a safe area, but was mistakenly shot by a sentry" (66). As far as I know, Winter had not read *And We Go On*, but his conclusion is significant for readers of Bird's work: "It is evident that soldiers' tales were important in deepening popular spiritualism, in that they added the prestige of the soldier and the weight of his experience to those who lived within or on the fringes of the spiritualist community" (67). Bird's memoir served to reinforce the findings of researchers like Dr. T.G. Hamilton, while the work of scientists helped to "normalize" the phe-nomenology of occult experience in war.

At the same time, Bird's narrative of paranormal events conforms to another social model where, in a masculine world of men at war, the role of women was to be mediums between the living and the dead. As Winter explains, women had long occupied a central position "in the spiritualist community. It is, therefore, not surprising that spiritualists were advocates of feminism and that the Roman Catholic Church repeatedly anathema-tized the movement and especially the women within it" (55). In *And We Go On*, after Steve's ghost appears to announce that he has died, Will feels an uncanny compulsion to stop and spend the night in an English village before going to the Front. In a scene that would not be out of place in a Dickens novel, he stands "by the ruins of an old water mill" where he suddenly feels "a strange chill [blow] towards me as if an unseen door had opened" (11–12). An English girl, Phyllis, who appears "like a phantom" is "very warm and real," but Will begins to feel a chill run down his spine as she stops speaking to listen to someone he can't hear, then tells him she is comparing his voice to Steve's. "We talked long there together and when we parted she told me that Steve had told her that I would come. I believed her" (12). Later, on his one and only leave to England, he learns from her grieving father that Phyllis had died in London on a bombing raid by German Zeppelins: "He invited me to take dinner with him – and he called me 'Steve.' The word shocked me. 'I'm not Steve,' I said, sharply. 'I'm his brother.' He peered at me, and I could see that he could not grasp what I said. 'Steve – that's the name,' he muttered. 'She went to meet Steve – her said it'" (98).

On the battlefield, Bird has more direct encounters with the marvellous, to an extent that even Tommy confides at war's end, "I steered clear of you. Did you ever stop to think about all the fellows who've been killed alongside you? Every time it's the other chap who gets it. I've thought about it and this time I wasn't taking any chances" (219). No other memoirist I have read recounts anything like the number and duration of Bird's uncanny experiences. Sassoon, who in *The Diaries* speaks of apparitions who come to accuse him while he convalesces in a London hospital, writes how, "when the lights are out, and the ward is half shadow and half glowing firelight, and the white beds are quiet with drowsy figures, huddled out-stretched, then the horrors come creeping across the floor: the floor is littered with parcels of dead flesh and bones, faces glaring at the ceiling, faces turned to the floor, hands clutching neck or belly; a livid grinning face with bristly moustache peers at me over the edge of my bed, the hands clutching my sheets. Yet I found no bloodstains there this morning" (161).

Sassoon has to admit that, "They are not here to scare me; they look at me reproachfully, because I am so lucky, with my safe wound, and the warm kindly immunity of the hospital is what they longed for when they shivered and waited for the attack to begin, or the brutal bombardment to cease" (162). Like the ghost of Hamlet's father, his ghosts come to accuse, like manifestations of Sassoon's own guilty conscience. Conversely, Harold

Owen, an officer serving at war's end aboard the British naval vessel *Astrea* off the coast of Africa, wrote of the vision he had had of his brother Wilfred: "He was in uniform, and I remember thinking how out of place the khaki looked amongst the cabin furnishings. With this thought I must have turned my eyes away from him; when I looked back my cabin chair was empty." From this visitation, Harold "knew with absolutely certainty that Wilfred was dead" (*Journey from Obscurity* vol. 3:198–9).

While Sassoon's ghosts come to accuse, and Owen's to inform, the ghost of Bird's dead brother displays himself far more purposefully, as if he were a battlefield scout on active duty. The first time Steve appears in the Vimy sector, Bird writes:

I was wakened by a tug at my arm. I looked up quickly, throwing back my ground sheet, and there stood Steve!

I could see him plainly, see the mud on his puttees and knees. He jerked a thumb towards the ruined houses and motioned for me to go to them. I did not speak. I thought that if I could do exactly as he said, and not wake the others, perhaps he would actually speak to me. He started to walk away as I gathered up my equipment and rifle and greatcoat, and when I hurried he simply faded from view ...

In the morning I heard fellows talking about a big shell that had killed two men. I jumped up and looked. They were digging from the shelter I had left the mangled bodies of the two lads who had invited me to join them. The shell had exploded just above their heads. (48)

On another occasion, waiting for an enemy patrol at Parvillers to "reappear I felt a light tap on the shoulder. I wheeled instantly. No one was there! 'Come,' I shouted, and jumped into the trench. Doggy [an enlisted man under his command] thought I had seen something and dived after me. As he did a Maxim opened fire from somewhere ahead and clipped weeds like a scythe in the very place where we had been crouched" (159). Typically, Steve's warnings work on a functional level to mirror Bird's role as a guide on night patrol or as a scout to attacking units. In consequence, Bird admits that

It was not physical courage that carried me, far from it, but a state of mind that words will never describe. Each night when I slept I dreamt of Steve, saw him clearly, and when awake, in the trenches at night, out on listening posts, FELT him near. In some indefinable way I depended on him. Ever since he had guided me in from that foggy unknown stretch at the back of Vimy I would go anywhere in no man's land. I knew with a – fanatical, if you like – faith, that a similar touch would lead me straight where I should go … I was always watching for him, waiting for him, trying to sense him near me. (67)

Bird's "faith" has nothing to do with conventional religion; it is more like the conditioned response of a behaviourist experiment, reinforced by results. It may best be described as a secular version of the religious imagination, where "faith" in his spirit guide lifts him out of the terror of the trenches. It is finally what gives Bird an enduring faith in life that is quite rare in Great War writing. Aboard the ship carrying the remnants of the Black Watch back to Canada, he recalls how, "Many and many a night when relaxed on outpost duty I had turned on my back for the moment and rested my eyes on the great star-lit spaces overhead until I felt lifted away from all the foul and cruel existence that we knew. Stars in the sky, twinkling stars! What a sense of the infinite they endow! It came to me as I watched them that even the war, the greatest catastrophe this world knew, was but a momentary episode, that Time and Space were limitless. And we go on. Where?" (229).

Ultimately, it is on this level of significance that Bird's title has its greatest reach. In the pre-dawn light, he stands shoulder to shoulder with "the brotherhood" of silent men waiting at the ship's railing to see the first lights of home, and realizes that, "We were prisoners, prisoners who could never escape. I had been trying to imagine how I would express my feelings when I got home, and now I knew I never could, none of us could. We could no more make ourselves articulate than could those who would not return; we were in a world apart, prisoners, in chains that would never loosen till death freed us" (231). And yet the small miracle of this book is that, at the limit of its own vanishing point, it finds the words that permit Bird and the rest of "the brotherhood," both living and dead, to speak the unspeakable to loved ones and to us, who know the things we have come to know because of the enduring eloquence of this remarkable Great War memoir, *And We Go On.*

AND WE GO ON

"Nothing except a battle lost can be half as melancholy as a battle won."
Wellington

Preface

In the trenches one night near Vimy Ridge I heard a newcomer ask our veteran sergeant, "Where is the war – what is it?"

The sergeant led his questioner to a firestep, and pointed over the parapet. Some yards in front, half hidden by the grass and weeds, was a skeleton, with the uniform rotted until it was indefinite. No one could say whether the shrivelled corpse were friend or foe. "That," he said, "is war."

The newcomer, a mere youth, looked startled. He stepped down hastily to the trench floor, swallowed hard, then asked. "How long have you been out here?"

"Sixteen months," said the sergeant.

The youth smiled and flung back his shoulders. Sixteen months! "Then," he said, "I guess I don't need to worry yet. We've all got the same chances, haven't we?"

It was quiet, one of those strange lulls in the shelling. The sergeant stood there in the gloom, looking into no man's land, and recited softly.

The Ball no question makes of Ayes or Noes,
But Right or Left as strikes the Player goes;
And He that tossed you down into the Field,
He knows about it all – HE knows – HE knows!

The youth looked up at him. "I don't know anything about poetry," he said, "but I had a queer feeling all the time we were marching up here. It seemed as if I was going to bump into something before I saw it ..."

Ping!

We buried him before it was light. The chance bullet had come from
some distant point, skimming the bags, missing the wire and the burly
sergeant, and dropping, with the trajectory of a spent missile, just enough
to strike the temple of the boy who had been two hours in the line. And
as we went to our dugout after stand-down the old sergeant repeated
more of his favourite poem.

And many a Knot unravel'd by the Road;
But not the Master Knot of Human Fate.

This story is an effort to reveal a side of the war that has not been given
much attention, the psychic effect it had on its participants. There existed
before all battles and even in the calms of the trench routine, a condition
before which all natural explanations failed, and no supernatural explanations were established.

Every human emotion ran its full gamut in that land of topsy turvy, and
prolonged tensity of feeling wrought strange psychological changes which
warped the soul itself. Never on earth was there a like place where a man's
support, often his sole support, was his faith in some mighty Power. All
intervening thoughts were swept aside. Unconsciously there were born
faiths that carried men through critical moments, and tortured minds
grasped fantasies that served in place of more solid creeds. The trench at
zero hour was a crucible that dissolved all insincerity and the superficial,
and it did more. It drew from even dulled and uncouth natures a perception that was attributed to the mystic and supernal.

Men glimpsed, or thought they glimpsed, that grim crossroads we all
must pass. It was as if for them a voice had spoken, a hand beckoned them
on. And at once there fell from them all frenzy and confusion. White-
faced, unsmiling, filled with a strange courage, they greeted that which
waited them. Was it all phenomena produced by war-strained imagina-
tions?

I have another reason for writing. We are being deluged now, a decade
after the war, by books that are putrid with so-called "realism." They por-
tray the soldier as a coarse-minded, profane creature, seeking only the
solace of loose women or the courage of strong liquor. Vulgar language
and indelicacy of incident are often their substitute for lack of knowledge,
and their distorted pictures of battle action are especially repugnant. On

the whole, such literature, offered to our avid youth, is an irrevocable insult to those gallant men who lie in French or Belgian graves.

This narrative is an attempt to give a balanced perspective; to show that the private in the trenches had other thoughts than of the flesh, had often finer vision and strength of soul than those who would fit him to their sordid, sensation-seeking fiction. It is but a personal view, I know, yet I only ask pardon for my crudity of diction.

My diary is not infallible. There were lapses in its compiling which I could not prevent, but as I am striving for a correct picture as well as accuracy of detail, those who discover any debatable point will please bear it in mind. Every case of premonition I have described is actual fact; each of my own psychic experiences were exactly as recorded. The reader may term them fantasies, the results of overstrained emotion, what he will; there are many who know he cannot explain them.

CHAPTER I

France and Vernon Carter

We sat huddled together in the wet tent, listening to those who plodded by in the ankle-deep muck between the lines. A single candle sputtered beside the tent pole and by its light we stared at Freddy. He was a slim, dark-faced, little man who seldom talked, but now he had started from his sleep and would not be stilled.

"I tell you I saw everything plainer than day," he repeated. "It was like a woman in white and it came right through that laced flap and went around the pole and pointed at you, and you, and you." He jerked a thumb toward six of the men who were in their blankets. "And I know," he went on, "that I'm going to get mine – I'll never see Canada again." There was something in his voice that stirred us strangely. He had had a very vivid dream – his voice and attitude told us how deeply he was moved – and Freddy was not a man who dreamed regularly.

"Aw, lay down and keep quiet," said big Herman roughly. "Give us a rest. You've eat too much bully, that's all."

Freddy quieted. He sank back on his tunic pillow and his eyes were fixed on Herman. "You," he said in almost a whisper, "was one of the six."

Long after all the others were snoring I lay there in the dark and thought about Freddy's dream. Was there anything in dreams? Why had he seemed so certain? And then I made a mental note of those six men he mentioned. Big Herman, a splendid specimen of manhood, over six feet tall and built in proportion; Ira, blocky built, strong as a horse; Melville, rugged, bony, red-faced, big-hearted; Arthur, a quiet lad, studious; Sam, a sour-souled middle-age miner, and boy-faced Mickey, only eighteen and looking younger.

We woke to a damp, chilly dawn, deeper mud, and a bawling sergeant outside the tents. "Fall in, in twenty minutes, everybody."

I looked at Tommy. He was always ready for anything impulsive. "Let's not go to the Bull Ring today," he suggested and I had seen him whispering to two or three of the others.

I nodded agreement. We were at Le Havre, or rather the camp outside, waiting to go up the line to join the Canadian Black Watch, and for four days we had gone, with all our belongings, up steep hills and winding, greasy paths to the "Bull Ring," a big area where the soldiers made the rounds of bull-throated sergeants, specialists in bomb-throwing, wiring, trench building, and bayonet fighting. It was all a mad game, supposed to put a keen edge to a soldier's spirit, to make him determined and bloodthirsty, and yet it was there that the majority lost the zeal that had been engendered by flag waving orators and throbbing drums. One week at the Bull Ring and the recruit was more or less a skeptic and his patriotism had vastly weakened.

Six of us left our tent and went up the hill to lines that had been occupied by a large draft going to join Scottish battalions. They had gone in the night and their tents were empty of all but a few blankets. We gathered those blankets and put them into one tent, well in the rear, and there we moved all the worldly goods with which we were endowed, and sat quiet.

We heard the usual wranglings in the muddy lanes below us and heard the sergeants shouting and haranguing, and then, through our tent flap, we saw the column march away. We looked at each other, and grinned. It was worth the risk. Four lay back in their blankets and slept the morning away. Freddy, one of us, sat writing letters. He was a changed man. He was more kind and considerate than he had been before, and he would not mention his dream unless we asked him about it. Never once did he alter his opinion. He himself, and the six others, were "for it."

I sat in my corner of the tent, there was plenty of room now, and began my diary, the first of four little books that were to carry all the impressions that I could place in words. As I wrote I looked around and thought of all that had happened in a few short months.

In August, 1914, I had enlisted, or tried to enlist, with the 17th Battalion. Their officer had turned me down with caustic comment. "We can get enough good men," he said, "without taking them we've got to repair." My defect was bad teeth, broken while playing hockey, and never properly attended. Later in the fall I tried to join the 25th, in which my youngest brother was a sergeant, but without avail. There was no mention of my molars, I was simply told that I could not join, and that the main reason was that my brother was with them and that it would not be fair to our widowed mother. I know now that Steve, my brother, had requested that I be turned down.

Disheartened by my failures I went to western Canada and worked there on different ranches. Steve and I had been more like David and Jonathan than brothers. We had fads in common, our likes and dislikes were so mutual that we could read each other's mind. We followed baseball and hockey in the big leagues and were such red-hot fans that we knew the batting averages of every leading player both in the American and National League. His favourite was Nap Lajoie and my hero was Ty Cobb. It was the same in hockey, he boosting Cyclone Taylor and I favouring Art Ross.

They would not let him come home on leave before the battalion sailed and so he stole out of barracks, avoided all the military police and rode blind baggage to a safety zone. The famous "Van Doos" were training in Amherst, our home town, and their police were checking all soldiers from the 25th. Two of them intercepted Steve. He talked frankly with them and gave them fair warning, but they were zealous M.P.'s and so he left them in the snow with sore heads as souvenirs. He was only eighteen years old but he weighed one hundred and eighty pounds and had the strength of two men.

He kept in hiding while in town but each day came to the little grocery where I worked, and there we talked long hours over the more serious things of life and when he left he said, "Bill, if there is anything I can do for you, just let me know, and if I don't come back maybe I'll find a way to come sometime and whisper in your ear."

He said it in his jocular manner, but knowing him as I did, I shivered at the time, and never forgot.

He went to France in September, 1915, and the next month was in a trench on Hill 60 that was mined by the Germans. Only fragments were found of him and a dozen of his comrades. I was working in a harvest field in Saskatchewan, pitching sheaves on a wagon, when Steve walked around the cart and confronted me. He said not a word but I knew all as if he had spoken, for he had on his equipment and was carrying his rifle. I let the fork fall to the ground and the nearest man came running to me, thinking I had taken ill. I did not tell him what I had seen, but I left the field, and never pitched another sheaf of grain.

All that day, and the next, and the next, I wandered by myself around the prairie, and then the message came, a wire, "Steve has been killed. Come home." I went back home, and could not rest. Three times I had been rejected, for I had tried to go with a Western battalion, and there did not seem a chance. But I went again to enlist as the Nova Scotia Highland Brigade was forming – and was passed without a question.

Fourteen years have not removed the rancor that bit my whole being. Why did they not let me go before? Now I had to go with men who had never wanted to join, to be a late-goer, and it was rank injustice. I went to camp in that mood and it was small condolence to find that there were hundreds of others in like position, big, fit men who had been more than once rejected by mosquito-brained recruiting officers.

It was a long summer, that of '16. In my soured frame of mind I was often in trouble with officers and non-coms, and I refused to take promotion. One stripe was forced on me at last and led to my being imprisoned in the "fox farm," a wired enclosure on a hill back of the camp. There I served a sentence that lasted till just before we sailed. On Friday, the 13th of October, on the 13th trip of the "Olympic," we left Halifax. A dozen idle onlookers watched our battalion march on board at dusk, and we left the harbour as if by stealth.

I was not long in England. There was leave, a six-day affair, a course in wiring, learning futile "apron" stunts that I never saw again, a few days fatigue at Witley, and we were away to France, a draft of men for the Black Watch. I had had more trouble to incite my bitterness. The medical inspector turned me from the draft on account of my teeth, and when I asked that they be put in order, he had replied that there was not time. Across the road a draft of the 134th Battalion was on dental parade. Going to one chap who was my build I offered to take his place. He assented gladly and I put on his tunic and balmoral. The dental officer looked at me grimly and told me I needed eight teeth pulling and filling. I asked him if he could not pull them all, and he seized his pliers. A few minutes later I was before our company commander requesting to be replaced on draft. He looked at my mouth, and agreed. I went that last evening to Godalming and had a decent meal, a good bath and an hour's enjoyment of fine music, then was seized at camp for being out of bounds. I went to France under open arrest.

Tommy was a queer chap. None had better intentions, and yet he was always doing the wrong thing; he was too impulsive. He yawned and stretched and sat up. "I can hear them canaries up in the Bull Ring," he said. "That Welsh sergeant is yapping like a fox terrier. Over at the bags the bayonet lad is spitting blood and telling the boys that the only good German is a dead one. He said yesterday that if he had fifty Germans in a row he could go along and cut the throats of every one of them. Did you ever hear such rot?"

The others awoke and sat up, and grinned. We had all had our fill of this "killing" stuff and we hated the whole game of Le Havre, from the French women and kids that ran alongside as we marched trying to sell "Apoo, choc'lay, orange," to the hollow-backed, hoarse-voiced, yellow-banded non-coms who stood at the entrance to the Bull Ring and barked "Press on your butts! Correct your slopes!" We went down to the "dining hall" and got our dinners.

One waded through slimy, filthy mud to the door of the long dirty hut. Inside, at the entrance, men *broke* up loaves of bread and the size of your hunk depended on your luck. Another poured you a tin of cold, greasy tea and perhaps you got a piece of stringy, odious meat in your mess-tin top. You went to long tables and ate your food from your fingers. Everything was dirty, and the food was nauseating, and the place hardly fit for a stable. Presently an officer and sergeant would enter the front of the hut, walking very rapidly. They would not look to right or left but hurry to the rear door. By it they would pause just long enough to shout. "Any complaints, men?" and then they vanished before anyone could reply.

No one found us in our retreat. The boys came back at night, cursing anew the "canaries" who chased them about the muddy Bull Ring. Everyone thought we had been detained for camp fatigues, and the look of the camp decided them that their lot had been better. A week more we stayed in our tent and then went up the line. We were to go to the 42nd Royal Highlanders, a sergeant told us, in the famous Seventh Brigade. "How famous?" we asked, and he told us that it contained the Princess Pats, the Royal Canadians, the Forty-Niners, who were a very fine battalion, and that the Brigade had done great work at the Somme. It had come to the Vimy area and we were to fill gaps in the Black Watch battalion.

The night before we were to go up the line I thought a long while of Steve, and of Phyllis. I had not mentioned her to anyone, not even to my half-brother, Hubert, who was in England. He had come with the High-landers but had not been able to get on the draft.

We had had two days in London, seeing the Tower, the Zoo, Crystal Palace, St. Paul's, Westminster Abbey, and all the other major features of that great city. The evening before we had gone to see "Choo Chin Chow." I was walking along the Strand wondering what next to see or where to go, when an officer spoke to me. As a rule I avoided all those who wore Sam Brownes, but one always obeyed a summons. He asked me about my Highlander's feather, and where I had lived in Canada, and what I was doing in London. I tried to tell him the part I wished most to see, and how I liked the "Old Curiosity Shop," and my visit to Stratford-on-Avon, and he invited me to come with him on a motor ride. I got a few necessities for an over-night stop, and went.

We went from Paddington through a sunlit country, past the turreted mass of Windsor Castle, over the shimmering Thames, in and out of Maidenhead and through an English part of England. There were green, shadowy valleys, sharp little hills, a countryside soft in the glow of evening sun, woods, trickling brooks, wide pastures, a long street of quaint, low red-tiled houses, an old tavern with an ancient sign, "The Black Boar." Something gripped me, held me. I turned to the officer. "If you'll let me out here, please," I said, "I'd like to stay over night."

He acceded quietly. "I hope you like it," he said. "I'll be going back to-morrow and I'll pick you up." Something had urged me to stop there. I had intended going with the officer to his home, but it was as if some person had pulled me from my seat. I went into the Inn and after some difficulty in getting myself understood, arranged for a bed and meals. Then, outside again, I strolled on through the village. A rambling, ivy-covered rectory, nestling in a rose garden and embowered in great sheltering trees, was within easy reach of a little, gray, weather-beaten church. A soft wind, an evening wind, almost imperceptible, brought to me the sound of running water, a humming droning music that fitted the harmony of the evening.

The street was very quiet with only a few children playing in a field and an old man smoking his pipe on the bench outside the Inn. I passed down a narrow lane and found the little droning waterfall. It was by the ruins of an old water mill, and as I stood there drinking in the scene I suddenly shivered. It was dusk, and a strange chill blew towards me as if an unseen door had opened.

I turned swiftly, and there stood a girl. She had appeared like a phantom, but she was very warm and real, for she took my hand and welcomed me to the village. "I am so glad," she said, "that you have come."

We talked about England, and her past, and a little about Canada, then she began to listen in a curious way, as if she could hear things a long way off. I asked her the reason, and her answer chilled me as the cold breath had done. "I am comparing voices," she said. "Yours and his."

"His?" I exclaimed. "Whose?"

She glanced at me impatiently. "Your brother's, of course," she said. "Steve's."

I did not start or cry questions, though she had not asked my name. It seemed, all at once, as if I had entered a different sphere of existence, that such a coincidence were natural and that it was not mine to either doubt or query. We talked long there together and when we parted she told me that Steve had told her that I would come. I believed her.

The next day the officer came and took me back to London. I had not asked a question at the Inn, and I knew nothing about Phyllis, except that she lived with her uncle in a cottage next to the rectory, and that she had met Steve in London. The officer chatted a little as he drove, but we were each preoccupied with our thoughts. He was a tolerant, easygoing fellow with Cambridge manners and that peculiar English drawl so often affected. I never saw him again.

We were glad when the train pulled out of Le Havre. In mud and slush and a snowstorm we had been paraded through an open hut, stripped naked save for boots that the muck tugged from our feet, and examined by a doctor who sat in the gloom beside a table and checked off names. He did not even look up as I passed by and went, growling and fuming, to dress again. Tommy was especially excited. "We're away from all that blasted outfit down there," he said, "and I'm sure they make it so rotten purposely, and then a chap's *glad* to go to the trenches."

A little party of us had stuck together, Tommy and I, the group I had mentally dubbed the "Fatal Six," Earle, a big-shouldered farm lad, Baxter another, and Laurie, my cousin. The train moved slowly and as it went we heaved from the window the body belts that had been issued, odd tins of bully, and enough ammunition to reduce our loads to a reasonable weight. That track from Le Havre must have been surrounded by such material, as each soldier dumped at least one quarter of his belongings.

We arrived at Rouen, and Tommy grew eager. "This place is noted for something, isn't it?" he asked. I reminded him of Joan of Arc, and we found the place where she was burned, and where William the Conqueror had died, and walked about admiring many buildings. When we got back to the train we were threatened for being away so long.

All the time we had been at Le Havre we had had no mail, and now as we came in sight of Mount St. Eloi a sergeant brought us a cartload of parcels. There were no letters, but all our Christmas parcels had arrived at one time, earlier than we expected, and while we were at a miserable overnight stand.

All day we had had little but tea and bully and we gorged on fruit cake and fudge and other good things.

In the morning a dull thudding, thumping noise woke us, and it continued. We sat up and looked at each other. It was very cold and we were shivering and shaking as we got dressed, while deep inside us there was a queer tightening, a funny feeling. Part of it was caused by too much fruit cake, but the rest was caused by the thunder of the guns. We wondered and wondered, and our parcels lost their importance. We drank the tea a surly army cook served us, and then went to the French house – we had slept in a barn – with all the things left over, chocolate and cakes and candy. Three skinny women and a swarm of kids almost fought over us as we gave them the lot.

As we passed Mount St. Eloi and its twin towers I dug up a little more history for Tommy. "The hill itself is over 400 feet above the sea level," I said, "and that is a seventh-century church occupying the site of an abbey built ages ago by the bishop of Noyon, whose name was St. Eloi."

He looked at me. "Where did you get all that dope?" he asked.

"In a little French guide book I bought in London," I said. "I've got it with me. What's the use of coming over here on a trip if you don't know what you're looking at?"

He grinned. "Tell that to Howard," he advised. Howard was a big-boned man who had been a sergeant in the brigade, and had reverted to ranks to come to France. He was one of the few men that the Bull Ring had not changed; he seethed with the fervor of platform patriots.

At Le Havre he had heard Tommy raving about the methods of those in authority, and how he intended dodging everything he could. "Be British," roared Howard. "What did you come over here for?"

Tommy looked at him in an odd way. "Damned if I know," he said. "Adventure, mostly. How did your ticket read?"

"Adventure!" blared old Howard. "I come to fight for my country, for the flag, and for the right."

"Good boy," soothed Tommy, "but how in heck do you know you're in the right?"

We had to get between them then, for Howard was ready to represent the British bulldog in realistic manner. He went to the trenches, and shortly after made close acquaintance with a five-nine shell. He was not seriously damaged, but his patriotism received a blow. He got back to England and held forth there on the glorious crusade on which we were embarked. It was much safer across the Channel.

At the transport lines we were lined up for an inspection. We had marched and trudged through mud and water, in a drizzle, until we were ready to collapse, and we all felt that it was well that there were no more Christmas parcels. A brick-hued, bulging officer inspected us. He looked as if he had been bred in the purple hielands o' bonnie Scotland, and he talked as if he considered himself the repository of the regimental honour. He told us that we must realize what great privilege was ours to come and fight in the ranks of such a company as the Royal Highlanders. He hoped, he said, that we would always do our best – and his tone implied that he thought our best would be pitiful enough – and that implicit obedience to all orders would be very much to our advantage. Then, before he dismissed us, he looked sternly at Tommy and said that he trusted that none of us would become a bar sinister on the famed Black Watch escutcheon, or words to that effect. Tommy had moved impatiently and said things under his breath. Inspections roused him, enraged him. They were, to men of spirit, a degrading thing. You were herded like cattle into fields or yards and there stood to await the pleasure of some be-ribboned personage who gazed at one as if he were really lower in worth than a good horse. You look straight in front and the steps come closer and closer as the mighty one and his retinue goes down the line, and then a cold, supercilious face is before yours, and with creaking, shining leather and immaculate khaki they pass as you try to thrust back at them a gaze of impenetrable indifference.

That night we went to Neuville St. Vaast and joined the battalion. Arthur, and big Herman, and Earle, and Laurie, and boy-faced Mickey, and Freddy, and Sam, and Ira, and Melville, and Baxter, and myself were shunted into a cellar in which were timbers holding shreds of wire that had once been bunks. Rats ran into holes as we lit candles and then came boldly back and stared at us. It was a cold and wet-smelling place. We sat on our packs and stared around. Not an order had been given us, we knew nothing about the lines, where we drew food, or what platoons we were supposed to be with. Some of the men were restless, and nervous. Tommy answered them sharply. "Let these Royal gents do the worrying," he said. "They know where to find us."

In the next cellar the same condition existed. Hughey was there, a hairy, thick-shouldered man; Joe, an ex-policeman; Charley, an old school mate of mine; Billy, a man who always complained; Glenn, a giant of a fellow bred beside the sea; Gordon, big-framed and good-natured; Christensen, a Dane; Eddie, an athlete from my home town; and Jerry, a fine, clean-living youngster away from home for the first time. There were a few others lined up in a passageway between, but these men were my friends. Tommy and I went above and explored our area. A path led around ruins to numerous other dugouts and cellars. We went down one entrance and looked around. It had splendid bunks and was fitted with hooks for equipment and rifles, and was heated by braziers. "They shoved us in that hole because we're new," blazed Tommy, when we were outside again. "It's the old army game."

"Sure," I agreed, "but in six months' time we'll do the same with other new ones."

"That don't fix things now," he growled, and we went on down a side path to where light glimmered from an odd corner. As we looked a man came out of the low entrance, and he dragged his pack after him.

"Are you chaps looking for a billet?" he asked.

"You bet," said Tommy.

"Go right in there, then," said the man. "There's bunks and a stove and extra blankets."

Ten minutes later Earle and Laurie and Baxter and Tommy and I were in that cellar. Our equipment was hung in place and we were reposing on our different beds. No one came to disturb us and we had a comfortable night, the best we had had in France.

Next day Tommy and I went outside and looked around. We saw signs, "Keep low. Use trench in daytime," and we went along the trench until we came to a Y.M.C.A. canteen. We had money and so we bought plenty of tinned goods and chocolate and went back to our little home. There we stayed all day. At night we went again and found the sergeant-major's place. He was a dour-faced man, very Scotch, but we knew instantly that he was a "white" man and never had occasion to alter our opinion. We asked for mail and he piled out letters, over sixty for the five of us. On the way back we met Mickey. "How did you like it?" he asked.

"Like what?" blurted Tommy.

"The working party." Then Mickey told us that all of his crowd, all of the draft but us, had gone to some distant trench and filled and emptied sandbags until nearly morning. It had rained and was beastly cold, and the new men were used like dogs, so he said. We grinned at each other and went back to our billet.

For three days we drew rations and stayed in that cellar and then, through Tommy being anxious to see what the front was like, we ventured out and "fell in" with the crowd. The sergeant in charge stared at us, but said nothing. He was a small man with a vitriol tongue and seemed to resent us. We were given in charge of a corporal, Stevenson, a veteran of South Africa, and went down a long trench until we were at the front. I thrilled. At long last I had arrived.

We had got used to the slamming roar of gun fire, and now we heard machine guns barking and snapping, and bullets came singing overhead to go swishing into the distant darkness. Some struck on wire or other obstructions and we heard the sibilant whine of ricochets. We had sandbags to fill. One man held them and the other shovelled in the gruel-like mud. When twenty or more were done, a man jumped up on top and emptied the bags as they were handed up to him. It was ticklish work and one often had to jump into the trench as bullets were humming about all night.

We got soaked to the skin. The cold slime ran down our wrists as we lifted the bags, and we stood so long in the mire that our feet were numbed, sodden things. All that next day we growled at Tommy for having caused us such displeasure, and at night Stevenson sought us out. We were to go, Tommy and Arthur and I, to an emplacement used by a big mortar they called the "flying pig."

When we got there we noticed a peculiar odour. All that shapeless ruin of Neuville St. Vaast stank of decay and slime, but this new smell halted us. A corporal stepped from the gloom. "Here's bags," he said. "Go in there and gather up all you can find, then we'll bury it back of the trench. Get a move on."

A flying pig had exploded as it left the gun and three men had been shredded to fragments. We were to pick up legs and bits of flesh from underfoot and from the muddy walls, place all in the bags and then bury them in one grave. It was a harsh breaking in. We did not speak as we worked. When we were done the corporal told us we could go back, we were through, but Tommy and I lingered in a bay and stared over the dark flickeringly-silhouetted landscape.

Over the tangle of wire in front lay the no man's land about which we had heard. Not two hundred yards away were the Germans in their trenches, and I wondered if there were Tommys and Arthurs and Big Hermans among them. Then I thought of Steve and wondered what it had been like up Ypres way when he arrived, and I thought of Phyllis, the last glimpse I had had of her face, cameo-like in the light of a window. A thin stalk of silver shot up as we looked, curved over in a graceful parabola and flowered into a luminous glow, pulsating and wavering, flooding the earth below with a weird whiteness. It was a Very light. We craned our necks and stared. Jumbled earth and debris, torn earth, jagged wreckage; it looked as if a gigantic upheaval had destroyed all the surface and left only a festering wound. Everything was indefinite and ugly and distorted.

We continued doing working parties, and gradually we got acquainted with the rest of the company. The men were not our equals in physique and, I saw, not of equal mentality. Given equal chances and we had no need to ask favours of them in any matter. The "originals" held themselves aloof, the others were fairly friendly.

We went back to Mount St. Eloi and were billeted in huts on the hillside. It was wet and freezing cold at night. There was little attempt to drill, for which we were truly thankful. At last we had reached a land where the most important items were not the correctness of a slope or the forming of fours by numbers.

After the first day of sleeping and resting the men grew garrulous, and we listened eagerly to all they said. The order against fraternizing with the Germans on Christmas Day was first jeered at, and then flying pigs and

"Minnies" were compared. We heard different craters mentioned glibly, such as Patricia Crater, Common Crater, Birken, Durand, and Vernon, and then we learned that an officer and party had rushed across at dusk on New Year's Eve and captured two German prisoners without incurring a casualty. They had slipped across no man's land without being seen and had completely surprised the two enemy sentries. I was thrilled as I listened. What adventure! Tommy could hardly remain still, and he whispered to me about it after the lights were out.

Across from me there slept a Scotchman who was always singing "Maggie frae Dundee," or quarreling with Stevenson, who had charge of the hut. Next him was a tall clean-built man, MacMillan, an original 92nd man. He and I became friends, and he told me about the Somme, and what he said sank in my memory.

We had been a month in France when we went back for our second trip in the line. It was the first week of January and the wind was raw with driving rain. Once more we were on working parties, this time in the "Quarry Line," cleaning trenches and helping with dugouts. At nights the Very lights soared like great soap bubbles and often there were salvos of shells near us. There would be a screaming, whistling sound, a clanging, crashing explosion, and clods of earth and chalk would come flying about, then smoke and fume would drift across the trench and sting our nostrils.

All this time we had not got to know an officer, and had seldom seen one. They were in better quarters, we knew, and would not come through the mud and rain to bother us. One night Tommy and I were detained by Stevenson, who was determined to finish a parapet before we returned. We were very wet and cold and the rations were slim, six men to a loaf of bread, and only a few hard tack and tins of bully to help out. The hot tea and occasional mulligan were very acceptable. We got our mess-tins from our bunks and went over to the corner where a sullen-faced man dished out "the dinner." He stayed in the dugout and heated it in dixies over a very "gassy" fire, and we did not envy him his lot, though he avoided all shell-fire. There was no tea for us, he said, and as we stood looking at one another Stevenson came and got his mess-tin full. I stepped forward and looked in the dixie. There was plenty more in it, and I said so very clearly. The cook looked up and snarled that we had better be in France five minutes before starting to run things, and Tommy took charge. He offered eagerly to make the fellow's face much less an ornament than it was, and gave him just one short minute to fill his mess-tin. The cook looked up and down, and gave us our portion. Later, when we were supposed to be sleeping, I heard the "oldtimers" discussing us. It was agreed that it would be a bad policy to try to "run" us, and the cook had little sympathy.

The next night there was great excitement. An officer and four men were to try to rush an enemy post on Patricia Crater. We waited tensely after they had gone. Not a sound was heard over the way, then; much later, they returned. They had gotten over safely without being seen, but when they entered the German post no sentries were there. Dumbfounded, they waited, and waited, resolving to capture the first Hun to pass along. None came and the moon began to rise, shedding too much light for a safe return. So they cautiously withdrew before any "goose stepper" came to their clutches.

We felt old soldiers as we went back to Mount St. Eloi that time, and "Maggie frae Dundee" rang out merrily. We ragged Freddy but he remained as inconsolable as ever. Big Herman kidded him continually. This time there were parades and we saw our company commander, a genial-looking gentleman whose appearance I rather liked. We were marched to baths, an old building the wind whistled through, and which was floored with muddy slime. There was a tiny trickle of water from overhead pipes, always failing when a man succeeded in soaping himself before he became too cold to endure the operation. We had little soap and we slipped about on the greasy surface and helped each other all we could. When we went to get dressed we found ourselves with shirts we could not enter, with unmatched socks, anything a bleary-eyed assistant cared to pitch our way.

When we went back to the line our sergeant told me that I would be one for Vernon Crater, and from the way he said it I judged that something was unusual. I asked questions and learned that it was a three-sentry post not usually held in daylight, and not over fifty yards from the German lines. We were to hold it for four days.

We went into the trenches heavily laden. It was bitterly cold and all the ground was frozen hard. We wore leather jerkins over our greatcoats and had socks pulled over our hands in place of gloves; there had only been enough of the latter to supply the oldtimers. It was very clear weather and every sound carried, so that we moved carefully and slowly. The main trench was a long black-shrouded ditch full of dark figures, scuffling, muttering to each other, and there were hissed curses when a steel helmet clanged against a rifle.

We reached a low-walled sap where a sentry stood and pointed to Smaillie, the lance-corporal in charge. Up we went, moving carefully, bowed over like skulking Indians. We were relieving the Princess Pats and four of their men came hurriedly by us and went on to the main trench. Our post was a wide affair, in three sections. In the right-hand corner, like an enlarged well with a firestep, two men were placed, a short lad, Dunbar, one of our draft, and Doucette, another. They were to take turns in doing sentry in that position. On the left, ten yards from them, was a similar post, and in it were Laurie and old "Dundee." I was at the centre post, a cup-like hollow, and MacMillan was my mate. Behind us was a roofed space about six feet square and in it Smaillie stayed. He had a seat there, and his flares and pistol, as well as extra bombs and ammunition. A blanket was hung over the rear entrance.

We prepared to meet the cold. I had drawn sandbags over my boots and tied them at the knee and ankle. We had on our woollen caps underneath the steel helmets, and little cloth gas bags to put our heads in in case of gas attack. They were frightful arrangements with nozzles to breathe through, and we were glad when the box respirators arrived. We had sandbags over our rifle muzzles, and kept breech covers on them all the time. Our rations, mess-tins, and haversacks were in the shelter with Smaillie.

MacMillan told me all there was to learn about sentry duty, and I did not duck when the first flares went up. We could hear plainly the Germans coughing in their trenches, hear them walking on frozen boards, and hear the creaking of a windlass drawing chalk up from some dugout. The first night passed uneventfully. At daylight we put up small periscopes on slivers stuck in the sandbagged parapet and watched in them till dark. Several times during the day we heard "fish tails" and "darts," German grenades, going over into our lines, but none came near us.

The next night I saw my first uncaptured German. I had looked at prisoners in the cages back of the lines, and saw their queer top boots and gray uniforms with the two buttons at the back of the tunic, but now I had seen a real enemy. He was only a boy, as young-looking as Mickey, and he was standing waist-high above his trench wall as one of our flares burst directly above him and placed him in dazzling light.

He did not move at first, but his face looked very white and ghost-like, and then I knew that he had seen me for I was standing as high as he on our side. Some wild impulse caused me to wave to him – later I would not have done it – and he waved back. The light flicked out and I jumped down as MacMillan cursed me soundly. After midnight I stepped back to talk with Smaillie and as it was bright moonlight pushed aside the blanket at the rear and looked out. Ping! A bullet embedded itself in the wooden post beside me. I ducked in again, very frightened. A few minutes later there were hurried steps outside. It was a corporal from the trench and he had come to see if I were hit or not. A new draft of men, mostly New Brunswickers, French-Canadians, had come into the line and had been placed on duty. One of them had thought I was a German, had been watching our post, and only his poor aiming had saved me. I felt shaky for a time.

The third night in we saw more Germans. A light snow had fallen and whitened the scalloped wilderness between the lines. There was a wrecked cart near the German wire, and I used the part of a wheel that was above the mud as a guide when looking in the periscope. As I peered at it in the night it blotted out, then appeared again. I told MacMillan and he was instantly alert. In a short time he had detected two of the enemy crawling towards us. We had visions of special leave and medals if we could capture those two prowlers, but we felt that if the rest were to assist there would be little more than a complimentary message from the colonel. So we prepared to catch the pair ourselves. We stripped our greatcoats and equipment with great haste, shed our steel hats and examined our rifles. Unluckily mine had been stood at the back of the post and water from melted snow had run down the barrel and frozen. MacMillan's had the breech uncovered and it was a lump of mud and ice. We could not use the Lee-Enfields, and we jumped for bombs. If the Germans had come to that post that hour they would have had an easy time. We could only use our bayonets. The bombs were little blocks of frozen mud, and we could not clean them in time to use them. We worked frantically with our army issue knives, and the Germans, after a few minutes crawling around, slipped back under their wire and disappeared.

When morning came we had cleaned our rifles and bombs and everything was in working order. We told Smaillie what we had seen and he sent up flares during the dark hour before dawn, fearing that a raid might be intended. I was quite excited and MacMillan was also nervous. Each morning a sergeant had brought in a rum issue just before it was light, and always there was a surprise because I did not care for mine. Six of our draft would not take it. This morning the sergeant was a little late, and an officer was with him. As they served the rum they talked to us and the officer seemed a very fine man. When I did not take my rum he told the sergeant to give my share to old "Dundee." Then he put his foot on the firestep and said he wanted to look over, as he had been told that our post was the nearest of any to the German trench. I told him it was not safe to look, that snipers had shot away my periscope not five minutes before. He said he would move quickly, and rose up. I was so close that I seized him without reaching and tried to hold him back. It was too late. Clang! His steel helmet flew back over the rear wall and lodged in the wire, and brains and blood were spilled all over the front of my overcoat and on my arms as the officer sank down at my feet. He had been shot between the eyes with an explosive bullet that had torn his helmet away, breaking the strap under his chin. It was the first death I had witnessed and yet I found myself strangely calm. I straightened the dead man in the trench, leaving just room enough to stand beside him, and placed a clean sandbag over his face. MacMillan was as white as paper and trembling.

We told the others what had happened and the sergeant rushed over from "Dundee's" corner, swearing wildly. There was nothing he could do, however, but go back and report, and we could not remove the corpse until it was dark again. The sergeant went down the sap on his hands and knees as it was getting lighter. Old "Dundee" was like a wild man. He cursed the Germans and proceeded to clean his rifle, swearing vengeance. I heard a report and rushed to his post. Laurie was standing there looking quite pale. "Dundee" had let off his rifle as he cleaned it and the bullet had gone under Laurie's legs and struck an iron post, splintering itself. One fragment had gone through the top of his foot and it stung him sharply. "Dundee" was shaking and wilder than ever; he had had too much rum. He suddenly raised up and put his rifle over the parapet. Crack! He fell back before he could pull the trigger. The bullet had gone in his cheek on one side and out his eye on the other. He threshed about in agony and blood poured from him. Laurie got out his field dressing and he and MacMillan bandaged the old chap as well as they could but the bleeding would not stop. We looked at each other. The orders were that no one was to leave the post in daylight, but could we let old "Dundee" bleed to death? I tore off my equipment and started down the sap as I had seen the sergeant do, and Smaillie did not check me. I was half way along it when I tired of slow crawling and rose in a crouching position and ran. Crack! A bullet burned the back of my neck just as a hot iron would have done. I dropped and crawled the rest of the way, and was very scared when I reached the main trench. A stretcher-bearer and our sergeant at once went back with me, taking a stretcher with them, and a runner was sent to make sure the doctor was at his dugout. We got back to the post without incident and got old "Dundee" on the stretcher. Taking him out was a terrible task. He would not lay quiet or listen to orders, and had to be forced down while the stretcher was worked along the sap, dragged and pushed by the men at either end. They were an hour getting him to the main trench. All day I sat beside the dead man.

At dark we were relieved by the Pats and I barely escaped being detailed as one of a party to carry the officer to the quarry line where the transport would get him and take him out for burial. We went to Neuville St. Vaast again and into caves there. It was weird to go down and down and suddenly enter a quiet that startled one. The place was musty and had a damp chill that was peculiarly depressing. Before morning we were called out, five of us, as a ration party, and I saw how easily a man might get a "blighty." We passed an old ruin with a long wall extending beyond it and light flickered through a small opening, perpetually shifting and stirring in a noiseless flighty dance. One aperture overlooked no man's land and the flickers were from the flares which rose and fell all night long. As we paused by the opening there was a sudden snapping of machine gun bullets overhead, but they were disregarded as the wall protected us. We filed by and the fifth man yelled in pain. A bullet had come through that brick-sized opening and entered his leg. We bandaged him and he went cheerfully "down the line." At the place where we got our rations I saw Freddy, and spoke to him. He was as wan and unchanged as ever, and told me, in dull voice, that one of our draft, a man from my own county, had been killed that afternoon.

When we returned with the rations I slept several hours and then was wakened and told that I was to take my pack and go with three other men to Mount St. Eloi. There we would meet a sergeant who would take us to a bombing school. I hated the idea, but made no objection. I had had my fill of talks on explosives, and had listened to dreary descriptions of the hairbrush bomb, the "lemon," the "cricket ball," and all the rest and I especially despised the wooden-handled ones with long cloth streamers, but it never pays a new man to argue with an oldtimer.

We met the sergeant and went down the hill and across the road to long huts and found ourselves with men from the other battalions of the brigade, and I discovered that instead of all those silly arrangements I hated that we were to be instructed only in shooting rifle grenades and throwing Mills bombs. I was pleased at once, and when I found the hours short and rations plentiful was very glad I had come.

The next day at noon as we lolled in our bunks there was a sudden shrill tearing sound, and a terrific explosion just outside. Pieces of shrapnel came through the side of the hut. We leaped to the floor and raced from the building and into the field. Wheeeee. A second one came, and there were cries of "stretcher bearer – stretcher bearer!" Four men were killed and several wounded by those shells.

To my delight I learned quickly the proper elevation for the rifle grenades and made a top score the first day I tried. Throwing Mills bombs was easy for me. I had played ball in Canada and soon got the knack of the overhand throw, consequently I was called in by the sergeant and told that I would be given top notch marks for my work. I thanked him, and thought no more of it. The battalion had come to the old huts at Mount St. Eloi and had it rather easy, as well as us.

When our six-day class was up I reported back to my platoon, and was astounded to find that I had been transferred to the battalion bombers. I, a new man, was to be among the grand selected ones, the specialty men. The others chaffed me and said I had pulled strings to get my shift, and I really disliked leaving them. Freddy was not a cheerful tonic, but the rest were splendid comrades. The weather had become even colder and we went into the front line again and once more relieved the Pats.

CHAPTER II

I Shoot a German

The bombers were kind to me, and I found myself paired with Sammy Sedgewick, a real gentleman. He was a very fine, clean-living fellow and we got on well together. He told me all that was necessary about my work, which was to be chiefly patrolling the trenches. It was possible that we might be called to bomb a post or assist with some offensive scheme, but on the whole there was no intimation of anything unusual. We had good dug-outs and plenty of rations, and our hours were much easier than in the company, where a man did six hours on and six hours off with monotonous regularity all the time we were in the line.

One came down from his post, chilled, half-dazed from lack of sleep, and pushed his way into the crowded underground to his chicken-wire bunk. There he could lay on his elbows and eat his rations, and consider himself lucky if there were any lukewarm tea to drink. The warmth of the men thawed the earthy walls enough to cause them to ooze water. Rats were everywhere, great, podgy brutes with fiendish, ghoulishly-gleaming eyes. They came at night on the parapets and startled one so that he thrust at them with his bayonet, or crawled over him as he lay under his blanket in his bunk trying to "shiver himself warm." The bombers had it much better than the company men.

We patrolled the crater line, visiting all the trench posts and in the stretches between paused now and then and sent grenades into the German front. Then we would hurry along and so escape any possible retaliation. Such a procedure naturally roused the ire of the men doing sentry, who could not leave their stations, and we were soon unpopular. Sammy and I agreed not to play such a game, and not to shoot grenades unless we were certain of a target. We got them twice. One sentry called out to us and pointed out dark blurs that were working about the German wire. We sent two grenades among them and a Lewis gun helped complete the job. Later in the night another sentry told me that he had seen two Germans working at something just opposite his post. It was very frosty and still and we could hear a thumping sound as if they were hammering posts. I set my rifle carefully and fired. The elevation was exactly correct and the red flash of explosion was over the very spot aimed at. The sound of the report had not died away before a long-drawn yell sounded. The voice seemed that of a mere boy and his agonized screaming could be heard all along the crater line. I had the sound in my ears all the next day.

The enemy sent over "darts" in reply but none fell near us. It was as cold as ever the next night. Everything had frozen and no working parties moved anywhere. The ground was like rock. We moved constantly while on our rounds, as it kept us warm, but the sentries huddled in their corners and grew stupid from the cold. Several of them went to sleep on duty. This would have been a serious matter in some places, but our officers and non-coms made allowance for a man's condition. We were well managed. There had been no asinine drilling in muddy fields while we were out of the line, only necessary parades concerning equippage and pay and baths. Our rifles had to be kept clean, and our feet rubbed with whale oil to prevent frost bite, but there was no shining of brass and buttons. At one point we found a Lewis gun crew asleep, every man, and for a joke removed the gun, hid it, and wakened them by throwing bits of chalk. I do not think they went to sleep again when on post.

I saw one of our draft asleep, and wanted to wake him, but the officer making his rounds reached him first. He shook the fellow and then talked with him in a low voice, telling him the usual penalty for such neglect of duty. That man never forgot his lesson, or the kindness of the officer.

The cold continued, it being the coldest winter France had experienced in years. During those hours we wandered from post to post I thought of many things. Something in the eeriness of the line, great tumbled heaps of chalk, and rifts that were trenches, made one feel that danger was always near. Away on the Somme and up at the other end of the Ridge there was always shelling, and here and there machine guns chattered, but often our part of the sector would be quiet for an hour at a time. Only the stamping of feet, coughing, or the pounding of arms told where the sentries were, and overhead uncanny wailings crossed each other under the stars as the "big ones" went seeking cross roads and other back area targets.

I thought of Canada and its people, sleeping snugly in their beds, with only vague ideas of what war really meant, of the French folk in their cottages, many within range of the German guns, trusting that no sudden death would be their lot before morning, that some day the Allies must be victorious, shrugging their shoulders and meeting every fresh calamity with their laconic expression the soldiers termed "See la gare."

I thought repeatedly of Steve, and now understood more clearly many of the letters he had written while in Belgium. Sometimes I stopped at Mickey's post, or Melville's or Charley's and talked with them of the home town.

The war had changed men, changed them mightily. Down in dugouts where there was hardly room to breathe, men who had come from comfortable homes moved without complaints to their fellows. All grousing was reserved for the higher-ups, the "brass-hats" and the "big bugs" responsible for everything. The men were unselfish among themselves, instinctively helping each other, knowing each other, each with a balance and discipline of his own. We endured much. The dugout reeked with odours of stale perspiration and the sour, saline smell of clothing. There was not enough water to permit frequent washing, and whenever we could get warm the lice tormented us.

The vermin were everywhere. We could wash and change our shirts as often as we liked; within a few hours we were lousy again. Men squatted in their bunks beside candles and picked the seams of their clothing, sought the crawlers, always fought them, but never, while we were in those dugouts at Vimy, conquered them.

I talked with Tommy each night, and his vigorous comment was refreshing. He said that we were as uncivilized as in the beginning, that we were nocturnal beasts, hunting each other in packs, with the same mercies and feelings as wolves. He talked about his fellows and said that it was curious to note the influence the front had on different men. Everyone was puzzled about himself, wondering, and yet an open book to his comrades. I did not agree with such a view. Fear, he said, was at the back of every brain, and our talk was but to camouflage it.

One afternoon I had to go on an errand that led me up a trench called La Salle Avenue. Another man was going ahead of me and as we hurried along I heard a "phew-phew-phew" in the air. The man ahead looked over his shoulder and yelled. Crash! I was hurled against the trench wall, slammed against it, and for a moment knew nothing. A million bells rang in my ears. Lights danced and sparkled and I could not get my breath. Hands tugged at me and I got up to stare at a gaping, smoking crater not ten feet from where I had fallen. A big "rum jar" had fallen between the other man and myself, and though he was much further away than I, he was seemingly shell-shocked. He was taken back to a dugout and never again did front line work.

I was sick for an hour and my head ached and throbbed, but otherwise I was not affected. That night was very quiet. At times there was no shelling on the flanks, and there would be oppressive silence as the Very lights dropped silently and intermittently, their eerie glow tracing queer moving shadows across the desolate waste of chalk and dirty snow. A solitary rifle shot was startling, and the heavies overhead rumbled like express trains. I went down the trench and talked with Fernley, a very quiet, easygoing fellow. He had stood his rifle against the side of the trench and was pacing up and down and beating his chest with his arms in an effort get warm. We chatted awhile and then moved on.

I was not ten yards from him when – ping – a dart burst on the parapet several feet from where he was standing. I had turned as I heard the missile and to my surprise Fernley sank to the trench floor like a wet sack. I hurried to him and spoke to him, but he never answered. He was dead.

There was not a mark on him. A dart must strike almost beside one before doing great damage, and I was completely puzzled. I got the sergeant and he examined Fernley, and was mystified. We carried the dead man to the dressing station and they began to strip him. I went back to the trench and looked around, looked until I noticed the rifle still standing there, and – part of its bayonet was gone. The mystery was soon solved. The dart had exploded beside the bayonet and had blown three inches of the steel toward Fernley. His arms were extended as he beat himself and the piece pierced an armpit and entered his heart. Not a drop of blood had issued from the wound.

We were in supports again, and then back to the front trench, and this time I was excited. I was to do a reconnaisance with one of the non-coms. We crawled out under our wire and moved by inches, worming between Durand and Duffield Craters. After each yard or so we listened for a time and it was an hour before we were in position to look at the enemy wire and judge its strength. When we got back to the trench the bombers told me that a raid was to be made from both our craters and from the Patricia posts. The next day the Stokes mortars pounded the German line.

The raid was on the 13th of February, and zero was at 9.15 a.m. Six bombers were taken to Patricia and there we were given sixty grenades and told to shoot them all in two minutes, beginning at 9.13. It was ticklish work. In our hurry it would be easy to make a mistake and cause a premature burst, but no accident occurred and we got our barrage away on time. Then we went down to a tunnel entrance and awaited the raiders' return. Buglers were stationed in the crater posts to blow the recall. One officer and five men were wounded, the officer severely, and two prisoners were taken.

That night we were relieved by the "Van Doos." I offered to guide their bombers in to our particular dugout and was given the task. It was the first I had seen of the 22nd since they were in Amherst, and my impressions were rather mixed. They lagged in the trench, talking loudly, making much noise, and one man even played a mouth organ. We hurried as fast as we could, getting out before the company, and shortly after the Germans gave our friends a house-warming in the shape of a "Minnie" bombardment. We heard afterward that there were many casualties before morning.

The next day we marched and marched and marched, going through several towns, of which I only noticed Houdain, and on to Division. After the long session in the crater line, with little exercise, it was a hard grind. My legs grew woodenly stiff, my back was numbed and aching, and my shoulders were raw where the straps chafed. We staggered into billets and I was sent back to the company and told that the "battalion bombers" were no more. A re-organization was to take place, each platoon to have its own bombers and machine gunners, and I was not sorry. I wanted to be with the old crowd again.

When I woke in the morning I could barely move myself. The boys brought me my breakfast and I lay in my blankets until noon. Then the medical sergeant, a prince of a fellow, came and examined me, and asked about my experience with the "rum jar." He said that I had undoubtedly suffered from concussion, and that I had better remain in billets for the day. The next morning I went on the sick parade and the medical officer, after a brief examination, gave me a paper and told me to report to a medical hut in Bruay. I went at once, for I was missing an inspection, a review by General Nivelle.

I was at the hut in Bruay for two hours before the orderly there took my paper. A dozen of us sat in a chilly room and waited for our turn. The man next to me had sore feet and I judged from my paper that my heart was to be examined. After waiting until one o'clock, four hours, a doctor came and snatched my paper and the one from the man with bad feet, then he yanked me into the room. Four officers were there. They ordered me to remove my boots. I started to protest and explain, and was told to keep quiet. They looked my feet over and told me to dress them again, then pushed me out by another door. I don't know what happened to the man who needed my examination.

The medical sergeant told me to report again to the doctor, but he was a gruff man who had little use for the "other ranks" and I felt that I could carry on. At once I was notified for guard. We were marched to an old brick barn and reached our quarters overhead by a shaky ladder on the outside of the building. It was terribly cold and the barn had a hundred vents for the wind. We lay on bare boards and tried to keep warm but it was impossible. The sergeant went out and after a long time returned with a jug of rum. Earle was on the guard with me and neither of us, as a rule, took our ration, but we did that night. We were trembling with cold and the sergeant gave each of us a cigarette tin of the liquor. I felt as if I could not swallow it and after a time things seemed to move, but I was warmed. It came my turn to go down and stand sentry by the ladder but I found it a very difficult task to reach the ground. Once there I clung to the ladder and watched the estaminet nearby go wheeling around. Earle had as difficult a time when he came down, but when we were relieved each of us went to sleep and slept warm until morning.

Christensen, the Dane, got in wrong with the noncoms on Sunday. He was told to prepare for church parade and would not do so, saying that he had no religion, that he was an infidel. They crimed him for it and ever afterward he was given sharp treatment. I was in a billet with Billy, the complainer, Earle, Laurie, Flynn, a quaint Irishman who had false teeth, and Theriault and Roy, two of the New Brunswick draft. We were in a house and slept fairly warm, but one night a rat stole Flynn's teeth from where he had lain them by his head and went down between the walls with them. Flynn roused everyone, but never recovered his grinders. Theriault and Roy were comical chaps and we got on well together.

The sergeant-major called me to his billet one night and asked me if I cared to be promoted or not. Up to that hour I had been fairly content with my lot, but somehow – though I knew he meant it well – his words brought back all my old bitterness against the army. I refused to consider such a proposition, and he was far more courteous than I had expected. He told me that our draft was the finest bunch of men to join the battalion, though the 92nd had been considered an extra class, and that he wished to get some good N.C.O.'s from among us. I said nothing, but I knew that some of our men were of the very finest type, as well educated as any of the officers.

The weather continued cold and one of our draft became sick. He was in a barn lying on straw and had little attention other than that of his mates. He was a college graduate, from a splendid home, and he died in hospital after being moved, having been neglected too long. Several of the boys were highly roused over it, Tommy especially, and it was rumoured that Christensen, who had become stretcher bearer, wrote a letter to the lad's parents, a letter which was not allowed to go through, and for which he was again crimed.

The new platoons were formed and we were shifted in our billets. I found myself moved to the other side of the village and teamed with a man named McDonald, an "original" 42nd man who had been in the transport section but had come to grief through some infraction of rules, and so was sent back to the company. He was a very likeable chap and we were soon good friends. Through him I got acquainted with several of the oldtimers: Westcott, a lance-corporal; Martin, a Lewis gunner, and Davies, our sergeant who was the finest non-com I met in France.

One very bitter morning as we went from our billets to the cook kitchen, a considerable distance away, we passed the house where our company commander lodged. As we went by his window we heard him complaining to his batman that his shaving water was *too cold*. Tommy, a chap named Jasper, Arthur and myself had had for several mornings to use snow as water, rubbing it on our faces in lieu of washing, and trying to force a lather with the same. Water was very scarce. Tommy stopped and gave voice to feelings that we all had, and we appeared for parade without being shaved. Our officer was one sent to the company as a supernumerary, and he took great delight in putting us "up" for company office. Our major asked us why we had not shaved. "My shaving water was too cold," said Tommy, and Jasper, and Arthur and myself.

The major reddened furiously, he glared, then grinned, and looked severe again, and finally sentenced us to dig a much-needed latrine near our billets, and to do it after the usual parades. When the time came, a burly police escorted us to the garden of a French miner, and ordered us to go to work. In a short time the owner of the place appeared, and asked, in French, what we were doing. Arthur could speak French like a native, and he explained that we were going to plant some doubtful bombs there. They might explode and they might not, but it was not safe to have them in our billets. The Frenchman went wild. He rushed at us and tore the shovels from our hands and he almost clubbed our gallant escort, who finally bade us to stand by for further orders. We went back to our billets and, very strangely, were never recalled.

The 42nd had a fine football team and it defeated the R.C.R.'s, then the 49th, and we were marched to Marle les Mines to watch them play. They won the divisional championship and were presented with a silver bugle. Sir Robert Borden came and reviewed us, then General Lipsett and finally General Byng. All the old hands said that we were in for a bloody slaughter, after so many inspections, but we did not believe them – we had grown accustomed to "cook house" rumours. We knew, nevertheless, that we were to participate in a big battle, for we were training daily over tapes that represented the German trench system on the Ridge.

We had got to know Divion fairly well, and knew where to purchase eggs and chips and, occasionally, French bread. The rations were better than they had been in the line and we began to feel more like living. I often went to the kitchen of my billet to write letters or jot notes in my diary, and soon discovered that madame and her family were not the least disturbed by my presence. Mickey was with me one cold Saturday evening when the two bony daughters of the household calmly bathed beside the stove, and then the father came home and madame scrubbed from him the grime of the coal mines.

I had had just fatigue enough one day to clear me from parade and was going back to my billet when I met a man who, I often thought, came nearest of any to guessing my state of mind. He was Sergeant Cave of the scouts, a tall, shrewd-eyed man who knew his business. He was going then to arrange targets to shoot at and asked me if I cared to go along. I went, and found that the targets were simply tin cans stuck on a hillside, but I surprised the sergeant. In Canada I had made good scores with the Ross rifle, and I could shoot much better than the average soldier. My father, an officer of the old 93rd Regiment, had been an expert marksman.

We shot, five of his snipers and myself, at tin ends on the bank, a small target. In ten times I never missed, and then I punctured one at one hundred and fifty yards. The sergeant was excited and asked my name and my platoon. I talked with him a time and then went back to Tommy and the boys.

The battalion moved to Dumbell Camp, a miserable swamp in a wood near Villers Au Bois. We bagged slimy mud and made shelters, walls three feet high covered with corrugated iron, or rubber sheets, or anything we could salvage, and camouflaged the whole with branches. It rained and was very cold and the rations were very scarce. Never in France was I as hungry as then, and I would have eaten anything in the food line I could find in the muck.

From that mess we were rushed to the front line. The Germans had blown a mine north and adjoining Durrand Crater, and a party of them had been repulsed by our "A" Company which was in the line. Thirty yards of front line had been destroyed and it was important that a new trench be made, with saps leading to new posts. The Germans shelled the Quarry line and all the back area as we marched in, and the mud made the going hard. In addition, we had not had enough to eat and were almost sick from exposure to rains and mud. We had been almost drowned out of our shelters. More new men had joined us and among them was a pair, Slim and Joe, that no one wanted near them. "Slim" was a tall, thin, bony lad, not over seventeen, uneducated, who had been living like a gypsy until the war, and who did not know his parents. Joe, his mate, was a French-Canadian, who also was uneducated, and who had no dependents. They did not get any mail, were very slovenly in dress and drill, and would not wash or shave unless forced to do so.

As we entered the communication trench Slim fell in at my heels; Arthur was next to him and then Laurie. An officer named Stewart took charge of us, and we filed from the cover of the trench to open ground. Sharp orders were hissed. We had to dig in along tapes and we were in range of both snipers and machine guns. The mud was deep and we did not know our location. Each man worked frantically. A brigade wirer led the way and it so happened that I was first man out and farthest over. All around us there was a clamour of shell fire and machine guns were rattling. It was quite dark and flares were soaring in quick succession.

Slim stuck close to me and I had to thrust him back in his position. We dug and dug. I struck barbed wire in tangles, and the brigade man heard me and came with his cutters. As he left he groaned and sank to earth, shot through the body. Bullets were snapping all around us and Slim got down on his knees and huddled close to the earth, yet never slackened his shovelling. I did not draw a full breath until I had gotten below my wire, then I looked around. Arthur was sitting in the mud. I thrust past Slim and went to him and asked if he were sick. He looked at me and shook his head and would not speak. I insisted and he said, so low I could hardly hear him, "Freddy was right."

"Are you hit?" I asked, and he shook his head, then got up and began to work. I went back to my place, puzzled. He had never acted queerly before.

Almost immediately there was a call for stretcher bearers and then came word that Lieutenant Stewart, a finely built man, had been shot through the stomach. He died that night. I worked on and Slim kept pace with me. We soon had our strip as deep as required, and at last came word for us to go back. We started and had not gone a dozen feet when Arthur pitched over on the bank, shot through the head. A chill crept over me, weakened me. How had he known?

It was daylight when we reached camp, but we sat about a time, cleaning mud from our legs, before we lay down to sleep, and we talked about Arthur. Freddy did not say a word; he had got so that he would not talk. Charley was deeply impressed, though he had not been one of the six. "None of us'll ever see home again," he said, as he crawled from sight. "We might as well go now as any time."

That night we marched out again, tired as we were. Near me was a lad named Gilroy, a plucky little chap whose boots had almost crippled him. He took them off as we rested by a road and the flesh was worn raw and bleeding. He would not report to the sergeant. Once more we worked under machine gun fire, but were mostly deepening the trenches and making posts, and none of our lot was hit. We staggered and stumbled back to our Camp at daylight, and hardly knew what we were doing. We were moving automatically, trying to follow the man in front, shaking with cold, dull, heavy-eyed in the gray light, every muscle clamouring for rest, for the torpor of sleep. Starved as we were, we would not take more than a drink of tea that waited us before we wormed, mud and all, into our shelters.

A third night we went, forcing ourselves into action, and the Hun shelled more fiercely than before. In the Quarry Line we came in contact with a line of mules going up with rations and ammunition. As our party took the near side of the embankment, the sides of the sunken road, whizz bangs began to erupt all along, and we crouched to cover. Twice we had narrowly escaped a salvo, and then, just before our trench, more shells came. I jumped ahead and squeezed between a mule and the bank. The brute knew as well as I the safety of the earth wall and thrust solidly against me, so that its dirty hide was pressing my face.

Whizz bang! Whizz bang! Whizz bang! Three explosions so near that I felt the "lift" of concussion. Yells. "Stretcher bearer – stretcher bearer!" A man was down on the rails behind us, and those in front were racing for the trench mouth. I tried to push past my mule and the beast sagged on me so that Tommy had to help get me clear. As I did so the mule dropped dead, and I found that my legs were bathed in its blood.

Up in the trenches we just worked when forced to by the non-coms. Every man was dead beat and nervous under the shelling and machine gun fire. I asked who was hit in the Quarry line and told that it was a man named Cockburn, not one of our draft. Again we reached our camp, and once more I started to worm into shelter, then remembered that I had not seen Laurie. I went over to the stretcher bearer's mud hole and uncovered him. "Was anyone beside Cockburn hit?" I asked.

"Yes," he said. "Laurie was hit, shrapnel near the spine, a place you could put your hand in. He'll not live."

Laurie and Baxter had been together since we had come to France, but Baxter had been sent to the Brigade Trench mortars. It seemed as if our little company was going fast, I went back to my place, and Charley was there. He looked at me, and he was an unhealthy colour. "Bill," he said, "how would a man know he was for it?"

"He wouldn't," I said vehemently. "That stuff is all bosh. What's the matter?"

"I saw something to-night," he said. "Just as we left the trench I thought a big white light flashed around me and that I was picked up on something like a flak car and whizzed away from here altogether. It was the queerest feeling I ever had and – I – believe I'm for it."

I argued savagely with him. Charley was not a thinker. He was one of the rough and ready type, rugged, used to fun and merriment. He went to his shelter, but I saw that I had not convinced him. McDonald asked me about him and when I told him of Charley's obsession he jeered and said there was nothing in it. That night we marched in and took over the front line.

No sooner were we established than the sergeant came and told me that I was to go to the sniping section and to report to Cave – I had been transferred. I raged. Smaillie had just arranged that I be on his post, with MacMillan, and I had the next six hours off duty. All the while we had been dragging our souls out through the mud and sleeping in the mud, without proper food, the snipers had been in their warm dugout having it much easier than we.

In that mood I reported. Cave was very kind to me and told me that I would work with Harry, an English chap, who was a reliable sniper. In the next bunk were Sedgewick, a brother to Sammy, and Smoky, a cranky-sounding fellow. They did not offer to make friends with me, and I saw that Smoky was one of the men I had beaten at shooting. Harry, however, was kind and we had long conversations.

The dugout we were in was very long and roomy, and to my delight several of our company moved into the other end. As they sat cleaning their rifles someone discharged his, and the snipers sat up and yelled curses. No one had been hit, but they talked among themselves of those blasted "herring chokers" and "soup eaters," and wondered why the battalion had not got "our own kind" of men. "Perhaps," said a voice, "the squaws wouldn't let them come."

It was Tommy, or course, who had come to see me.

For a moment there was a challenging tensity in the air, but Tommy was not answered, and soon the matter passed. It was not the first time we had heard that outbreak. Many of the "oldtimers" resented us, for in all the company competitions our men were easily outstanding. The sharp-tongued sergeant had become outspoken on the matter, until one day at Divion he loosed his spite when only men of our draft were with him. Hughey promptly caught him up like a schoolboy and shook him till his teeth rattled. "You're not enough man to hit," he said, "but I'll slap your pretty little face for you," and he did. The sergeant was white with fury at first, but calmed when he heard all present tell him very plainly what he might expect if things went further. He reported Hughey, however, but gained small satisfaction. The men were the only witnesses and they stuck to the story that the sergeant had attacked Hughey.

Curiously, the "originals," and they were very few, seemed to dislike us because we did not seem to care for hard liquor or the red lights of Bruay. Most of the lads played poker when in rest billets. Very few of them ever got drunk, or bothered with French women. Quite a few of us had books in our packs and read when we had an opportunity. The old "hard" men could not understand us.

That night the Germans bombarded our trenches but no one was hurt. "Rum jars" put our candles out and brought down showers of chalky earth, but the roof held. In the morning Harry and I went out, as soon as it was light, to a sniping post on the crater line. A steel plate was placed on a high point, and camouflaged on the enemy side with wire and rubbish. We swung back the small plate that covered our observing slit and watched for a victim.

It was interesting to lie there and scan the German lines through a glass that brought everything to you with startling clearness. I could see their coloured sandbags, spades lying on the parados, tiny curls of smoke from a dugout, and several times a big pot helmet bobbed along the trench, just high enough for us to get occasional glimpses. Keen to spot a Hun, I lay there until I was more cramped and chilled than I realized, and then went back to the dugout. What a change! We simply went, whenever we felt like it, and got a drink of hot tea and had something to eat. In the afternoon we went again and I studied a tangle of wire and stakes away over on the left, and had as my reward a momentary view of a gray figure flitting to cover.

Sedgewick and Smoky, I gathered, were scouts, and did their work at nights. I heard them reporting their prowl of the previous night, and thrilled as I listened. Scouting appealed to me more than anything else, and I talked a little with Cave about it after they were in their bunks. He eyed me sharply, as if doubtful of my ability, and explained that it was a grim game, requiring special qualities of character and training, nerve power, and instinct of hearing, and the sense of direction in darkness. Often a man was required to play a lone hand in a tight situation, and always he must be prepared for the unexpected. I simply replied that I was sure I could do as well as the others.

Harry and I went out a second day, and never had a shot. He was a cool-going fellow, and never seemed hurried or impatient. He told me that he had shot over eighteen Germans and expected to get many more. Then, on the third morning, I got my fill of such sport. We were in our usual position when I saw a German in full pack rise almost waist-high in a place in their trench. I was so amazed that it took me a moment to discover that during the night our guns had blown in the parapet. The German apparently was a new man to that sector, or else had grown careless of danger. He did not hurry and I tingled all over as I scored my first hit. It was not a great shot, the distance was not one hundred yards, and I had cross-hair sights, but at last I had really killed a Hun.

Harry was tickled. He rubbed his hands and noted down the facts in his book but had not finished when a second German, also in pack, rose in the same place. I shot him as soon as he appeared, as I was excited and taut on the trigger. Hardly had he fallen than a third man stepped on the piled earth, and stared all around. I shot him very carefully, aiming directly at his left breast, and through my telescopic sights could see his buttons. As he pitched down beside the others, two more Germans appeared, but they had thrown off their packs and big helmets and they flung themselves down by the broken parapet and peered toward me. One had an immense head, round, enormous, and he glared like a bull. His mate was very dark and his hair was close-cropped. They remained with their chins resting on the bags, as if watching me, and Harry gripped my shoulder, "Shoot, man," he rasped in my ear, "you won't get a chance like this again."

A queer sensation had made me draw back. I handed him the rifle. "Go ahead yourself, if you want," I said, "I've had enough of this bloody game."

He seized the Ross and took quick aim and I saw the dark flush that spurted over the face of the bigheaded man. He sank from view, his fingers clawing and tearing at the bags as he went. His companion ducked slowly, just escaping Harry's second shot. Then over on the left by the wire tangle, a German got up and walked overland and he carried a big dixie. It was a cook, and it clearly proved that a new battalion was in the line. Harry shot him with great satisfaction, and then potted a third man, an officer, who stepped up on the blown-in part and waved to a working party. When he fell he first stepped back, then ahead. No other Germans came in sight, though we could see their shovels as they cleared their trench. Harry shot at a helmet top several times, and twice a spade waved a miss. Then he led the way back to the dugout and told me that unless I explained myself to Cave he would have to report me.

The sergeant looked at me oddly as I told him I had had my fill of such butcher work, and he said he would see about it when I went out. He said that probably it was too big a kill for my first time, and that if I had just gotten one man in a day I would never have minded. Then he informed me that there was to be a raid the next day, April 1st, between Durrand and Duffield and that I would be with snipers who were to get on top and shoot any Germans who fled overland.

The raid was in the morning and a box barrage was laid down. We climbed out of the trench as soon as the raiding party went over. I had been hot and tired the day before and had not slept much that night. I could not eat and as I got out of the trench I was almost dizzy. The Stokes battery put over their part of the barrage and several of their shells fell short, dropping very near us. An officer shouted to me to watch out, but I did not care what happened. I could not understand my condition and knew I must be sick. Two Germans were captured, one a little short man, and they came hustling back our way. The rest of the enemy had gone into their dugouts as the barrage opened and our men threw bombs and Stokes down the stairways and killed them in their hiding places. The short German got excited as he ran. He had his hands up and was slipping and falling all the time. Getting out of one hole he changed direction and ran to our right. A new man was on post there and when he saw the German appear he shot him.

The other man got over all right and the raiders withdrew without a casualty. I was last man down from our position and an officer, the one who shouted at me, came and smelled my breath. "That man acted as if he were drunk," he said.

I did not say anything to him, but sat on the firestep resting before I could follow the other snipers to the dugout. Several sentries were grouped near me and they were much excited over the raid, and the fact that the Germans had appeared so easily subdued. Martin got up at one post and said he would pot the first squarehead to show himself.

Crack! Martin slumped back, dead. A sniper had got him in the temple.

I watched them put a blanket over him and carry him away and then saw our medical officer going along the trench. As he passed me he stopped and stared, then felt under my ears. "Why don't you report when you're sick?" he bellowed. "Do you want to spread that stuff all around?"

I was dazed. "You've got the mumps, man," he roared. "Come along."

He took my rifle and laid it on the firestep, yanked off my equipment and slung it there, then took me by the arm and started me out to the Quarry Line. When I reached his post I was all in. The medical sergeant got me a hot drink and was very kind. He put me on a trolley that ran back to Mount St. Eloi and away I went. An ambulance took me to some clearing station and there, as soon as my tag was read, I was hustled to an outbuilding. It had been a stable or pen and had a strong door and foot-square windows. As I reeled into it the orderly snapped the door into place and fastened it securely. I was locked in.

For the moment I hardly knew where I was and then I found that I had company. A man with several day's growth of beard on his face, and red-shot eyes, was on his hands and knees, going around and around in circles on the stone floor. He ignored me entirely and kept muttering to himself. In a split second I forgot my weakness. I got to the door, which had an open grating and yelled to a soldier who was by a cook wagon. He came over and I was cunning enough to tell him that I was very hungry. I showed him a five-franc note and told him he could have it for a mess-tin full of mulligan. When he brought it he released the door and extended his offering. I kicked as hard as I could, sending the hot food into his face, blinding him. He yelled and pawed at his eyes and I ran from the place without looking back. In the front an ambulance was just starting away. I piled into it and discovered it only had one man on board, and he seemed unconscious.

We swayed and rocked along the road and a snowstorm began. When the ambulance stopped I climbed out and walked to a tent where an orderly confronted me. He read my ticket and asked me who had sent me there. I made no definite answer and he said that Canadians were for some other hospital, but he led me to a marquee that served as a mumps ward. A dozen men were there, some of them huddled around a brazier. I was shown my "bed," a stretcher resting on two high benches. Under it was at least an inch of water and drifting snow that had come in the tent door.

The blankets were made up so that one could only get into bed near the pillow and thrust feet first down into it. As the benches were easily tipped over this required careful work, and I was glad to get in safely. One of the men told me that an orderly would come for my khaki and put it through the "mill." That meant a steaming plant, and that my tunic and trues would come back to me in a wrinkled mass that could never be straightened. So I folded them and thrust them under my blankets, next to the stretcher.

Shortly afterwards the orderly came, and I told him another man had taken my uniform. He went away and I went to sleep. I woke next morning, and snow had blown in on my bed and melted so that one shoulder was damp. Not a doctor or nurse had come near, and none did till nearly noon. Then the medical officer came and asked a few questions, said something to the nurse with him, and passed on. After he had gone the other patients told me that he would not likely be back for two days, and that I was in the most slip-shod hospital in France, an Imperial outfit at St. Pol.

Three of the men got up and dressed and brought us something to eat. These three had been well for over two weeks and had simply stayed in the marquee, slipping out whenever the doctor was making his rounds. No one bothered them and they had a good time. An orderly, an Englishman they called "Spike," came and told me that I had better move into the next ward. He was a fine young fellow, had been two years at college, and was very bitter against all those in authority at the hospital.

I moved to a bigger tent and stayed there six days. The doctor never looked at me again; was only in the tent once in that time. The nurses came seldom, except one, a Canadian girl, from Ontario, who, when she found I was Canadian, used to come and talk with me. She was on night duty and would come with her flashlight, making the rounds. She told me that things were worse than I could realize and that her only hope was to get away from the place. I had had the worst of my sickness in the dugout and no complications set in. Easter morning we were surprised to see an officer and orderlies come into the ward and start laying oranges and cigarettes on the tables. The officer gave us strict orders not to touch them. "There is to be an inspection first," he said. "After it is all over we will come and tell you and you can help yourselves."

None of us had had enough to eat in the place, the food was very scarce, and no smokes could be obtained, so that we lay and feasted our eyes on the good things. Presently a retinue of red tape and bombasity passed through the ward, glancing at the exhibit. No sooner had they gone than in came the officer and orderlies again, with their same baskets, and before more than two or three of us had gotten our cigarettes and oranges they had seized our supposed treat and taken it, never giving a word of explanation. Spike came in and told us that they had pulled the same stunt in nearly every ward, and that the doctors and head nurses would have a big blow-out in their own quarters.

That evening I moved to a third tent. They were making ready for the casualties of the 9th, and were putting more patients in one ward. There were eight of us in a much smaller tent and I found myself next a man from the 7th battalion. He was a middle-aged fellow and well-educated, and we talked for hours at a time. The sniping business preyed on my mind so that some nights I could not sleep yet I could not mention it to him. I was much better, and as darkness came on we thought of the boys in the trenches up in the crater lines, waiting for the morrow.

I thought of Freddy, and wondered what he was doing. I felt that if he did not get sent back on some job or get wounded he would lose his reason, for he rarely spoke to any one. Big Herman tried to humour him, but the rest left him alone. I thought of Charley, and his premonitions, of little Mickey and his boyish face, of Earle and MacMillan and McDonald. How lucky I had been to get clear of the attack, and yet I wished with all my heart and soul that I was there. In spite of all the bitterness I had brought to France with me I had got to like the battalion, to be proud that I belonged to it, and I liked our sergeant, Smaillie, the sergeant-major and our company commander. They were all "white" men.

At midnight the ambulance brought in a soldier whose face was so swollen that he could not speak. He had crawled in mud from a listening post, unable to walk, and his hands were raw discoloured hooks. Spike put the man to bed and he lay very quiet after getting a hot drink. In the morning he was dead. He had died without making a sound, absolutely worn out with crawling in the mud, back and forth from post to trench, without enough to eat, and suffering all kinds of exposure. He seemed to be quietly resting when we looked at him, and one felt rather glad that the poor chap was through with all the mud, and rain, and snow, and rats, and lice, and discipline, and discomfort; he could rest a long, long time.

Towards morning I lay awake and listened for the barrage. I could picture the boys in the trench, tense waiting, staring over the parapet. Mud would be everywhere, plastering their clothing, gripping their feet. Our last trip in had been a nightmare journey and the deep trench in the dusk looked like the bed of some dirty river, suddenly gone dry. The barrage was like rolling thunder. Even where we were we could hear it so plainly that it awed us, kept us quiet. As it grew light I saw men go by the tent carrying something wrapped in a ground sheet, with muddy boots sticking stiffly out, eloquent of an ended journey. Spike came in and said the man had been brought down in the night, a scurvy case, and that they had not tried to put him in a bed.

No one brought us any breakfast and so I got up and dressed – I had managed to keep my khaki with me – and went among the tents until I found the kitchen. I gave the number of our ward. "How many?" barked the cook. "Twelve," I said, and was given hot cocoa and bread and jam and margarine. scant enough rations for our eight, but the best meal we had had. Then I got in bed again and talked with the 7th battalion man, while out on the roads motor lorries droned and rattled without ceasing.

We talked of patriotism. He said it was not a password in his company, that loyalty was a word they sneered at; discipline, with the death penalty behind it, a canker we could not cure. Then he derided the caste of the nation and cursed the propaganda passed out by preachers, editors, staff officers and platform patriots of both sexes. He seemed emotional and told me that he was an original member of his battalion, and so I humoured him, though not condoning all his violence. We agreed that the war was, in some indefinable way, our duty, but that those "patriots" were to be detested as our handicaps. We were sure that had they been as sacrificial and sincere as the soldier the war would have been over, or would never have been begun.

I thought of the way some of those platform shouters had ranted about the Germans, and their "hate," and how different it was in the battalion. All uttered hate was at the "higher-ups," and outside of a certain derisive jesting at old "Heinie" the German was seldom mentioned in billets. Given a dirty night at the crossroads or an undue strafing in the trenches and there would be bitter vows of vengeance and Fritz and his methods would be luridly described. Twenty-four hours later the orator would give a prisoner a cigarette and grin at him.

We talked about discipline, the cruelty of cartwheel crucifixion, which I had seen on the parade grounds of the R.C.R.'s below Mount St. Eloi. Men, volunteers, spread-eagled to cart-wheels, tied there for hours in a biting, bone-chilling wind, all because the fellow had not shined a button or given some snobby officer a proper deference. I had seen men laden with their packs and rifles, overcoats and all, marched back and forth, twenty feet each way, to the barking of a bristled non-com, a sheer process of fatiguing the man until he was almost a wreck; and these men who had left good jobs and homes and had come, as the orators said, to fight for right and loved ones.

We were all, the 7th man said, at the mercy of authority-crazed, over-fed, routine-bound staffs, old fogies with a tragic lack of imagination and a criminal ignorance of actual warfare. Spike came in and sat a long time on our beds, talking about religion. He was a thinker, and it was his theory that we took from this world our memories and affections, and he wondered what visions of the war we would carry. His ideas held me. If, I thought, the cosmic law is based on logical principle, then memory and affection ARE indestructible and personality persists beyond that which we call death.

The 7th battalion man proved even more of a thinker than Spike. Life, he said, was an uncreated thing, co-existent with Him who is life, and Time is not, never was and never will be. Memory and affection might be indestructible, and we are much greater than we know, component parts of that Spirit that is undying. He looked at me and said solemnly, "You'll find, Jock, that the greatest moment here on earth is when you leave it."

Privates in a dirty, wind-blown, rain-soaked tent, unshaven, strangers to each other, with sick men on either side, discussing topics that cause any man to sober. I think of Spike and that 7th man every time I read of the "sodden cattle" of the dugouts.

All that day I wondered about Steve and what it had been like at Hill 60. It must have been another region where mine craters grew and multiplied and sprouted machine gun posts and saps, but what had those first fighters thought of the war? Had there been rats up there, those obscene creatures with their glittering eyes, had they to endure the same post duties, six hours on, six off, in all weather, under all fires, all dangers, and with the wraiths of no man's land peeping over the parapets in the lonely hours before dawn? And the more I thought of these first comers the more I wished I had been with them.

I woke next morning and heard strange guttural voices. Dressing hurriedly, I went into the next tent and found it filled with wounded Germans. They stared at me, some of them friendly, some indifferent. One chap with a turban-sized bandage on his head was sitting up, stolidly eating bully as though it were an occupation instead of a meal. A man beside me said something, repeated it, and I gathered that he wanted a drink. I got my mug and water bottle and he drank thirstily, then thanked me. Spike came in and asked me to give him a hand in feeding them, and I enjoyed it. The stolid man with the bully was the exact replica of a New Brunswicker with us, who only asked for plenty of hard tack and his rum ration. Given those, he was content, and a double issue seemed to make a feather bed of his chicken-wire bunk.

An officer came that night to see the Germans. He was one of those eye-glass youngsters, full of "pip-pip" and "tootle-oo" stuff, which fizzed from him as he talked to the nurse accompanying him. I did not know whether she was there out of curiosity or as his bodyguard, but they went away again without doing anything to help a sufferer, leaving only a trail of "right-os" and "cheerios." Spike came afterwards and ground his teeth. So far as we knew he was the only person to attend those wounded Germans all that night.

I was just sixteen days at St. Pol, then coolly walked away from the place and got on board a train.

No one halted me or questioned me. I never had seen a doctor again, and for five days I drew rations for our ward, washed sick men's faces, and fed many. I had a bath at the bath house and even drew a new tunic from the quartermaster I unearthed, and a badge. As I left, a Scot – a bandy-legged chap – who had been hanging around one ward six weeks, dodging doctors, looked at my balmoral and said seriously, anxiously, "Ye'll no disgrace the tartan wull ye lad?" I looked him up and down and walked away.

By devious ways I reached Mount St. Eloi and there to my astonishment found Melville. He had been down the line with mumps the same as I, had taken French leave from his ward and was very anxious to get back to the boys. We went over the Ridge just at dusk and found it a jungle of old wire

and powdered brick and muddy burrows and remnants of trenches. We
went off the main track that was being used and sat in a big crater to rest.
Melville spoke sharply and I looked. Three dead men were reclining in the
place, lolled back to the muddy wall, gazing incuriously before them, their
faces turned black. We rose and climbed away from the place and almost
stumbled over another dead man crouched in a shell hole, his rifle in his
hands, squatted as if he were ready to spring.

In the twilight, just before darkness, we stood and looked down over the
Ridge on the enemy side. The first flares rose, in scattered places, and we
could not distinguish the lines. The air was damp and chilling, an un-
earthly feeling predominated. The dead man, the solitary flares, the captured ground, gave me a sense of ghosts about, and one realized the
tragedy of the stricken hill. Many, many men had died on that tortured,
cratered slope.

We found the platoon, and hardly recognized it. The sergeant was there,
and MacDonald, but the rest were strangers. They told me that the 73rd,
of the Fourth Division, had been so cut up that they had been withdrawn
and the 85th Nova Scotia Highlanders had taken their place. The remnant
of the 73rd had been divided between us and the 13th. I got MacDonald to
one side and asked questions. It was far worse than I thought. The 42nd
had gone straight through to their objective despite the sleety snow and
mud and confusion, had driven back all opposition and seized their objective. But on their left the Fourth Division had been held up, and a flanking fire had taken heavy toll.

Freddy was gone, he had predicted truly. A big shell had landed beside
him, killing him and burying him. Charley had fallen in the first rush, riddled with bullets. Joe, the ex-policeman, had fought through to the objective, and had been killed by a sniper on the flank. One shell had wiped out
Stevenson, Theriault and Roy, as they grouped by a captured gun.
MacMillan had been shot in the stomach, and had died after waiting
hours in a trench. Billy, the complainer, had fallen as he charged a machine
gun, keeping on until he was almost within reach of the gunners. Little
Gilroy had been killed, and Westcott, and Smaillie had been wounded.
Hughie, and the sergeant he had defied, had been wounded at the same
time, and had been taken away together. Big Herman was missing. They
located his body a month later. That morning he had shaken hands with
Freddy, said goodbye to him, and then when he had got going had run

amuck. He was found almost at the bottom of the Ridge, near a battery position, with eight dead Germans about him, four of them killed by bayonet.

In the other platoons, besides Tommy, Slim and Joe had survived, and Ira and Sam, and big Glenn and Eddie, and Mickey and Jerry. They sat in the dugout that night, after a hard day of re-building roads, each man suffering from bodily fatigue, and crawling vermin, and the clammy chill of mud-caked clothing, their faces brooding, enigmatic, even Mickey's curiously odd, only their eyes moving. They would not talk about the fighting and seemed utterly worn. Six months ago we had marched to Mount St. Eloi, eagerly, bravely, our tin hats askew and with a cheeky retort for every comment, hiding whatever secret apprehensions we had, not knowing the heavy ominous silence that follows the burst of big shells — and the cries of the wounded; not knowing what it is to scrape a hasty grave at night and there bury a man who has worked with you and slept with you since you enlisted.

CHAPTER III

The German Officer

We left the top of the Ridge and went to Vimy village, relieving the C.M.R.'s there, and doing working parties, digging trenches near the front line. I came back alone the first night and two of the new men asked me to go with them to a shelter that they had made in the railway embankment. It was a snug bivvy and there was plenty of room for the three of us. We were soon asleep, but about midnight I was wakened by a tug at my arm. I looked up quickly, throwing back my ground sheet, and there stood Steve!

I could see him plainly, see the mud on his puttees and knees. He jerked a thumb towards the ruined houses and motioned for me to go to them. I did not speak. I thought that if I could do exactly as he said, and not wake the others, perhaps he would actually speak to me. He started to walk away as I gathered up my equipment and rifle and greatcoat, and when I hurried he simply faded from view. I was disappointed. For at least ten minutes I stood by a path, waiting, watching, listening, hoping he might speak or whisper. Nothing happened, and I grew cold, so I kept on to the nearest ruin and there lay on a rough earth floor and went to sleep.

In the morning I heard fellows talking about a big shell that had killed two men. I jumped up and looked. They were digging from the shelter I had left the mangled bodies of the two lads who had invited me to join them. The shell had exploded just above their heads. All that day I thought of how I had been saved, and I resolved that if ever again I saw Steve I would do exactly as he motioned; he had saved my life.

Earle had transferred to the Brigade Trench Mortars, and so I did not see him, but McDonald and I slept together. After two more days we were warned to fall in at dark to march back over the Ridge. The officer in charge was the supernumerary who had been with us at Divion, and he seemed very unused to his work. When the time came to fall in, the Germans began shelling, using gas shells. We put on our respirators and waited in the ruins until there was a lull, as the gas shells could penetrate the walls. Finally the officer called us out, and at that moment the shelling increased. I had been told to act as guide and was with the officer, and I shouted that everyone was to follow me.

The platoon started after me on the road that led over the Ridge, but the officer called us back, reprimanded me, and made us fall in in two ranks. Shells were dropping everywhere and we had to put on our masks again. Yet he yelled for us to NUMBER, and to FORM FOURS. It was a ghastly business but we made a semblance of obeying. He would not hurry and turned to see if we were properly in line, then gave the order to move in single file. McDonald was next to him. I had slipped in third and Melville behind me. A shell came over the officer's shoulder and struck McDonald full on the chest, breaking in pieces as it did so. The impact killed him instantly and drove him back with such force that Melville and I were knocked off our feet and sprawled into the ditch. The liquid in the shell splashed over the legs of the officer, burning him badly. He lay on the road and called for assistance.

Melville and I jumped up and examined McDonald, but could do nothing. We laid him to one side, on the bank, and left him, then hurried to the nearest ruin for shelter. The others had run there as McDonald fell. A sergeant of the 73rd, Oron, had taken charge of the platoon, Davies being with company headquarters, and he came shouting at us to go and get the officer. Not a man would volunteer, and he had to give stern orders and name his men to get them to move. We all knew that McDonald had lost his life through the arrogant stupidity of that major.

We left the ruins at the first lull, and I led the platoon as quickly as possible. I had my own mask off and saw a short lad, Hayward, pitch headfirst into a water-filled hole. I yanked him out and then helped old Sam up the hill, as he was sick from the effects of the gas. Finally we reached Grange Tunnel and there a lad, Kennedy, of the 73rd, shared with me a tin of beans. They were delicious and he and I were friends at once.

Next day we got out into the sunlight. It was perfect weather, clear and warm, and the grass was yellowed with dandelions. Larks sang overhead and in that same sunny blue aeroplanes wheeled like great hawks, the early sunlight glinting on white wings as a deadly duel was fought. The sergeant-major came to me and told me that I was to go back to Cave as a scout, and that I would be transferred as soon as a re-organization was effected. I went to see Earle and was told that he had been wounded in the arm by shrapnel and had made "Blighty." Another of the old crowd gone. We had one more trip in the line before my transfer was made, relieving the Fifth C.M.R.'s and doing several working parties. I was out one night on covering party, and then was warned for patrol.

Sergeant Oron was in charge and we worked our way out too rapidly. The flares had stopped and it was dark. He got mixed, and then, after we had been out longer than we intended, he whispered to me, asking directions. I started to crawl the way I judged we should go and when I veered I felt a touch on the arm, so swung around. On we went. A heavy dew had fallen and wet weeds brushed my face like dead fingers. The guns had stopped firing and every tiny sound was magnified by the gloom. Again and again as I crawled I felt that guiding touch and wondered why Oron, if he knew the way, had made me crawl ahead. All at once wire loomed before us and a very Canadian challenge was given. I felt thankful to slide into our trench, almost where we had left, but I turned to the sergeant. "What," I asked, "was your idea? Why did you have me go ahead when only you knew the way?"

He stared at me. "What do you mean?" he snapped. "I just followed you, I didn't know where we were."

"Didn't you keep tapping me on the shoulder to go right or left?" I was completely bewildered.

"I never touched you," he said. "I was behind you all the time. What are you trying to put over?" He could not understand me, but all at once I knew it had been Steve again. I said no more, but got away from him, and later heard that he had regarded me as "queer."

The last night in we were to put up wire in front of a "jump-off" trench some yards ahead of the main line. Our officer had come from the 73rd, was in poor health, and did not seem very capable. Twice our party of twelve men were led out into no man's land and we had the wire and screw stakes ready when flares went up and machine gun fire flattened us to the mud. Each time we were brought back into the trench and told that we had made too much noise and to wait an hour. It was the truth all right, there had been considerable clamour, but it was made by new men and we could not help it. We talked among ourselves as we waited, and when a drizzling rain began Tommy and Melville and Mickey and I told the officer that we would put up the wire without a covering party or any one else out there. He agreed eagerly and we went out. We worked swiftly but carefully, making a good "fence" and came in again without being disturbed. The rain came heavier then and our relief was a long time coming.

When it did arrive the officer ordered us out over the back of the trench to let the relieving party file in. As we stood there in the rain flares went up and our wet ground sheets glistened. The Germans saw us and we had to flop in the soft mud with all our equipment of haversacks and messtins. We were soaked, chilled, mud-plastered, when we got up, and the officer led us out by an overland route. He got mixed, would not wait for a guide, and we wandered away over on the left. It was pitch black and the rain poured in torrents. There had been casualties among the Lewis gunners and the extra "pans" of ammunition were passed back among the platoon men. We carried them in turn. Just in front of me "Old Bill," a night blind veteran, stumbled along with a pair of the "drums." The connecting strap was over one shoulder. We came to a wide, shallow trench crossed by a plank. The farther end of the plank had sunk down the opposite bank until it had quite an incline, and successive feet had muddied it until it was slippery. The officer flashed his electric torch and showed "Old Bill" the way. Two steps – and his feet shot from under him. His kilt flew up and he sat down hard on the plank and shot, as if it were greased, to the far end, bringing up so heavily that the "drums" of ammunition crossed and the strap nearly strangled him, while his steel hat dropped over his face. As soon as "Old Bill" got air he gave voice and in fiery language denounced all wars, the Great War in particular, all battalions, the 42nd especially, all officers, his present company NOT excepted.

The officer tried to subdue him, but "Old Bill" only subdued when his breath gave out. We went on, and got more lost than we were. Finally we halted by another trench, so soaked with rain that we cared not what happened. "Try to make yourselves comfortable," said the officer. "Wait here and I'll find where we are." And he was gone.

The trench had a foot of water in it, and there were no shelters. Melville and I explored, then, at a narrow part, pulled in the sides with our entrenching tools until we had soft earth heaped high above the water. We spread a ground sheet on it and lay down. It was a very tight squeeze but we lay there side by side, lengthwise to the trench, with the other ground sheet over our heads, and the rain poured down. We slept in spite of everything as we were utterly worn, and an icy touch roused me. I woke to find that all one shoulder was under water and that I could not move. I soon understood. The sides of the trench, loosened by our work, had slid in more, and had almost buried us, while the water in the trench, dammed by our block, had risen until it was ready to drown me.

Never will I forget those few minutes. We could not move an arm or leg, were absolutely helpless, and the rubber sheet over our heads smothered our calls. But we yelled and yelled for help and at last, just as my ear had filled and my nose was blowing bubbles, Tommy found us. He ripped up the sheet and dragged us out, and for a time we could hardly speak. Then we moved off, trailing two miles back to where we should have gone. Old Bill had stayed up all night, sitting on a firestep with a rubber sheet pinned across the corner above him, dozing. He heard a moaning, shuddering sound, he said, and went to investigate. One of the men of the other section was sitting in soft mud, had been there all night, shaking so that his teeth chattered, and making an awful moaning. Back near the Ridge we found the officer, a desperate-looking figure, and then, as we went up the hill, we had to pass a large crater. It was slippery and there were loose wires. "Old Bill" tripped on one and went head over heels, slithering and clutching at things, clear to the bottom. The officer hurried back and stood peering down in the gloom. "You poor fellow," he called. "Did you fall down there?"

"Old Bill" removed a lump of mud from one eye, shook old wire from his ears, and looked up. The air was brittle. "No," he blared. "I was here WHEN THE BLEEDIN' HOLE WENT UP."

The morning cleared the skies and we went back to Villers Au Bois. The weather continued perfect, and Tommy, who had been rather quiet, began to be his usual self again. A draft of new men had come to us and I made several new friends. One was Tom Mills, a pale-faced youth, and rather reserved, another was Dykes, a very heavy built man, who liked to talk about the French. I also got better acquainted with "Old Bill," a cockney, ten years older than any of us, and a regular old timer. He had joined the battalion at Ypres, had fought all through the Somme and its terrors, and yet was night blind. After dark he could not see any distance or with clearness. He did odd jobs about the company, kept the billets clean when we were out of the line, and looked after the dugouts and trenches when we were up front. But always when there was a "scrap" on, "Old Bill" was there. He was a man of very clean habits, careful of his personal appearance, and had a nice tenor voice. All the boys thought the world of him but I had not got to know him well before that time.

The scouts and snipers were re-organized, and five new men joined them, Hill, a short, thick-set man; Jimmy, a tall, observant, quick-tempered lad; Bulmer, a big husky hockey player, and myself, all from our draft. The other was an easy-going, mild-mannered "pipe-puller," Brown, one of the "originals."

Before he could make a trip with them Bulmer had some leg disease that crippled him and sent him back to Canada. The rest of us were initiated into the mysteries of night work, shown how to crawl around the German lines without making a noise, how to make a report, to read a compass. McLeod, a fine-looking man, as big as Herman, was friendly with us and Cave was just the same as he had been. Wilson, a 73rd man, came in Bulmer's place and he and I were teamed together. He had had considerable experience.

I got a day's leave before we went back to the trenches and had extraordinary luck. As I left my billet a big car slowed down and the driver asked me for a light. He was an officer's chauffeur, his "boss" being one of the head signallers stationed at Houdain, and he asked me where I was going. I said I had the day. We went to Bruay and then he took me all around the country, to Ferfay where the divisional school was, and to Olhain Chateau, surrounded by a moat and of 15th century construction. It was a wonderful treat to me. The sky was summer blue and sunshine made whiter the cottages with their red-tiled roofs. The hedges were in bloom and fruit trees were white with blossom. We had a real dinner at Houdain and he brought me back to my billet.

We went back over the Ridge and relieved the Fifth C.M.R.'s at the railway dugouts. Everyone was excited with talk about a brigade raid. It was to be on the night of the 8th of June, and the German front line trench was to be taken and held for a time, and then vacated. Just why this was to be done we did not know. All details were gone over in the companies, but we at headquarters were left severely alone. Cave told us that there would not be anything for us to do.

At dark we left the embankment and moved over to another dugout. I went with the company and had a chat with Tommy as I looked over the few left of the old crowd. We were moving along through a trench, talking and calling to each other, when – crash – crash – crash – three shells landed close by. We hurried for a distance, then eased our pace, and as we did another salvo came and one shell struck directly in the corner of the trench. I saw men go down and heard the shout for "stretcher bearers." There was no need of them. Poor Slim and Joe had been together, lagging a little behind the others, and both had been instantly killed. As I looked at them I thought of the way Slim had dug on his hands and knees his first night in at Vimy.

Tapes were laid to the front line, white lines that led to the first aid station, and guides for bringing back prisoners overland. They looked, in the dusk, like a pathway for ghosts. The barrage was sharp and heavy and we got out of our shelter to watch it. No orders had come for us and so after a time Jimmy and I quietly left the place and went up to the boys. We had our rifles and equipment. The objective had been taken when we reached it. Several dead Germans lay around, but there had been few casualties among our men. Just where we got in the trench a stout-looking "Heinie" lay huddled in one corner. One of the last draft looked at him. "It can't hurt a dead man to stick him," he said roughly. "I'm going to try my bayonet on that chap. I want to know what it feels like."

He poised his steel, ready to make his thrust – when the German yelled and leaped to his feet. The "sticker" jumped back in amazement, and Jimmy took charge of the prisoner. In a moment we had tested all the other dead men, but no more "live corpses" were found. The Germans were sending up orange sprays, red rockets, green flares, golden chains, all the varieties they had, but there was little retaliation. None of our old crowd had been hit and they were all feeling good. The raid had been a grand success. Over thirty prisoners were taken.

As Jimmy and I went back we found an officer in our front trench. He was helplessly drunk and had never left the post he was in. We said nothing about it to anyone as the others had not mentioned him. Before we could get back to our dugout we met two signallers. One of them told me that I was to go back up to the front with him, and to observe there all the next day. His companion had a reel of wire and they were running a line to the front trench.

I went with him and found that he was correct. We were to get between the lines, if possible, any good spot, and report all that the Germans did as they returned to their trench. Luck favoured us. We found a well-like hole not many yards in front of the enemy line, almost in reach of the wire. It had not been used for a long time as weeds were thick on the rim and we were careful not to disturb them. We got in the hole, made sure that the phone was in working order, and waited. I had a revolver, two Mills bombs and field glasses. The company had returned to their own trench.

For a long time there was not a sound, and then we heard the Germans moving in the outskirts of Avion, a village just back of their front line. It was an hour later before they were in their front trench, and was getting light. The first thing I saw was a dead man to our right. He was stretched out on his back, and as we looked at him we heard the Germans getting into their trench. They jabbered among themselves as they examined their dead, and then, to our amazement, we heard a dozen voices calling for help. All the time we had waited there had not been a sound and yet those wounded Germans had been lying just back of their trench, wherever they could crawl.

I made small openings among the thickest weeds so that I could watch all sides. The signaller remained squatted at the bottom of the hole and did his talking in a low tone. Suddenly a head shot up in the trench just in front of me, a broad face with a very blunt nose. The German stared beyond my hiding place and then scrambled over the bags and through the wire. I slipped the safety off my revolver and told the signaller to be prepared to beat it. But the German had not seen us. He crawled out to the dead man, a 49th soldier, and took his boots and puttees, even his socks, and then went back.

It got lighter and soon we could see the Germans coming from Avion. A brick wall was over on our left and we saw that it concealed the entrance to a dugout. Many of their wounded had crawled out on the ground between their first and second trenches and in order to get them in, the stretcher bearers would be fully exposed. An officer came from the dugout and after many harsh words, which we could hear, he made an elderly-looking Hun tie a white flag to a pole and climb out of the trench. None of our fellows shot at him, and soon the stretcher bearers were following. They only had three stretchers and the rest were carried in in ground sheets, doubled like jack-knives, bumped along the rough ground so that they groaned piteously.

All that day we stayed there and watched the Germans. There were two officers in charge and we picked out the three different ways by which they came from Avion; saw where two more dugouts were placed; estimated the number of dead they carried away and the strength of the trench garrison. Then, at night, we stole back to our lines, and as we went found an old shallow trench, with a place in it that the Germans possibly used for a listening post.

The "new men" did not get on well with the "old men." All the veterans seemed to resent our intrusion. They held aloof from us and would not talk with us at all, with the exception of McLeod and a chap called Farmer. It did not bother me in the least, but Jimmy was hot-headed and often relieved his mind within their hearing. The last afternoon we were in the line I went out in daylight to have a look at the shallow trench. Tommy and Mickey were together on post and let me use it as a sally port. The old sap was reached without much exposure and I went down it till I found an enlarged space with a trip wire around it. Undoubtedly the place had once been used, but weeds were growing in it. As I crouched there I saw a slight movement in the tall grass farther along the trench and then glimpsed a red-and-grey pillbox cap. In a second I had hidden back of the old post, and lay watching.

Very quietly a head was raised, and then the shoulders of a German officer. He was a young man with firm, even features and a brown mustache. His eyes were blue and he had a very friendly look. After a moment's watching he crawled along and came into the post, worming under the trip wire. I lay perfectly still and released the safety of my rifle. It only needed the pressure of my finger to kill the fellow, for his head was in line with the muzzle of my Lee-Enfield.

The German lay still a long time, listening, and I knew by the way he acted that he was alone. He had a Luger in his hand, but placed it on the ground as he removed some old wire from under his knees, and when he crawled on he forgot his pistol. He came on the length of himself before he remembered it, and then, as he turned to reach for it, I raised up so that he could see me.

I'll never forget the look that was on his face. He was so surprised that he seemed paralyzed. A long minute passed, and then another. Neither of us moved. I had my finger crooked, ready, and he saw that I had. He whitened, turned red, paled again, his eyes watching mine, and then he smiled!

I had fully intended taking him prisoner, or shooting him, and yet, as he backed away, smiling at me, I did not do a thing. Back he went, foot by foot, watching me closely, and smiling. He passed the Luger and never looked at it. Back, back, he went, and I crawled forward. I did not know what I was going to do, I wanted to stop him, and yet that smile of his had me hypnotized. I kept on until I had picked up his pistol and he slipped back under the wire and to where I had first seen him. If he had picked up a bomb, or hurried, or done anything but what he did, the spell would have been broken, but he backed and smiled his way down the sap until he reached a bend, and there he stopped – and saluted me!

When he was gone I hurried back. I was bewildered at myself, called myself names, and yet I did not say a thing to Tommy or show him the Luger. All that night I thought of that German and alternately was sorry or thankful that I had let him go. I said nothing to Cave about it, or to any-one, and we were relieved by the 58th Battalion.

We went back to the line on the 2nd of July and found the front trench in Avion. The scouts were established in a cellar and as we looked about in the morning we spotted a lovely bunch of roses just in front of the German wire. Some of the platoon were in splendid dugouts, places with carpets on wooden floors, real beds, and clocks and stoves and mirrors, furnishings looted from French homes. Sedgewick and some of the others watched a house that was well over toward the German lines, and talked about using it as an observation post.

We had no orders, however, and when it was dark I got out of the trench and crawled through several gardens until I reached the roses. It was a longer crawl than I had expected and when I reached them a voice startled me so that I almost jumped and ran. Three Germans were just inside their wire and apparently they were considering a venture into no man's land. I lay within ten feet of them and saw them point and gesture, their huge helmets silhouetted against the distant glimmer of a flare. They talked there at least ten minutes before they got down and I could get my roses.

When I reached our dugout again, a royal row was in progress. The "oldtimers," after a long and careful reconnaissance, had reached the house they wished to use. In it, they had listened a time, and then had been badly scared by having Jimmy's voice, a few feet away, ask them if they thought it was all right. He was seated by a window watching the Hun lines, and had gone there as soon as it was dark. Sedgewick and his mate claimed that the Germans must have heard Jimmy, there had been considerable machine-gun fire soon afterward, and he derided them for taking so long to get to a place. McLeod made both parties keep quiet, but there was hostility in the air. And Jimmy and I wore roses.

An hour after, the Germans began pitching "Minnies" into our lines. Our cellar opened on to a street through which one could walk in safety from machine bullets and as I went on a message to a company headquarters I saw the red trail of a "Minnie" in the sky. I stopped and looked. Two men were coming along the street behind me. I watched the big shell and decided that it would go back of the house, so dodged in front of it then changed my mind and ran around the house. My last decision was correct. The Minnie dropped in front of the building, falling on the cobbles, and there was a tremendous explosion. Stones and bricks flew everywhere, crashing among the ruins. I ran around to where the two men had been, for I had seen them standing as if undecided. They were both lying on the street, two officers of the Princess Pats. One, Major Molson, was dead, the other a captain, had his leg blown off. I ran for help and we got him on a stretcher after binding the stump, and, strangely, he never lost consciousness and actually seemed calmer than those helping him.

Next day Cave sent Wilson and I over to the right in front of a company headquarters to where an old ruin extended into no man's land. He told us to get into it, if possible, and observe. We found the place rather exposed but reached it and found we could get to the upstairs part without showing ourselves. It was a badly shattered ruin but enough room remained to give us hiding. Beside where we lay was an opening large enough to allow a man to step outside. We were not there five minutes until we knew we had the finest observation post in that sector. In that time we had counted over forty Germans in view. We watched a carrying party going across a field, sheltered by an embankment, and a party of twenty were working busily, building what we supposed was a "Minnie" emplacement. They were mixing concrete and carrying timbers, a big non-com directing the whole. By using our glasses carefully we could see even his expression, and the screwed-up look on the face of a fat fellow who was trying to light a clay pipe.

I wriggled out through the grass again and reported our find and within the hour had an artillery officer up in the house with us. He had brought a phone with him. Wilson and I were tingling with excitement, but I had apprehensions as to what might happen. The workers were busy as ants around their construction when the first shell dropped among them. It was the nicest aiming I ever saw. The officer had had his battery fire a first shell far over into a field, then a second to the right, a third a little nearer, and had then made his calculations, and he scored a direct hit. When the smoke cleared four men were lying inert where they had worked and two wounded ones were just crawling from view. No others were in sight. The officer had that one gun remain registered, and then began sniping at other targets. He sent the carrying party, then on its second trip, diving into a dugout entrance we had not noticed, and he made two more kills, one a chance hit on a lone messenger, blowing the fellow into the air, the other on a party of three that had emerged from the embankment and were staring our way.

Two Germans showed their heads near the emplacement, and both had binoculars. We knew that they were getting suspicious and the officer kept his guns from shooting. Then came bold steps up the stairs behind us, a quick voice. Izzy, an impetuous officer of "A" Company, wanted to know what luck we were having, and before we could stop him he had stepped full-length into the opening beside us and stood calmly surveying the German lines. One scoop gathered our glasses and tunics which we had lain on the floor. Wilson and I made it a dead heat until we reached the company houses and the artillery officer was not far behind. He never bothered with his phone. Izzy stared at us, then started down, no doubt bewildered by our conduct. Crash! A shell went through the top of the ruin, blasting out the entire corner where we had been and covering Izzy with a deluge of debris. It was a miracle that he was not killed. We saw him come into the open and dash blindly toward the company headquarters, and we kept on, far along the side of an old railway track until we were back to our cellar. The Hun smashed that ruin to powdered brick and he kept right on and levelled all the houses where the company officers were, they remaining in the cellars, unable to get away. We heard that Izzy received the colonel's compliments. The battalion was relieved and we went back to Chateau de la Haie.

No sooner were we in billets than I went to see the boys in the company, and was astounded to learn that Ira had got into trouble. During the heavy shelling of "D" company's trench at Avion he and others had been ordered to dugouts. They had stayed there for some time when a shell blew in part of the entrance and showered chalky earth on Ira who had been halfway up the stairs. Probably he was shocked by concussion. At any rate, so Tommy told me, he had been shaky for some time, brooding on the fate of Herman, who had been his friend, and thinking of Freddy's prophecy. When, later, an officer came and ordered them back to their posts Ira would not go. He told the officer that he could not do so, and he was crimed. They sent him to join the road-making gang for twenty-one days.

There was a queer old chap in the company, one of the last draft, a short, bow-legged fellow, Bunty. He had made himself a bivvy under the parados – because it was easier digging –and so constructed it that he had to sit in it like a Hindoo. He was a heavy sleeper, and very scared of shells. Tommy found him asleep there one morning, sitting cross-legged, and took a dud shell to the place. He made a cleft in the parapet directly in front, then scooped out the earth between Bunty's knees, without waking him. He pushed the dud into the hole, and then threw a Mills bomb into the grass just back of Bunty's parados. The explosion, of course, wakened the little man, but there was no outcry, not a sound. Tommy hiding around the traverse, was obliged to go to see what happened. Bunty was there, rigid, sweat streaming down his face, unable to move or speak. Fright had almost paralyzed him. Tommy removed the shell and never let Bunty know it was all a joke. Melville also had got into trouble. A German airman had the habit of coming each morning, just as it was light, and flying very low above our trench, shooting at the men. On the third morning Melville was ready for him. He had two rifles beside him and he pumped lead like a machine gun, causing the airman to swerve from his route. The boys all claimed that Melville hit him, at any rate the flyer never returned, but an officer who had seen the shooting had Melville on the carpet. The orders were that no man must even look up while an enemy airman was overhead, and never shoot at them.

During our stay at Chateau de la Haie the private war between the "old" and "new" scouts waged merrily, though I had little to do with it. At every opportunity Tommy and I went to other units, visiting them, and I talked with all the interesting strangers I met, making notes of all unusual stories that I heard. One evening we went to the old crater line at Vimy and I looked over from Vernon post to where the German front had been. It seemed incredible that we could have remained so close to the enemy, for one could almost have thrown a bomb from one post to the other. Then we went and looked down over the plain. The moon had risen, casting its spell over all the hillside, blotting out harsh lines, tinging all with an eerie sort of beauty that held us, unspeaking, a long, long time. I thought of some rare moments there, quiets at midnight when we talked of home and things near the heart, fugitive minutes, never to be forgotten. As we went back Tommy pointed out French graves near Souchez, with "Mort Pour la patrie," on the crosses, others with but an inverted bottle holding all the particulars, and told me that he and another had found a dreadful spot, a little area of unburied dead, mostly Sengalese, rotting, rat-picked bones, with fezzes, faded red sashes, and brass-studded belts among the skeletons.

We moved to Berthonaval Wood and there we went for scout instruction to a small glade that seemed remote from war. Dashes of blue cornflower, scarlet poppies, and yellow mustard added a vivid touch to the sun-drenched grass. All around was a background of glossy sheen, a wall of still green trees. Then the expected happened. The "umptyumps" and the "oldtimers" clashed. Jimmy gained victory, though not much damage was done, and the next day all save Brown and Wilson were sent back to their companies. Headquarters did not want the turbulent bluenoses about. They disturbed the tranquility, disrupted the even tenor of headquarter ways. Brown would never be troublesome. He was a quiet, inoffensive plodder, and would be a good billet orderly. Wilson was impulsive but had the making of as good a scout as any there.

We went back to Lozingham and were billeted in a barn. A new officer took command of fourteen platoon, Mcintrye, one of the "originals" who had been a sergeant. He was a rough and ready Scot, and a splendid soldier; we all liked him. We had an ideal vacation in that village. The weather was wonderful, glorious summer, dazzling sun and very hot, but cool and starlight at night. There was an aerodrome at Auchel, just above us, and at all hours the planes were roaring overhead. I chummed with

Melville. He had never for a moment believed any of Freddy's predictions, but scoffed at them, and he was a good man in the line. Beside us were Mickey and Jerry and Tommy, of the old gang, and Eddie was in another billet. Hughes, a 73rd man, was our corporal, and I found him a splendid fellow, a little too easy to maintain discipline, but "white" to the core. Christensen was stretcher bearer in another platoon and I got acquainted with our man Stewart, the kind-voiced fellow who told me about Laurie. Laurie, however, had recovered. We had had letters from him. He was still in hospital and would never come back to the trenches. Sam, the miner, looked more sour than ever, and the surly cook would not speak, but I loved being with the company.

McIntyre started at once to re-build the platoon. He got three of the poor men transferred to other work, and looked after us like children. He came to see our rations, our meals, our quarters, and made us drill and act smartly on parade. Every man was solidly for him. In my section were four of our draft, Barron, an athlete; Sambro, a dark-faced lad who had not missed a scrap since joining; Hale, husky; and Hayward, whom I fished out of the water hole at Vimy. The others were Luggar, a late arrival, Johnson, an English lad, and Orr, a lanky fellow, an "original," who had been, until then, on a job in London. He was a sort of comic singer, and "Old Bill" took a great delight in imitating him, while we all called him "oldtimer."

Jennings, a big man from the 73rd, was in the platoon, and he did not like the French. The boys were better singers than any of the various canteen choirs I heard and the two ladies next door were very appreciative, bringing us offerings of coffee whenever a special selection was rendered. Melville always said that they were bribes for us to stop singing and Jennings backed him. He did not want to see them at all. Orders were issued that we were to have "physical jerks" before breakfast. It was an idiotic arrangement, but persisted for a short time. The bugler roused us and we were to don shorts and hurry to the training field where for half an hour we were supposed to go through snappy workouts. No one would move quickly. We wanted our tea and bacon and the goo that made Scotland famous before we could feel like jumping or running. The first morning McIntyre raced in the lead away down the field lane, calling us to follow him. We did, but at a distance, and he turned and loosed his tongue, calling us cripples and babies and all kinds of soft pets. Melville gently reminded him that we were not officers, that we had not come from ten months of good living in England, and that even now we had not four-course meals awaiting us, and batmen to serve us, when we went back from our workout.

McIntyre took it all in good part. Then turned us about and offered five francs to anyone who could keep up with him on the way back. I had done considerable running in Canada, it was in the family, Steve having a cup for the eighteen-and-under hundred-yard championship of the Maritimes, and I trimmed the officer without trying extra hard. Barron also got in ahead of him, and McIntyre did not know what to say. In a day or so the before-breakfast foolishness was eliminated. It was announced that a prize would be given for the best-drilled platoon in the brigade, and at once McIntyre set to work. He took sole charge and in a short time we were like a well-oiled machine, and really took a pleasure in the work. Any soldier must like to belong to a smart unit. We met the other platoons and defeated them easily, one by one, until we came to the finals for the battalion championship. Tommy heard a rumour that morning to the effect that some were getting a day's leave, and that the rest of the company was being taken to a good show in Auchel. That decided the issue. When we took the field we purposely made a few mistakes, and lost our chance. McIntyre, we expected, would be raging. Instead he stood and gazed at us, then grinned. "You blighters let me down," he said. "You could beat those others without trying, but, I'm glad you did. I want to have a good time myself."

No officer ever met a difficult situation more diplomatically, whether he was sincere or not.

Melville got acquainted with the madame next door and often milked her cow and did other chores. He was like a big kid, always carrying on. One night Hale went to help him and as they teased madame, Johnson thought they were going too far. He was rather odd, a quiet lad, very fair-skinned, and resented anything said about the French. There were words, then blows. He and Hale were in a wild scrap, and Hale knocked him out. Madame explained volubly that the men were not doing any harm, but really helping her.

Two more "originals" came to the company – Captain Grafftey, who took command, and Clark, a sergeant. Davies was now sergeant-major, though the original S.M. was still with us. He had the Distinguished Conduct Medal and the Military Medal, and was to go to the Depot as an instructor. We marched to Cite St. Pierre and did a short trip in at Hill 70. There had been hard fighting there by the Canadians but our share was nil. Beyond enduring the terrible stench from unburied bodies in August heat, and considerable shelling, there was little to record. A second trip at Fosse 10 was but a routine tour. That sector was a zigzag warren of old trenches and enormous slag heaps, rusting wire and rotting sandbags. The slag heaps dominated, grim, shell-pounded hillocks, sombre sentries in sombre landscape.

CHAPTER IV

Passchendale

We went to the trenches in front of Mericourt and there "A" Company captured two German patrols in a few hours. The battalion put out a party in front to cover the relief of posts. It was in charge of Izzy, and his Lewis gunner was one of our old draft, Leslie, a big six-footer, whose helper was Jackson, another of our men and just as big. They saw the Germans coming toward them, a small patrol, and lay low until they were close, when Leslie rose with his gun ready. There was no fighting, the Huns surrendered. When they got the prisoners to the trench they questioned them and found that a second patrol was expected. Izzy took his men out again and bagged the second lot, led by a lance-corporal. For such good work Izzy received the Military Cross and Leslie and Jackson got the Military Medal.

McIntyre told me that I was to go with him on a patrol and we went far over toward the German lines, remaining out three hours. I think he wanted to get a little glory for himself, and we certainly tried to find a few goose-steppers. Melville was always with me. He was a splendid scout, cool as ice, ready for anything, and could move like a great cat. War was a game wherein those trained were often the most like novices. We had a newcomer who had specialized on scouting and could read a compass like a sailor, yet he was useless, bewildered in no man's land, while Melville could go anywhere with an uncanny sense of direction.

We went out a second night and I got acquainted with "the Professor." He was a quiet-voiced man, sandy-haired, unnoticed in the platoon, but had held an important position in a college. We crawled out slowly, then separated in three parties of four each. There had been a magnificent sunset, a flood of exquisite colouring, opals, pinks and crimsons, and I had remarked about it in the Professor's hearing. He crawled beside me as we took up a position where we were to remain for an hour, hoping to trap a patrol, and shivered each time the flares went up. The Hun was having a little fun all by himself, sending up red and green lights as a change from the regular white ones. The red glows made some small pools of water look like big blots of blood, and the green lights gave everything a ghastly, corpse-like sheen. At one spot we disturbed a bunch of rats, and they rustled through the grass and over old rubbish, their snaky tails dragging after them. Their little eyes were malevolent as they watched us and one shuddered when he remembered what they were seeking.

"Are you nervous?" I whispered to the Professor, and as we lay in our position he seemed glad to talk.

"I'm really so frightened that I could jump up and bolt like a wild thing," he said. "How on earth do you chaps stand it?" Melville and Tommy were on the other side of him.

I tried to convince him that it was only the nervousness of the first night that gripped him, but he argued against me, and, to my surprise, Tommy agreed with him. For the first time I heard my closest friend admit that his heart was in his mouth as he crawled into the region between the wires. "Bird's like a bloody machine," he said. "I've been beside him for ten months out here and when there's been chaps killed near him, and I've never seen him act shaky. He hasn't got nerves like the rest of us."

I changed the subject then and talked of other things in order to soothe the new man, and was surprised to find him so well-educated; he should never have been a private in the ranks. He, in turn, told me that he had been surprised. He had been in a rather rough Ontario battalion, and its members had made a specialty of carousals while they were in England, the canteens being their main entertainment. He had expected things as bad or worse in France, and had found our company as fine a group of men as he had ever met. During all that summer I had not seen a dozen drunks in our billets, but the fact had not impressed me before. The Professor then talked about the sunset and asked, rather curiously, how I could be interested in such things, and at the same time intent on killing my fellow men. He spoke of the beauty that belongs to sunsets and dawns and high mountains and still waters and moonlight, and pointed out the incongruity of a star gleam in a stagnant pool beside us. Everything about us, he said, should be horrible, distorted, repulsive.

No Germans were abroad in our territory and after a long time Melville and I wormed ahead through the grass, on and on, until we were so close to the enemy trench that we could see its wire barriers and the cruel length of the barbs. Then we went back, and long after I was in my bivvy, listening to the heavy hammer strokes of a battery back of Canada Trench, I thought of the Professor's words. It was easy to misjudge character. Men whom no one credited with heroic qualities, revealed them. Others failed pitiably to live up to expectations. There was, I was sure, a strength or weakness in men apart from their real selves, for which they were in no way responsible. And who could know the Professor's calibre? Snobbishness died miserably in the trenches. No artificial imposition could survive in the ranks where inherent value automatically found its level; all shams of superiority fled before such an existence of essentials; but a man's endurance under that which he most dreads was something we could not gauge.

The Professor was a dreamer, which made it harder for him. His imagination led him twice through every danger, tried him cruelly. For every medal earned by the martinet type of soldier, a dozen were deserved by the dreamers. But when I tried to measure myself I failed. It was not physical courage that carried me, far from it, but a state of mind that words will never describe. Each night when I slept I dreamt of Steve, saw him clearly, and when awake, in the trenches at night, out on listening posts, FELT him near. In some indefinable way I depended on him. Ever since he had guided me in from that foggy unknown stretch at the back of Vimy I would go anywhere in no man's land. I knew, with a – fanatical, if you like – faith, that a similar touch would lead me straight where I should go. In the trenches, on posts, in any place, I was always watching for him, waiting for him, trying to sense him near me, and in the doing I missed the tensity of dragging hours, and easy fears that seized the unoccupied mind.

I liked the keen damp air of the mornings of September. At stand-to each man would have a glowing cigarette, each have his collar turned to his chin, his shoulders hunched, and would be pacing the hard-packed trench floor. When he stopped and gazed over the bags he would doze a second – start guiltily, and doze again. The east would shoot with crimson. Birds would twitter. Then, like magic, the sun would glitter on the dew-covered weeds and wet wire. There would be mists in the hollows, often extensive, so that the distant slag heaps would appear dark islands in a woolly sea. Gradually the sun would gain strength, and the vapors would dissolve. Then we went back to our shelters and odours of tea and bacon made each man happy.

On the third night our patrol was divided into two parties. McIntyre was not with us, and the officer we had was "windy." We did not go out nearly as far as usual, and when I took him to a spot near three trees where there was a short sap with German greatcoat in it, he was alarmed. He led us over to the right and left Melville and I to "guard" his flank. There was a length of low ground, almost ravine-like, through which an enemy patrol might pass and he told us to stay on its banks. We lay there in the grass. It was quiet and we were tired. It was our third successive night of crawling, and so Melville took a length of fine wire he always carried and made a neat trip string at the head of the long pocket. Then we relaxed, relaxed thoroughly and slept.

Fortunately I woke just before the officer and his men reached us. They were hurrying and the lieutenant was panting with excitement. "Where was the German patrol?" We sat up and grinned at them. There had been no patrol. "Yes, there was," hissed the officer, "and it came right into this hollow. Where is it?" We argued earnestly then and had a difficult time. They assured us that six Germans had filed by them and that only a lucky move had kept them hidden. At last the controversy ceased, with honours even, and we went in, but not before Melville slyly inspected his trip-wire – and found it broken. We talked afterward about that Heinie patrol. How could they pass us without seeing us?

We made a second trip into the same front and I got to know no man's land like a back yard. McIntyre was more nervous as the lines were much closer than where we had held before. He had several listening posts out and constant patrols. The only change in work I had was a covering party to protect engineers who examined a road that crossed our trenches. Word came that we were to be relieved by the 22nd Battalion and I was sent out as guide. With me were Hickey and Egglestone, two men of the 73rd, both good soldiers. They were to take in the other platoons. We had a long wait for the "Van Doos" and there at the top of the Ridge talked and smoked, and as we watched the ten mile arc of Very Lights glimmer and sink before us, we saw a German attack on the battalion to our left. The flashing of bursting shells along our lines was a winking chaos of crimson, and then we saw our flares looping, our S.O.S. soaring aloft. Within a minute red flashes marked the German front, a fury of explosions that lasted twenty minutes. Meanwhile the din of bursting shells and machine guns came clearly to us and we could even see the bursting of Mills bombs. At last everything regained its normal appearance, and our men arrived. The attempted German raid, we heard afterwards, did not reach our trench.

The French-Canadians would not be hurried and their officers humoured them like children. They were a great battalion, carried a fine reputation, and seemed conscious of it, which was natural. Slowly, and with long halts every half mile, we wended our way down the Ridge and out on the plain. The "Van Doos" smoked in spite of all cautions about being spotted and I was very thankful when, at last, we arrived at our trench. Our lads moved away with amusing alacrity – the veterans had recalled another time at the crater line – and soon the trench was handed over. No patrols covered the relief and to McIntyre's amazement all his listening posts were ignored. No more sentries were posted than we used in daytime, and the only remark the officer made was, "If he wants to come over – let heem come."

It was now October and we moved away to Magnicourt. Rumours had come that we were going to the Salient, that graveyard swamp of mud and slime, to the long agony of Passchendale, and the men were restless. For the first time some of them began to look on the "vin" when it was "rouge" and one man, Giger, had to be carried to his billet. His like was not elsewhere in the Corps. His appearance was a reminder of what Mother Nature could do when she was in an angry mood; he had scarcely any forehead and could neither read nor write. He had come in a late draft and had been sick for several days, giving up everything but his oath of allegiance. We laughed to weakness the night when at a barn billet a calf got its head through an opening and licked his face. Poor Giger howled with fright.

Our billet was a coal shed. Around the wall ran a brick ledge and around the ledge ran mice and rats, three generations of them, so that we moved our quarters to the loft of a barn and slept on the straw. In the night I heard men marching and went down. Many times when out at billet I had risen quietly and slipped outside, drinking in the moist air, looking at the moon-bathed fields and hedges, picturing the same night across the water. It was dark and uncanny when I left the barn. One heard nothing but the steady tramp, tramp, tramp on the road as the shadowy files marched past in a cloud of dust like river mist, silent and half asleep. They were, like us, headed Ypres-way. Bulky ghosts loomed alongside the column, the non-coms, watching for stragglers, but there were no shouted orders. The only sounds were the thudding shuffle of feet, the dull creak of equipment, a muttered curse as someone trod on another's heels. All at once the men halted, and slumped down on the roadside without waiting for the "fall out" order. Mostly the men sprawled, motionless, on their packs, but here and there a match flared as a cigarette was lighted and there were glimpses of tired, sharp-lined faces.

After the battalion had gone I wandered along the road. It was warm but a shower threatened. A dozing sentry of the guard leaned on his rifle. Back from him, under two big trees, several soldiers were sleeping on the ground. I walked away down the road and to my surprise met McIntyre. He had probably been visiting officers in another battalion – there were many moving our way – and he was feeling talkative. He asked me sharply what I was doing, and then gave definite hours that I should rest. I mentioned the Salient and he swore and cursed it, and then broke forth about his gallant boys, his splendid men. He knew every man, his faults and weaknesses, and was kind to them all. At times he seemed strict, but never without reason, and there that night he almost broke down as he talked about us, and I sensed that he that afternoon had had to censor the company letters, perhaps more poignantly inarticulate than usual. It began to rain as I left him and I went back in the mysterious silence, listening to the steady beating on the cobbles. The bent still figure of the sentry had not moved, but under the trees the sleepers were stirring and muttering as drops from the branches fell on their unprotected faces.

The next day we moved on and seemed to leave the main route for we stopped at a little village prettier than any I had seen. Trees shaded all the little homes and a brook flashed and gurgled its way among them, crossing under a quaint old stone bridge that must have been hundreds of years old. The company seemed changed, the men more restless. At the estaminet they found one of those crazy penny-in-the-slot pianos and there made merry, singing too boisterously for harmony. Giger got drunk again and semaphored to a mademoiselle until he became incapable of motion.

I watched the men as they got their evening meal, and they were all flushed, unnatural. Even little Mickey was shrill, and I looked at the boy. He had changed, was different, and I feared for him. His nerve was leaving him. On our last trip in a whizz bang had made bloody work of two gunners and an arm had been left lying in the trench. His post was nearby and I saw him walk by the place hurriedly and then, with a sudden cry, seize the arm and hurl it over the parapet. Afterward he had given me a glance of dog-like entreaty and I had stayed and talked with him for more than an hour. He smoked continually, those army gaspers, Red Hussars and Bees-wings, and his hands were not steady.

That night was the wildest of any I had seen in billets. Half the men had had more liquor than they could carry and all were shouting ribald songs and indulging in horse play. It was all fun, and their delight seemed in making the Professor cringe. They had got to know him and it was rumoured that he was such a granny that he even considered a knowledge of French immoral. They shouted about the three kinds of "cases" there were, walking, "sandbag," and "stretcher," and asked each other grisly questions concerning "religion" and "next-of-kin." There were pledges about "V.C.'s" or "wooden ones," and more of like kind. All of it was but a reflex of their own inner thoughts.

The Professor and Tommy and I helped many of them make their beds that night, and then I went out in the village to the old bridge and sat there listening to the water. The moonlight fell flat on things and gilded them, and there was the night's faint moist smell of trees and grass and brookside. I thought of that long ago when we had come to France, those first nights filling sandbags with Vimy slime, Freddy's white set look, his premonitions; Arthur sitting in the mud, dazed, stricken, five minutes before the bullet was to hit him; Charley at my water-logged bivvy in Dumbell Camp, pleading for something to change his convictions; poor ape-like Slim and his pal, Joe, always together, in trench or billet, and together in death. What waited us up in the Salient?

A man came down the street, walking slowly, quietly, and sat beside me on the old stone wall. It was Stewart, the stretcher bearer, and he spoke softly as a woman as he talked about the beauty of the night. Then he rambled on, telling me of his boyhood in old Scotland, of his going to Canada, of all he had done, and intended to do, intimate things which only old friends mention. I listened sympathetically and over an hour we sat together, then he walked on up the road. I looked at my watch. It was one o'clock in the morning.

Before I could leave another came, the Professor. He had been lying down and could not sleep, and now he unloaded his mind. He thought that some one should shriek from the high places about this awful, stupendous folly in which we were engaged, that the few sane men left on earth should combine their efforts to stop the carnage. He hated war, loathed it, feared it, hated everything connected with it, even to those gaily-woven silk souvenirs and postcards that played havoc with our five-franc notes. Our existence was, he said, an ugly nightmare, and Heaven must shudder in protest. We walked back slowly, and in the garden by our billet found Mickey lying on the brook bank. One roll would have dropped him in a deep pool, and there he lay on his back in a drunken stupor. We carried him in and I could have hugged him; sharp lines were cutting into his boyish features, altering him, aging him.

We moved to Hazebrouck. Sitting in the "40 Hommes" coach I watched the boys. They were normal again, but different. They sang a long time, old songs, in harmony, and then were silent; there was none of the usual jesting. I had looked at each in turn, "Old Bill" with tissue paper on a comb, one of the orchestra; Sambro beside him talking to Barron; Big Glenn, reading a letter; Melville, Ira, Jennings, and Hughes singing lustily; Stewart, smiling at them; old Sam, as sour as usual; Hickey and Egglestone with a lance jack named Alway, a nice fellow; Kennedy, Bunty, Johnson, Luggar, Dykes, Flynn, and Eddie, all singing. I sat with Mickey and Tommy by the door, and Tommy talked of the marching battalions he had glimpsed on the road. The Professor came from a corner and joined us. He was talking again about the war, calling it a ghastly paroxysm of civilization.

Mickey stared at him, wide-eyed, and I tried to ease the condemnation, pointing out that war was not new, had always been. I got out my little guide book and tried to divert Mickey's thoughts as I read about the history of the country. Arras, Boulogne, Cambrai, Verdun, had all been towns under the reign of Julius Caesar, and a German invasion was nothing new. Attila and his heathen Huns had poured into France when it was Gaul, burning and plundering and had lost 160,000 men before they were driven away. I read about King Edward at Crecy with his expeditionary force of thirty-two thousand, facing three times his strength of the finest French chivalry. The English held strategic position on a slope, with the sun at their backs, and their bowmen shot down the mounted Frenchmen who attacked with their lances. Thirty thousand men of France fell in that battle, twelve hundred knights and eight princes, so why should we consider we were entangled in an original catastrophe.

"How many knights and princes are going to be killed up in Passchendale?" asked Tommy, cynically. Then he raved about the officers, the gilded staff in fine chateaus and billets, waited on hand and foot, living like lords, travelling in cushioned cars, stroking away – with careless pens – thousands of lives. The Professor and Mickey did not speak.

I turned the pages and read to them that when Louis XIV was waging wars, taking four fortresses on the Rhine in four days, the pomp and splendour of his equipage rivalled that of fairy princes. Every campaign ended in a sort of royal pageant. There were coaches of crystal and gold, horses draped in cloth of gold, courtiers and conquerors dazzling with diamonds, ladies in silks and plumes and laces. Old King Solomon himself was outshone. "So you see, Tommy," I said, "there's really nothing new. The old boys had their big parades and banquets and probably their W.A.A.C.'s to wait on them."

"That's all right," said Tommy, doggedly, "them old chaps were bred for wars, it was all they knew. They didn't think about anything else."

The Professor had been looking at my little book and now he snatched it from me. "Listen," he said tensely, and read, "… the code of chivalry was completed by an education that began at the early age of seven years. Boys were sent to the castle of their father's overlord, where, in return for their breeding, they rendered domestic service, no matter how lofty their birth. At twelve they learned to ride and use arms. Then they went on adventure, on horse, carrying shield and lance for their leader. Between sixteen and twenty they were made knights and put on, for the sacred fast and vigil of arms, the white tunic, a sign of purity; the red robe, which symbolized the blood he must shed; the black jerkin, betokening death, a close companion of all knight-at-arms." "They were soldiers," he cried, "we're not. They wanted war, we don't."

"It's all the same through history," I said weakly. "There has always been war and will be. We can't change things, we just go on."

The Professor argued firmly that such reasoning was piffle, stank of the fatalistic. Chivalry, he said, had long been buried, purity had become a strange word.

I tried to stop him, but it was no use and Tommy took up the argument, declaring that we were really worse than they were in the Dark Ages, and that anyone who had been drilled to fight and kill from the time he was seven was different. We were simply civilians in soldier's clothing, and war was a mess of grotesque murder. He stopped, finally, when I could give him a nod that Mickey could not see, but the lad had absorbed every word. He sat staring at us and through us, seeing things, fearful things. The Professor stilled as soon as he noticed him.

At Hazebrouck, Melville and Ira and I went to have a feed of eggs and chips, but discovered that we did not have enough money amongst us. As we looked in the windows of the shop we saw big, good-natured Gordon sitting alone at a table, and at once went in. He could not speak French and we were able to make madame understand that he would pay the bill. As we ate I talked with Ira, and found him changed. He was quiet, thoughtful, kind in manner, and never raised his voice as he calmly told me that everything was all right with him, he had got hold of himself. I dared not ask him what he meant, and he told me without asking. He was going to his death, he said, and would meet it like a soldier, and there was that in his voice that told me any argument of mine would be futile. My skin was pricked with goose flesh as he talked.

Melville heard all he said and was impressed. We all forgot about our empty pockets until Gordon had risen to go, and we were in a predicament. He looked at us, then grinned in his usual manner. "I'll bet you guys were planning to stick me," he said. "Just to let you have your joke, I'll go ahead and pay." And he did. He was a big-boned man, sometimes a little awkward in his work, but no bigger heart than his beat under khaki.

It began to rain that night and continued all the next day. We went to Ypres and waited there four hours. Tommy and I went exploring and found our way to a lane that led to an old ruin half-hidden by piled wreckage. We scrambled over debris and got into a long, shadowy passage with a film of moisture on its walls, ending at a door as cold and stiff as a thing dead and rigid. I pushed it in, wondering what we might discover, but it was only a large inner room, the windows completely blocked so that little light crept in. It was a place of dull mystery, shadows and watching darkness, and the stillness of desolation brooded over it. Tommy shivered, and so did I, and we hurried out into the drizzle and stared around.

I told him how in 1382 the Bishop of Norwich had landed at Calais with sixty thousand men and marched to take Ypres – and failed. In my little guide book I read descriptions of that part of Belgium. "White villages glistening in warm sunshine, orchards teeming with golden fruit, here and there a gleam of water. The land is highly cultivated. Waving cornfields overshadow the soil, the homes are ornamented with ivy, the honeysuckle, rose and vine peep from groves of poplar or willow; and placid waters – the slow streams and still canals, which intersect that land in all directions – sparkle and glimmer. Yet this landscape of mild earth, so lovely in an aspect of repose, has been the theatre of almost all the sanguinary wars which from time to time have desolated Europe; that luxuriated crop has been manured with the best blood of the brave, the gay, the virtuous; those sleeping groves have responded to the storm of slaughter – and may yet again."

"Cut out that stuff." Tommy spoke sharply and I put the book away. I could understand his irritableness; it was on all of us. The atmosphere of the Salient had gripped us. Before us, all around us, in the fan of a great wheel, it lay, Pilckem, Wieltje, Railway Wood, Hooge, Sanctuary Wood, Mont Sorrell, Hill 60, Hollebeke. Among the veterans I had visited in other battalions I had heard of numerous Farms, Lancashire, Turco, Argyle, Hussar, and Essex. And there were Cottages and the Willows, and Admiral's Road, and Hellfire Corner, and Crab Crawl, the Spoil Bank, the Bluff, Maple Copse and Zillibeke Lake. We peered around us as we marched out into that flat world of mud and water, a desolation racked by explosions, fetid with slime of rotting things, gray and gruesome beyond description.

We went to California Trench, relieving the 4th C.M.R.s, and found it a dreadful ditch with makeshift shelters. The rain continued and we stood about like wooden Indians or arranged some sort of roof to shed the drizzle. There was considerable shelling from all angles and at dusk the Salient seemed a mighty ghoul, something invisible and vengeful, blood-seeking, watching. All that night we sat in such shelter as we had and were soaked by constant dripping, chilled to the bone. Dawn came slowly and with a clinging penetrating mist that made even the rifles clammy to the touch. We got out and moved off in small parties and an officer came to INSPECT that swamp hole in which we had cowered, to see if any cigarette butt or rubbish had not sunk in the mire. Wheeeee–ump! A shell, probably a stray, came with a heart-stopping suddenness and exploded in the very niche Melville and I had excavated, leaving the lieutenant a bloody pulp.

We moved to tents in St. Jean and left our equipment there. It was still raining and we were taken through the mud to battery positions. Horses and mules had drowned there as they tried to move the guns and so ropes were used, and thirty men tugged on each one. We could not pull the guns in the usual fashion as the mud gripped the wheels, so we turned them over and over until they were in new emplacements. It was tremendous labour. We wallowed often to our armpits in mud and water mixed to porridge thickness and the only thing solid underfoot was a dead man or his equipment. As we got the guns in their new places big black-winged Gothas came overhead and dropped bombs on us, or the track that was some hundred yards away. There ammunition-laden mules were packed in line and I saw direct hits made on broad rumps or on the shaky planks of the "board road." More carcasses were piled beside the way, more legs to stiffen toward the skies, more bodies to distend and afford footholds for rats. Shambles of heads and heels and entrails were shovelled into the mire and the procession kept on. None of our airmen were in sight.

Then the Hun shelled us. The battery had not loosed a round before one gun was wrecked by a direct hit and two gunners killed. We went away, back to our tents, sodden, shaking with cold and exhaustion, and were cheered by steaming hot tea and mulligan. But we sat at night in the rain-soaked tents, huddled in sitting positions on floors that were pooled with icy water and the shelling kept on. We sat there in the dark, unmoving, without speaking, our brains numbed by the awfulness of everything, trying to reach a comatose state that answered for sleep. Again we moved on, this time to an area dotted with derelict rusting tanks, and on the way met remnants of relieved battalions, men who looked like grisly discards of the battlefield, long unburied, who had risen and were in search of graves in which to rest. A German airman came over, flying deliberately, one of those hawks of the Black Cross, swooped down and sprayed bullets at one of the sausage balloons above Ypres. There were forked flames, billowing smoke, a meteor of fiery fabric, charred fragments, and two swaying figures attached to parachutes. They dangled a moment and then sank from sight.

Some of the men slept in tanks. We went to one, Melville, Tommy and I, and could tip it with our weight. Water was underneath and as we rocked the monster, a head squeezed out in the muck, a face without eyes, the skin peeled as though from lard, a corpse long dead and frightful. We left the place and found a mound of solid earth, enough to make our bed, and there we stayed, between sandbagged walls, with a roof of salvaged corrugated iron. Not far from us was an old trench revetted with German stick work, blocked at one part with broken wire and the black dead of forgotten fights. At night we were called forth and led to a dump and there laden with sections of new-made "bath mats." All around the giant horseshoe of the Salient there were red flashes and winking glows and the misty light of flares.

We went toward the front line, past water-logged trenches, a nightmare of scummy holes, an indescribable desolation, on and on. The sky was illumined by strange flickering lights, the reflection of a thousand gun flashes, and quivered with the passage of shells. As we neared the end of our duckwalk a few flares soared up ahead of us, alarmingly near, and their fitful gleams cast strange moving shadows over the swamp. A machine gun fired nervously and bullets buried themselves with vicious thuds in jagged, fang-like stubs nearby. We hurried, then met the foremost carriers without their loads. Each man, as he came to the end of the narrow "bath mats," threw down the one he carried, butting it to that one on which he stood. Thus the path went on with amazing speed. But the boards were new and their whiteness was detected. Suddenly a hurricane of shell-fire was all about us. Fortunately I was just at the end and I threw my load down, jumped around and ran. Others heaved their sections wildly and all was confusion. High explosive rained all around us – stunning, stifling, ear splitting; everywhere there was a dead smell of gas and mud and blood.

One man went down as I pushed by him and then we were all away. It was a miraculous escape, but the shelling followed the walk. I left it and plunged through mud a distance and gained another pathway. Someone seized my tunic, someone who wheezed dreadfully. It was "Old Bill," night blind, up there with his load, and he had finished putting it in proper place before he ran. I walked with him, helped him back to solid footing, and back to our shelters.

We went on to Abraham Heights and relieved the the R.C.R.'s. It was soft ground and we easily dug a trench and took shelter in it. Sambro was

on one side and Melville on the other. As we worked together our rations
came, very slim, and dry socks, and – wonders of wonders – mail. Melville
had not talked since we moved and I watched him closely. He took his pair
of socks and placed them in a corner of the bivvy he had made. "Bill," he
said quietly, "remember this pair and get them when you come back."

"What are you talking about?" I asked.

He tried to grin, big red-faced Melville, who had been with me through
a hundred ticklish corners, and then he said simply, "I'm not coming
back."

I tried to argue with him, asked him questions, but he never told me
whether he had had a dream or what had given him his premonition, and
he was not afraid. He had received a parcel containing some of his
favourite chewing tobacco, "Napoleon," and he gave it all away to the other
men of the platoon, saying that he had more than he needed.

Sambro and I looked at each other and talked together. There was nothing we could do. Melville had joked many times about Freddy's "fool
ideas," and now he ... As we stood gazing over the morbid ground there
was a distant report, distinguishable above the others, and a shell came
over us with a rush that made me perspire. It was a high velocity gun that
was strafing us and that first hit was not fifty yards from where we had
dug. Whii-iip! Another. Across from us Hickey and Alway had dug a short
bed-length shelter and that shell caused them to duck low. Before they
rose the third one came – and burst just beside them, burying them deep.
We rushed to the place, choked with fumes, and dug with all our strength.
It was of no use. We found Hickey first, and he had been killed by the blow
of the explosion. Alway was doubled beneath him.

Once more we moved, in the darkness, up Grafenstrafel Road and halted by shell holes occupied by the 49th. As they left we dug in, connecting
holes, then cut places in the trench side and hung ground sheets over
them, and there boiled mess-tins of tea. One lot and our water was gone,
and we were almost famished for hot drink. I crawled a distance in the
muck and found a hole deep enough to dip from and filled my mess-tin.
Twice more I went and we all had plenty of reviving tea. Then a low
moaning sound in front caused us all to stand steady. It was repeated at
intervals, sometimes faintly, and sounded like a man in agony. Once at
Vimy, while over on the left of our company talking to members of the
adjoining battalion, I had heard a man moaning in no man's land, and had

seen a sentry go out to help him. There had been a shot, and the sentry managed to crawl in, badly wounded by a German sniper, who had simulated suffering in order to lure a victim over the parapet. I thought it another trap and said so, but Sergeant Oron and Clark went out. They found a German in the swamp. He was badly wounded, had lain in the muck for three days and gangrene had set in. He hated us, bared his teeth, snarled like an animal. A stretcher party took him to the nearest dressing station, struggling for hours in the mud, and left him to await his turn in the line. Before it came, a shell dropped between him and a wounded officer and blew them to atoms.

Clark told me I was wanted at the end of the trench. An officer was there and told me I was to go on patrol with him. His men were all of another platoon and I did not know where we were, but I went gladly. Action helped me in the Salient. It was the deadly waiting, helpless waiting, that was unnerving, for always it seemed as if swooping Death were just above us, hovering, or reaching tentacles from dark corners. There was much whispering among the men and mention of a pillbox at Furst Farm. We moved out slowly, cautiously, through a farmyard, slimy, nauseating with putrid filth and stench, and crept along a hedge toward a road. All at once I froze. Directly in front of me I could see the outline of pot helmets. German heads, close together. A patrol seemed bunched there, waiting for us. The officer did not know what move to make and as we peered I saw that the helmets had never tilted a fraction. They seemed fixed, immovable, and two of us crept forward. Every German was dead.

They were in rifle pits and there were many more we had not seen at first. They had been killed by overhead shrapnel and were so wedged in the mud that few had fallen over. We floundered all around them and did not find a live German, though we fancied we saw a working party in the gloom, and then made our way back to the trench. I was covered with foul mud, sickened with smells and my kilt had worn my legs raw. Melville had tea ready for me but he was strangely quiet. Ira was with him, and beyond them, seated on the firestep, was Mickey.

Gradually it grew light. Rumour had come that we would be relieved at night and many of the men were glad. "Old Bill" and Bunty had had a fearful time in the mud, up that horrible road where one tracked the highway by dead men strewed like spilled bundles. Sambro wanted some tea. He had been on a message to company headquarters in a pillbox, and he was wet and cold. I crawled out to the water hole again, and as I dipped it was light enough to see. Just below my mess-tin, in the water, was a huge dead rat. Every other pool near it was discoloured with worse than rats, so I said nothing but boiled the tea an extra time.

All day we huddled, dozing, waiting for relief, and then came word that an attack was to be made that night. We were to try to capture a strong point, a Farm ruin, called "Graf House." McIntyre came when it was dark and gave orders. There were to be seven parties used and he was taking twenty-five men with him. We were to work up a road as quietly as possible as it was to be a stealth attack at two pip emma, without a barrage. The Stokes gunners would lend assistance once we were started. Melville shook hands with me as soon as McIntyre finished talking, but he did not say a word. Then Ira came and whispered that he was glad we were on our way.

The men chosen went to the pillbox headquarters and there we were given a rum ration, those who wished it. There seemed to be plenty of the liquor and breaths were reeking as we crept out and into the beginning of the road. I followed McIntyre and was to take back messages as soon as our objective was reached. Behind me was Luggar and next him was Hale. As we crawled I took particular notice of each object in the gloom, and as I peered over the bank on our left I saw a German raise his head, not twenty yards from us. I seized McIntyre's foot to signal him, and he yanked it from me and spoke out loud. The German fired instantly and the bullet grooved the top of Luggar's head slicing the scalp, and causing him to be temporarily insane. He threshed about and Hale and I held him down as a perfect stream of bullets was passing over us from the left. Other hands helped us and we passed him back to the rear to be bandaged there. I tossed a Mills bomb in the direction of the Hun and after it had exploded I crept ahead a few feet and raised carefully to look over the bank. Crack! A rifle was thrust up and fired only inches from Hale's head. The bullet split his scalp and the concussion broke his ear drums. Blood streamed over his face, blinding him, and I helped him get started back to Stewart. Then I pitched a second bomb, close in. Meanwhile McIntyre had not halted. He had rushed on and Sambro and I half-raised as we hurried after him. A machine gun blazed at us from a spot on the right and we dove into the mud. Crash – slam. The Stokes gun was at work but its shells dropped short, falling almost in our path. We rose again as the Maxim stopped firing, then – a flaming white-hot instant – oblivion.

When I recovered consciousness my head was splitting with pain and a terrible nausea had seized my stomach. The Stokes shell had dropped beside me, throwing me bodily into the mud, and Sambro was stunned as well. He was lying in the slime, and feeling his limbs, certain that he was wounded. All around us was frightful clamour of guns and bombs and rifle shots. I heard McIntyre's voice shouting "Five rounds rapid," then it stopped, but my nose was bleeding and I was too dizzy to stand. We crawled towards the sound, then halted. There was a great plunging in the murk, and two dim figures came towards us, puffing and blowing, tugging at something. They were Germans, big men, and had a machine gun and tripod. They placed it just in front of us and one man yanked at a long cartridge belt. I pulled the pin from my last bomb and heaved the missile at a count of two. It burst just beneath the tripod. One man went down like a huge tree, the other struggled a moment before he stilled.

We went by them, making sure the gun was ruined, and in a new-made crater found a man of "A" Company with his wrist almost severed. We bandaged him hurriedly and sent him back, and were rising to go on when Clark came stumbling through the mud, and yelled at us. "Come on, give them ..." His shout was cut off. He pitched, dead, in front of us.

A man scurried by with a stretcher as we went over to the bank where we could see men moving. It was a Lewis gunner, and he said McIntyre had been shot through the stomach and was dying. They got him on the stretcher, but we went on to the short bank in front and found "Old Bill," Mickey, and Johnson crouched there, shooting at a German gun that streaked sparks not more than thirty yards away. Sambro had bombs with him and he and I hurled them. The bursts seemed right on the gun and it was silenced. I stared at the other men on the bank. They were all dead. Melville and Ira and Jennings, lying there together, rifle in hand, all shot through the head by one sweep of the German gun. "Old Bill" had seen it, and stayed there after, trying to pot the gunner himself. The fourth dead man was poor old sour Sam, at rest at last.

We looked around and found that all the rest of the party had gone, but another fit of sickness seized me and I could not move for a time. Sambro stayed with me. When we did go back we had to crawl a distance to avoid machine gun fire, but the main fighting had shifted over on the left. A light vapour was stealing over the ground making it harder to see and I stumbled over a body as we found the road bank. It was the Professor, riddled with bullets, dead. He was covered with mud, had lost his steel helmet, had evidently got lost in the darkness, and there he lay, after years of study and culture, with glassy eyes and face upturned to the sky, a smashed cog of the war machine, with not a hope of burial excepting by a chance shell, and the mist thickened and rolled sullenly over him. A few paces beyond we saw some person on the bank itself, stooping over something. It was Stewart, the stretcher bearer, and we called to him softly, telling him to get down into the ditch. He was in plain view of any Huns left along the low ground. He did not answer but went on bandaging a wounded man, and not a second later came a sharp, heavy report. Stewart pitched across the man he was binding, headfirst, so that his kilt fell over his back and there he lay, dead, while the Germans shot again and again, a fusilade of bullets, as if venting their hate, and the man beneath Stewart stilled. We had not a bomb left but we wormed to the bank at a spot farther along and fired at the rifle flashes until the shooting stopped. Then we crawled on until at last we came to old trenches near company headquarters and there I suddenly lost consciousness.

When I woke it was late in the morning. I was lying in the corner of a remnant of trench and Mickey and Sambro were with me. I had been sick again and then had lain as if in a stupor. There had been a terrific shelling all about us and the acrid reek of explosives stung my nostrils. None of the other survivors were near us, not a runner had come into view. We huddled there together and listened to the thunder of the guns until it was noon. Then I roused and peered from our refuge. A few yards away were three green-scummed pools. White, chalky hands reached out of one – hands that were spattered with lumps of clay, and from the farther one a knee stuck up above the filthy water. In another bit of trench, where the parados had disappeared, a soldier stood rigidly, feet braced apart. He was dead, had been killed by concussion, and his body was split as if sliced by a great knife. Looking back I could make out the bank of the road and there distinguished Stewart's body still humped over the man he was trying to assist. Some dead Germans were over on the flank and one, bareheaded, was lying as if reclining on his elbow. A shell came as I looked up and erupted almost under the body, and the dead man stood straight up a moment, as if saluting, then tumbled down on the other side. I lay down again and saw that neither Sambro nor Mickey had moved. They were asleep as they hunched there side by side, mud-splattered, wan as ghosts.

Night found us still crouched in our cover and I got up and went around the shell holes until I found "Old Bill" and Johnson. They told me that a relief was due and that there had been no orders. Sergeant Oron had been wounded and Hughes was not with us, having gone on leave from St. Jean. We did not know who would have the platoon. As we talked there was suddenly a small barrage of fish tails. They whirred from the sky and several fell near the standing dead man and toppled him over. Then a corporal from another platoon came and called to us to follow him. We were to go back to Ypres, the 16th Battalion was relieving us. We went and met the incoming men by our old trench, were joined by the remainder of the company and heard that big Glenn had been killed, that Izzy had died gloriously in the fighting at the "Graf House."

All that long drag back was a hideous nightmare. The track was worse than when we had come in and the shelling was incessant. We moved with infinite slowness, every step a struggle, a tearing physical effort, and a vast noise was over all, a thundering, rolling clamour that dulled our thinking, mercifully smothering some of our agonized impressions of the night before.

We went back to the Watou area and there lay about and were given trousers to replace our soaked and muddied kilts. A big draft came and refilled our ranks and then came the dread word that we were to go back to Passchendale again. The November rains were chilling us, freezing us, our feet were always soggy and we were almost despondent. All that time we had been out we had talked but little. Each man seemed busy with his own thoughts, disinclined to speak to another. There had been too many of our friends killed, the men we had been with for months. I found that McLeod and Farmer had died in the mud, that Egglestone had been wounded and placed on a stretcher and then he and his bearers were all blown to fragments by a big shell. And poor old Flynn had been killed. We seemed to move in a daze, to do things as if we were automatons. One of the draft, Upham, a lad who had been out before, made friends with me and stayed by me. Sambro was with Barron, and Mickey and Tommy were together. Jerry was missing.

Once more we went to California Trench and hated it intensely as we all remembered the gory death of the inspecting officer. We went on the next night through a fearful shelling up to an abomination of desolation, finding curled tangles of wire in absurd places, men squatted in the muck,

silent, staring, stiff-moving men, who muttered as they got up and vanished in the gloom like mud-swathed phantoms. It was daylight before we
could find where we were to dig in and Captain Grafftey came among us,
the first officer we had seen up there with the exception of McIntyre. He
told us to dig for shelter, but no more, as we might move at any time. Orr
and Hayward had been wounded on the way up and one man killed.

As we worked the Hun began to shell our position with whizz bangs
and some of the men grew panicky. The captain climbed through the
mud, from shelter to shelter, speaking to the fellows. Tommy and I
watched him come near us. Just a few feet from us, in the next shelter,
Dykes was working. He straightened to speak and at the next instant a
shell cut the top of his head away, leaving but the jaw and neck. The body
rocked a moment as if in a wind and then toppled backward. The captain
saluted as he passed.

When it grew dark we moved again and formed a new line. The Hun
spotted us and started shelling while machine gun fire raked the ground.
Upham and I were together and as we started digging I saw a body just in
front of us, a big man with his equipment over his greatcoat. "Catch hold
of that stiff," I said to Upham. "Pull him back here and we'll use him for
part of our parapet."

He stared at me. "Don't," he yelled. "Don't touch him."

I seized the corpse myself, rolling it over and into place, and Upham
sprang from where he had been spading and commenced a new hole over
to the right. A salvo of shells came and exploded. Whizzing fragments
were all around me but I was not touched. Upham fell and was dead when
I reached him. There was a strange cry further on. It was the sergeant-
major who should have gone to the Depot, the old original. He had insisted in coming for one more trip and his jaw had been carried away by
shrapnel. He died before morning. Two other men were down, Johnson
and Barron, both wounded. The shelling continued all that night and the
next day. We had dug deep V-shaped pits, connecting some of them, and
there we crouched, gray faces under muddy helmets, red-rimmed eyes,
staring, dazed, wondering, our brains numbed beyond thinking by the
incessant explosions. One of the new men pitched down between our
shelter and the next one. He was pierced in a dozen places and one arm
had been sheared from his body by shrapnel. Mickey sat beside me shud-

dering, half-stunned, staring unseeing, his limbs twitching convulsively at each concussion.

A shell flung equipment in the air. A steel helmet struck into the parados. Then a haversack came hurtling into our trench and fell apart. We gazed stupidly at the contents, a pair of sox, a towel, a toothbrush, a razor and a tin of bully. Another new man came sprawling into our shelter. His helmet was gone and he had lost his rifle. He shook as with ague and crouched in the mud, grovelling and making almost animal noises. He had been literally blown out of his pit and his chum was killed. Then Davies came from the other direction, stepping on the armless body in his path. I shouted at him, asking some questions about the battalion, but he never answered. He sat down close beside me and I was wedged there between him and Mickey. There were continuous explosions just behind us. Mud showered down on our legs, buried our Lee-Enfields, but we stayed in our huddle. Then came a tremendous shock and the narrow through which Davies had come was blocked by an upheaval and the dead man slid toward us, slithered down until his one arm was out-stretched beside our boots. There was a watch on his hairy wrist and, strangely, it was going. I looked at the time. One o'clock. Each hour had grown to be a grim possession, something held precariously.

The new man recovered enough to huddle on the other side of Mickey. Fear had relaxed the muscles of his face and it had become like dough; his mouth dribbled; I could not look at him. All that afternoon we sat there and, oddly, it seemed but a short time. Nothing was clear to me. Explosion succeeded explosion, a concentrated clamour, slamming and pounding, until the noise beat on the brain itself, and when the firing lulled to solitary shells it became the torture of dripping water. I stirred, and found that my arm had been around Mickey all the while and that Davies and I had gripped hands. We got up, freed our rifles from the mud, shook ourselves and Davies went to find Grafftey. We hoped that we would soon be relieved. A message came for me. The Hun had been driven back on the left and we were to move our line forward as soon as it was dark. I was to go with an officer in advance and help stretch a tape where the company was to dig in.

CHAPTER V

Thou Shalt Not Kill

The shelling abated somewhat as we ventured into the no man's land that lay beyond our battered line. The officer was nervous and plunged through the mud so blindly that he lost his direction and it took me some time to get him convinced of his mistake. Then we swung and went forward and whizz bangs began dropping quite near. The officer jumped at each explosion, and yelled something at me. I paid no attention for I had just located the old stub we were to use as a guide. As I made the tape fast to it I looked up and saw my man racing away like a wild thing. Fear had mastered him. He had hurled the tape from him and was gone before I could do anything, leaving me there alone in the dark and the shelling, and with the company moving up in a few minutes. I snatched up my rifle and fired at him, forgetting in my rage that I might shoot some of my own fellows, forgetting everything, but before I could press the trigger a second time a quiet voice spoke to me so clearly that I could hear it above the din. I jumped around and there was the captain.

He had come out there alone and he calmly helped me with the tape as though it were his usual work. We had it in place as the men arrived and he did not threaten me nor reprimand me for what I had done. We dug in as swiftly as we could but there were wild cries in the dark and I rushed out with Tommy to find Christensen over a wounded man trying to bind his hurts. The fellow had become frenzied and would not lie still and we had to hold him by force until he was bandaged, then tie him on the stretcher. All the while Christensen never hurried or ducked as bullets snapped by. I never saw him flinch from a shell. He was the only real fatalist I knew. "When my time comes I'll go," was his creed, and he lived up to it. He had been shipwrecked twice and almost drowned, and several times he had had narrow escapes from shells. But he never showed fear. I have seen sergeants order him to stay in the trench as he passed to another part of the sector, and several times he had walked overland. He never ducked or hurried in exposed places, claiming that it was of no use. "My time is set," he would say. "When it comes I'll get mine wherever I am, and until that time I won't be hit."

A runner came through the murk and said we were to go with the battalion beside us in an attack on a pillbox. Corporal Hughes was at a place farther along and when I found him he knew nothing of such orders. Then we saw men advancing near us. There was no time to look further for verification and so Tommy and Mickey, Gordon and Sambro and I scrambled out of our trench and followed them. Three more men came after us. The rest did not come. We had heard names mentioned, Virtue Farm and Vocation, but did not know our front at all and so simply followed the others. All at once the strong point loomed through the murk and a Lewis gun hammered its rat-tat-tat-tat. Others joined in and cries of "kamerad" were shrill above the noise.

We plunged through the mud excitedly and found that a relief was on. The first attackers had reached the spot just as all the old garrison was outside their concrete fort, and before the new garrison could get in. Both garrisons were laden with full packs and practically helpless, and in five minutes those not killed had surrendered and we were in possession. The new Germans had thermos bottles filled with hot coffee and never did a warm drink taste as good as it. Tommy and I each got a bottle. No one seemed to know where we were to go and so we went back to our trench. Tommy and I were flanked on one side by a tall lad called Murray and his chum, Babson; on the other side were Bunty and Mickey. Farther to the right was a Lewis gun post, and Hughes and Gordon were beyond it. Then there was a stretch of twenty yards without a person in it, a short trench with men of another platoon, Sambro with them, and a small ruin with a roof over one end. On the left there was no one for fifty yards, and then another Lewis gun post. Barney, a big man, was in charge and his crew were "Red," who was red-haired; McPhee, a cheerful, always-grinning lad and an eighteen-year-old Newfoundland boy named Russell. On the other side of them was another gap in the line, then a battalion of Camerons.

At daylight a thick, clinging mist obscured everything. Not an officer had come near us and we had no orders. The only sergeant in the trench did not know any more than we did, and we had had no rations and were ravenous. I peered around and made out a hillocky sea of mud in the rear, and crawled out among the mounds and hollows, finding a number of dead South Wales Borderers in full pack. I looked into their mess-tins until I found a tin of MacConachie rations, a tin of jam, and, in a pack, a loaf of bread. It was green with mold but we cut away the outside and ate the centre. We had "tommy cookers" with us and boiled tea and heated the meat rations. While we did so Babson saw, in front of the trench, a dead officer who had on high boots of splendid workmanship. He went out to get them and Bunty begged him not to, saying that robbing the dead would bring disaster. Babson went and tugged the corpse about in the mud until the boots were released; then he calmly stripped his own feet and put them on.

When our meal was ready Murray and Babson and I sat together on the firestep I had made. We were just finishing our tea when I heard the unmistakable report of a high velocity gun. An instant later the world seemed to come to an end. There had not been a sound of shell but I was hurled against the back of the trench and buried under an avalanche of mud and debris. In that heartbeat all sound of gunfire was deadened and all I could sense was a vague thumping. Then I heard voices. I had been pitched so that my head was beside our rifles, which had been together leaning against the trench wall. They formed a sort of vent up through the piled earth and I could get air. I heard Bunty's voice, high-pitched, telling the sergeant that he had to help get me out, and I wondered why he did not mention Babson or Murray.

Then came sounds of digging, spades thrust frantically, and I suffered an agony of apprehension, fearful that a shovel would slice my jugular as my head was twisted around. Fortunately for him, Murray was buried least of any, and he was soon uncovered. He was shell-shocked by the concussion and was sent down the line, never to return. While getting him out they saw my legs and unearthed me without doing damage. I had been buried four feet deep but was not hurt beyond a severe shaking-up. When they reached Babson it was too late. He was buried deepest of any. Bunty looked at the long boots on his legs and shook his head. "Just what I told him," he croaked.

Another of those high velocity shells came and wiped out the Lewis gun crew to the right, and also shattered the gun. The mist cleared and showed us how thinly our line was held. Gordon saw the ruin and declared he was going to have a sleep in it. Water had seeped in where he had dug so that he had no place to lie down or even sit. Tommy and Hughes took the machine gun post, pulling the dead men to one side, and Bunty and Mickey and I remained in the centre of our trench. More shells came, and more of our trench was blown in. A wounded man on the right, blinded by blood and crazed by his hurts, got out of his place into the open and German snipers began shooting at him. Tommy and Hughes squirmed overland to get him, but were forced to take cover and the fellow was shot in the head.

Gordon had got in the ruin and possibly had lain down when there came another of the high velocity missiles. It exploded inside the wrecked building. Gordon would never know what happened. All the rest of day we sat there with the dead men beside us, the dead officer in front of us, and dead men lying in the mud at the rear. In my head was a queer little singing noise that the din of the shelling augmented. But I minded most the stench that dominated everything. It seemed to penetrate one's inmost being, that awful stench of death, a foul thing, a filthy thing, its reek was sickening. Mickey became ill and we persuaded him to work his way to the right and to try and reach some shelter where he could sleep.

As the dark came, early and foreboding, only Bunty and I remained in that bit of line that fourteen platoon had held. All at once I roused. I had seen something moving directly in front of where we were. We watched and made out a German patrol of ten or twelve men. They would remain a considerable time in one place and when they moved seemed uncertain of direction. We examined our rifles, and they were clogged with mud so that we could not use them. Every bomb had been buried. We could depend only on our bayonets.

For an hour Bunty and I watched them and then as they crawled far over on the left Barney's Lewis gun chattered and they came back our way. I looked about, standing up in the wrecked part, and could not see any of our men, then spotted a file of blurred figures coming in from behind us, over the boggy ground where the dead Welshmen were sprawled. They came directly to us and the officer in the lead was a young fellow. I told him of the Germans crawling towards us and he gave quick order to his men, telling them to get into the trench. Bunty dragged himself away towards the right. He was too all in to want to linger.

The officer told me he belonged to the Black Watch and that they were to relieve the Camerons. I pointed the way he should go but he asked me to go with him and help rout the Germans. It was a weird mix-up. The Huns seemed bewildered, apparently thinking that we were their own men for they did not start up until we were almost beside them. Then they fought sullenly. The mud was deep and the Scots could not rush them very well, though four or five men seemed very anxious to get at them with bayonets. The officer shouted to the Germans, telling them to surrender, and he shot their leader with his revolver. Two bombs changed the situation, though only one German fell, and then I made my first and only kill with cold steel.

It had been all like a bad dream to me. I was too sick of the mud and dead men and lack of sleep hardly to realize what I was doing, and I had kept with the officer. He, seemingly, expected the Germans to put up their hands when he spoke, and when one lunged for him he was taken off guard and only escaped the thrust by falling to one side. Between his assailant and myself was the body of the feld-webel killed by the pistol shot, and as, half-dazed by the bomb explosions, I flourished my bayonet, intending only to bluff the German into surrender – for I had always a dread of such fighting – the fellow drove headlong at me. He tripped over his comrade as he came, but I seemed paralyzed. I could not move to avoid him. I tried to ward his weapon and then instead of tearing steel in my own flesh I felt my bayonet steady as if guided, and was jolted as it brought up on solid bone. My grip tightened as my rifle was twisted by a sudden squirming, as if I had speared a huge fish. Then I tugged it free and saw that the other men had killed two more Germans and the rest had surrendered.

I was weak with the shock of excitement, and could hardly answer the officer as he asked me questions. I had pointed out to him the gap that would exist if we left and he told me he would look after it, but wanted my name and regimental number. He seemed to think that I had saved his life and said that he would recommend me for a D.C.M. It meant nothing to me then, I was so utterly weary that I only wanted to get away. I had not meant to kill the German, had not wanted to do anything, and I was glad when I got over on the company front and saw that our relieving battalion was arriving.

I did not stop there as all the rest were leaving, but went with Mickey and Hughes, whom I found back of the ruin. Mickey was ghastly white, and the corporal was tired. We floundered through mud to a pillbox that served as a dressing station, and I saw Bunty there, sitting on two dead men covered with a rubber sheet. He told me that he was not going to hurry and that he wanted a shot of rum before he went on. Out on the road we met incoming men going to other points, and as we stumbled and waded past each other there came a deluge of shell fire. In an instant all was confusion. Men blundered into each other, knocked each other down. There were stunning, smashing explosions, gusts of concussion, terrible cries. Wounded men fell in the mud and were tramped down to join the old dead. The others in their panic stepped on them, did anything but stop. It was death to do so.

I had Hughes by the arm and fairly dragged him through the mire. Twice I slipped on dead bodies, and then came to a ruin where a man sat a fragment of wall. I went to him and asked if he had water. Both Mickey and Hughes were begging for a drink. The man did not answer. He was not dead, or even wounded, but so absolutely all in that he did not nod or speak, and I took his water bottle from his equipment, took it to Mickey and Hughes in turn, and brought it back and replaced it. I thanked the fellow then, and still he never changed expression. We went on down the road and there came another salvo. As the last of the crashing, soul-tearing smashes rang in my ears I saw Mickey spin and fall. I let go of Hughes and jumped to him. He had been hit in several places and could not possibly live.

"Mickey – Mickey!" I called his name and raised him up and he nestled to me like a child, his white face upturned to mine.

"At last," he murmured, "I'm through." Then his whisper was shrill and harsh. "I never had a white tunic or a red one," he said. "I didn't want – to kill people. I hate war – and everything. Why did they do it – why – did – they?"

He seemed delirious and I tried to soothe him, but he would not listen. He talked about what we had read in my little guide book, the way boys trained for fighting, the soldiers killed in France and Belgium, the other wars that had been fought, the futility of the endless repetition. "And we just go on and on," he finished. "Doing things because – because – "

His voice sank so low I could not hear but his lips still moved. Little white-faced Mickey! I held him there, held him tight, and tried to comfort him as he grew weaker and weaker. Then he twisted, strained in my arms, "... and we go on – on – on – on," he shrilled, and stiffened.

I laid him there by the roadside with his rifle upright at his head, and took his belongings from his pockets. Hughes stood all the time, wavering, watching, yet never stepping from where I had left him and I suddenly knew he was in a worse condition than I had supposed, for he had thought the world of Mickey. "Come on," I said roughly, and led him away and he never spoke.

We reached the long duckwalk and all around us were flashes and glows of fire, the great Salient's maw, a huge death-trap, with shells whining and rushing through the air. There were red and yellow flashes, and streaking sparks of fire, and flares, ghostly, looping, falling, unreal, now and then silhouetting a straggling line of steel helmets and hunched shoulders; bewildered men in the dark, bone-weary, shell-dazed, treading on old dead and new dead, and slipping in the foulness of slimy ditches.

Somehow I kept going. Hughes had become querulous, resisting. He hung back, whispered that he wanted to sit down. I had taken his rifle and equipment, and I urged him on, knowing the fate of so many exhausted men who had stopped to rest in that ghoulish area. I took out my entrenching tool handle and menaced him with it as one would a child, making him go on and on and on, until at long last, in that blurry darkness just before dawn we reached tents that were to shelter us. The quartermaster was there to meet us. He took Hughes from me, led him away to give him hot drink and put him to bed. I staggered on, headed for the nearest tent – and pitched head foremost into a crater filled with stagnant water. Both rifles I carried were embedded in the clay and I left them and Hughes' equipment under the water. I was shaking with cold, shaking so that I could hardly speak, drenched, blinded with filth. Tommy came – he had got in ahead, and led me into a tent. There I stripped naked and lay on a pile of blankets while he heaped others over me, a dozen of them. We had plenty of room, plenty of blankets – so many did not need them – and the quartermaster came with his rum and gave me a great mug-full. When I woke it was the next afternoon.

We went in buses to Bourecq and there we were billeted in a barn. The entire company did not muster the strength of a platoon and we sat around, unshaved, unwashed, staring at nothing. At night I sat up and looked around. I was bathed in perspiration, though the night was cold, for I had been feeling again live flesh sliding over my bayonet, seeing again Mickey's white face close to mine, while his blood seeped from him and warmed my knees.

The men were muttering in their sleep, turning, twisting, straining. Tommy lay with his hands gripped, huddled, whimpering, all the terrors that he had fought back during consciousness flooding over his soul when the barrier of his will was lowered. Courage, in the heat of battle, is an animal instinct. There's a certain gregariousness in it, the instinct of the herd, the eyes of the other fellow on you; but the courage that kept a man in his place in those terrible late November days at Passchendale was the straining of the soul, the last limit of human pluck. Twice I woke and found a man on his hands and knees, gazing about him, wakened by the horrors of his own mind, unable to comprehend that at last the Salient stench had left his nostrils.

The first few days in Bourecq were easy ones. The captain was kind to us. He came on the ground as we formed up the first time, our pitiful ranks, and gazed at us without speaking, and I saw in his eyes things of which no man speaks – the things that words would kill. We had little drill, but rested, and slept and had good food and finally were more like human beings than we had been, but every man who had endured Passchendale would never be the same again, was more or less a stranger to himself.

A draft arrived and Earle was in it. I was glad to see him, more glad than I could say, for there were few of the old boys with us, only Christensen and Tommy and Sambro and Eddie: Earle had heard in England that I had been killed, and the rumour reached Canada. Those with me the first night, when I had been knocked out with the Stokes, had reported me killed, and again when I had been buried the story had gone. We went for a feed together. When we were returning we heard high voices in an estaminet and went in. Red was there confronting one of the "originals." "Red" had been with the 73rd, and was a good man in the line. The "original" had been on jobs back in safe areas but had got in wrong with authorities and had been sent back to the battalion. He had had a few drinks and now was declaring that Passchendale was nothing, that all the real fighting had taken place before the blasted "umpty-umps" came over. "Red" grinned at him, and said he was not trying to belittle those mighty warriors, the "originals," and dodged a swing at his chin. Plunk! The "original" went down for a long count, and when he recovered his friends took him outside.

There were few new men in the draft. Almost all had been wounded at Vimy or the Somme and had belonged to the 73rd or 42nd. I made friends with many of them. Sykes, a dark-haired fellow who read books whenever he could and who could make good rissoles of bully, onion and hardtack; Boland, a neat-built boy; Thornton, slightly deaf, always humming songs; Lockerbie, a tall, well-built man; Williams, another of fine physique. We had a new officer, a man new to France, and he had difficulties. We numbered in French the first morning he paraded us, and he flushed and scolded in a manner that delighted the mischievous. Battalion orders carried the information that the 42nd were now privileged to wear the red hackle; it seemed to be some sort of battle honour. Tommy snorted. "Red Hackles," he said. "What are they to us! What about Mickey and the Professor and Melville and all the boys? Red hackles, bah!"

I said nothing to him. Everyone's nerves carried too fine an edge to permit argument. A team of the rifle grenadiers was organized and entered in the divisional shoot for the Lipsett shield, and no one seemed surprised when it came to us. Suddenly my leave came through. Leave! I had not thought of it in the last hectic weeks, though "Old Bill" and a few others had mercifully escaped the second trip to Passchendale by having theirs come due.

Leave – I could see Phyilis! I caught a lorry and went to Boulogne and saw the leave boat in the harbour. It had left five minutes before. Those with me swore furiously but I had a stroll around the streets and, after looking up the history of the place, was quite entertained. Then I ran foul of one of those creatures I had always avoided, one of the peacock variety of nincompoops in shiny Sam Browne and cream-coloured breeches.

I had been reading that Mark Twain said France had neither summer nor winter nor morals, that Napoleon's monument outside of Boulogne had been erected to celebrate his triumphant invasion of England, and was walking slowly as I read. My lordship was walking by several feet from where I stood and I never saw him until his rasping voice requested me to "Drop that damn book and salute an officer."

The book was thrust into my tunic pocket and I gave my snappiest salute. It was not good enough. There had been an appreciative twitter from the blonde charmer at his elbow.

"As you were," came the rasping voice. "Three paces backward, march. Now then, try again. What regiment? Oh, the Black Watch, quite a lad aren't you? As you were, three paces backward, march. Try again, cut your hand away, my man, don't let it fall beside you."

My man! My blood boiled. Four times I had to pace backward, advance and salute that smirking monkey, a weak-chinned lieutenant, and then he dismissed me with the sharp warning to look out when I next met him. And he a Canadian, at least he wore Canadian badges!

That night I slept with the leave crowd in a big barrack-like room, and talked till midnight with men from the Second Division, lads who had been at Hill 70, who had indulged in raiding parties. The chatter was interesting. There were bitter denunciations of the folly of Passchendale, and one lad confided to me that he had a scheme he was going to work out while in Blighty. "I'm through holding bloody ditches for King George and Art Currie," he said. "I'll be in the States in three weeks' time."

Others talked of their officers and to my surprise I found myself telling what "good heads" we had in the 42nd. One surly-looking fellow of the Sixth Brigade said that he never set eyes on a good officer, he hated them all, and sergeants as well. His own words gave us his status. I thought of the officers with whom I had come in contact and decided that they were exactly the same as the men, good, bad and indifferent, with very little, if any, difference in the average. Their actions when we were out of the line declared their mentality, and in the line they had the advantage of the men. The weak-kneed ones used S.R.D. to fortify them in shaky hours, the soldier had not the opportunity. I had met our adjutant and found him a gentleman, emphatic in his praise of our draft. Everyone liked our colonel, and our regimental sergeant-major, McFarlane, was one of the finest men I met.

As a rule the average officer did not see more than a third as much of raw, undiluted war as did the men under him. The men stayed on post, six on, six off, and saw relays of officers, one at a time, doing two hours out of twenty-four, and that a hurried tour of the trench. The men carried rations, barbed wire and ammunition from dump to front line, in all weathers, under all conditions, and the officer that led them usually had the job once during that trip in the line; the soldier went each night. The men would stay on post and endure all kinds of strafing, dig out dead and wounded comrades from blown-in places, stick it and carry on, and their officer would not be seen while it lasted. During the two worst days at Passchendale I never saw an officer except Grafftey. Perhaps they were in as dangerous positions as we were. I do not know. Yet, given the same chance, many of the men, probably the majority, would do just the same as they. Officers were simply men in uniforms designed to make them look better than the privates, and they had responsibilities that we did not realize. I never envied them, hated them, nor regarded them any differently than any of the other men. Some were of much finer intellect than mine, most of them had come from finer homes – at least those in the 42nd had – and still there were some I regarded as my inferiors. The general opinion seemed that none of the "brass hats" were better than pole cats with the exception of McDonnell, Lipsett and Byng.

Victoria! Leave men thronging everywhere, hungry for a change of food, for girls who spoke their own tongue, for the welcome of their homes and a clean bed. Men straight from the trenches, lousy, mud-crusted, with the echo of guns in their ears and the smell of dugouts in their nostrils. I pushed through the milling crowd and checked my Lee-Enfield and equipment, then got into the street. Two hours later I had a complete uniform, clean underwear, soft boots, Fox puttees, Bedford cord breeches, a well-cut tunic, a Glengarry and an officer's British warm. I found a fairly clean place on Vauxhall Bridge Road and there I had a hot bath, luxuriated in it, and put on all my clean clothes. Then, after the barber shop, I went to a good restaurant and ordered a meal I had long pictured, and ate it leisurely.

I went back to my room and got ready for bed. It had been so long since I slept on anything but hard boards, trench mud or chicken-wire bunks. Yet something urged me to go out into the murky streets, to walk down the Strand again, one look about before I retired. I refused to go. Clean sheets and a soft bed were mine and I was going to enjoy them. Even then I could not fall asleep and I made plans for the next day. After a good breakfast I would get a taxi and drive through that English part of England and see Phyllis. I remembered her smile as I had left, the last glimpse I had of her face.

When I did doze someone came thundering at my door and I heard sirens. "The Zepps are over," the fellow shouted.

Zeppelins! After Passchendale! "Go away and leave me alone," I said. "What's a zeppelin." It seemed all a joke to me, that panic over a few airships. I watched a moment, long fingers of light in the sky, seeking the raiders, and listened to the rattling crashes of the anti-aircraft guns, then went to sleep again.

In the morning I had a delicious breakfast and heard that two Gothas had been brought down and that a number of civilians had been killed. It seemed a very minor affair to me. I was feeling like living again; there had been no dreams of a Boche on my bayonet, no others near to mutter in their sleep little sobs and moans and incoherent profanity.

I hired a car and went out along the same route that the officer had taken me more than a year before. It was not such pleasant weather and winter rain had made the country drab, but it looked lovely to my eyes. I lolled back in the seat, thinking how lucky I had been. It seemed only two hours since I had been trying to keep myself alive till the next day.

We rolled into the little village and when we reached the Inn I paid the driver and sent him back to London. I didn't want to have any link connecting me with sordid things that seemed so remote from "The Black Boar." The Innkeeper recognized me, and the fact was a thrill in itself. I was given my same room and then went to the little cottage where Phyllis lived. She had only written a few times and I had not let her know I was coming.

An old man opened the door, the uncle, and his wrinkled face was grooved with grief. "Come in," he said gently. "Her said 'ee might be too late."

"Too late!" I exclaimed, startled. "What do you mean? Where is Phyllis?"

He shook his head. "I'll tell 'ee," he said in his gentle way, and related how Phyllis had told him that I was coming back to England and that she would go down to London to see me. I interrupted to tell him I had not written her, but he shook his head again and said, in an almost reverent way, that Phyllis had "gifts," had no need of letters, she knew by some mysterious sixth sense. I had found that out when I met her, and I grew impatient.

"Where is she at now?" I broke in. "I'll look her up in London."

Again the slow shake of the head. "'Ee be too late," he said, and thrust me a crumpled paper. It was a wire from London. Phyllis had been killed by a bomb dropped by the German raiders.

Killed by a bomb! I remembered the urge I had had to go out in the streets. If I had gone I would have seen her … The old man rambled on, talking about her, her little ways that he knew so well, how she hated war, would not read the papers or listen to him talk about it. Then he startled me, chilled me. He invited me to take dinner with him – and he called me "Steve."

The word shocked me. "I'm not Steve," I said, sharply. "I'm his brother."

He peered at me, and I could see that he could not grasp what I said. "Steve – that's the name," he muttered. "She went to meet Steve – her said it."

We sat at his humble table, the old man and I, silent at times, now and then speaking about the war. "'Ee have been in battle?" he asked.

"Yes," I said. "Passchendale."

"Aye, I have heard it were a fearful fight," he said, admiringly. "'Ee have lived in a great day."

"I don't think so," I said bitterly. "This war is wrong."

"Aye, the Kaiser have something to answer for." The old man nodded vigorous assent. "But 'ee have a chance to do a bit for England, for England. He raised his old bent figure from his chair and pointed out the window at the countryside. "'Ee have something to store, to tell 'ee children."

I was silent. "'Course there be parts for forgetting," he went on, "but the rest do make up for it. 'Ee have lived in a great day."

We talked awhile about Phyllis, then when I was leaving he gripped my hand with his horny one and said gravely. "Lad, 'ee have much to be thankful for. Mine isn't for complaint, but to be young now would be the nearest thing to Heaven I knows of."

All the while he called me "Steve," and when I got outside I was glad I had not told him different. It seemed to please him that I had come and I knew that Phyllis had never told him that my brother had been killed. But – she had gone to meet Steve!

It was a lovely afternoon and as I went by the old church I saw that people were gathering for a service, and I went in. It was unforgettable. Through the stained glass windows of the old Norman church the sun's rays fell on altar and choir stalls, flooding the place with a riot of colour. The vicar, in white surplice and crimson stole, had an appealing voice and in his prayer seemed pleading with a God whom he actually confronted. The reverent people, the dignified service, the sunlight on the oak carvings, all touched me curiously. I felt that I was a rank outsider.

At the Inn I asked what the service was for and learned that a series of special meetings had been held for more than a month, intercessions for aid to British arms on the western front. They were asking God to make England and her Allies victorious, pleading that right should conquer, that the German and the devil be defeated. And in my haversack was a belt buckle I had taken off a dead German. Its inscription was "Gott Mit Uns."

I went back to London and from there took train to Retford, in Nottinghamshire. The girl I left in Canada had been born in that district and I was going to visit her people. They made me welcome and I had a wonderful time exploring the villages, especially Gainsborough and Lincoln. The old Roman wall in Lincoln, and the cathedral, were marvellous to me. When I went back to London I went down to Bramshott and saw my brother, who had been in England as a musketry instructor. Stanley, the big, broad-shouldered brother of my fiancee, was there at the depot of the 85th Highlanders. He had been seriously wounded at Vimy and was anxious to get back to France.

They asked me what it had been like at Passchendale and I said "Not too bad," and changed the subject. That which I noticed in others had come to me. No soldier who had been in that fighting would talk about it at all.

When I went back to the battalion it was still at Bourecq and I traded my finery to the quartermaster for a regular issue. He cut a dashing figure in my British warm. A dozen times I had been saluted while up in Nottinghamshire and when other lads at Bramshott donned my rigout to have a picture taken I realized that if we all were given the same uniform many officers would be in the background

A few days after my return we moved to Lieven and relieved the 16th Battalion there. One experienced an inexplicable thrill in being back again in dark, smelly confines and frost-bound trenches, where only Death was sure of his billet. We were to do carrying parties up Cow Trench, that long, crooked trail known to so many Canadians. Soon we were as lousy as ever and having a hard time to keep warm. The new officer proved conscientious and when I asked that "Old Bill" be allowed my rum ration the favour was refused. We made several trips each night, laden with barbed wire, "A" frames, corrugated iron, anything the engineers could load us with, while they walked along and gave orders. Tommy got a particularly evil burden the third night, some frame work an engineer was using to build an O-pip, and he expressed himself in no uncertain terms when we reached our destination. "The front line soldier," he orated, "does more

work than any man in the labour battalions, gets less food than any soldier, does three-quarters of the engineers' work, is used like a mule, bed-
ded and freighted like a horse, and officered by asses." Hughes had a hard
time quieting him.

On Christmas eve a few of us were in a cellar under a ruin. Our bunks
were a mass of broken wire and foul sandbags. We had no fire and the
rations were very slim, and it was so cold we could not sleep. Tommy set
a candle on a long board and each man produced the biggest, most active
louse he could locate on his person, and we raced them, three heats, the
length of the board, the winner to take all the prize, three dirty paper
francs. After that sporting affair was over we shivered and huddled around
until in desperation we tore down the bunks and made one common bed
on the floor, piling all the bags on it. There the six of us lay as close as we
could pack, our greatcoats over us, and slept, warmed by the heat of each
other's body. Shortly after day-light there were steps on the narrow stairs,
then flashlight beams. We sat up, expectant. Rum or rations? It was the
officer. "Merry Christmas, boys," he chirped. "Aw, go to Germany," said
Tommy. The rest of us never spoke.

We stayed in the line, relieving the 49th. I went out with an officer of
one of the other platoons, under barbed wire furred with frost, and got
acquainted with the no man's land of that sector. The next night we were
in the brick cellar used by the cooks, waiting for a mug of tea, when there
was a shout of "gas." We rushed out and found that gas shells were dropping everywhere, long slim containers that simply broke as they fell. The
officer wheeled. "Follow me," he snapped, "and put on your mask, man."

I put on my respirator and followed him as well as I could, but it was
fairly dark and I could not see well through the goggles. Before we had
reached the last company post he was away from me. He waited there, and
said something. I pulled off my mask to hear. "Can't you keep up with
me?" he repeated. I looked at him. He had not had his mask on at all.

"Not with such a handicap, sir," I said. "Give me equal chances and I can
stay with you anywhere, anytime." Perhaps I said it sharply. At any rate he
was nettled. "Is that so?" he sneered.

"It is," I answered. "You ordered me to put on my mask and left your
own in the carrier, then expected me to follow you. That," I said, "is unrea-
sonable."

"And so," he sneered again, "you're as good a man as I am?"

"Absolutely," I shot back, "mentally or physically, and only too happy to prove it any way you like."

"If you say anything more I'll have you arrested," he rasped, and turned away. He never talked to me again. I never understood what had made him so ugly that night. He was a good man in the line, better than ordinary, but at times he seemed to carry a grouch. If it had been some of the other company officers I would have been in trouble.

I spent New Year's eve on a listening post, cold and hungry, watching the Very lights trace their patterns in the sky, wondering what 1918 would bring, and whether or not I would see another New Year. The battalion moved back to Souchez when relieved, into miserable huts half the regular size, with vents to admit the cold wind, without stoves. With me was Pete, a 73rd chap who had been up to Passchendale. He had been an athlete, was a splendidly-proportioned man, but had lain too long in the water and slime. He was racked with fits of coughing, was too weak to go on parades, and finally they sent him down to hospital.

On the second night in the huts Tommy and I got up. We could not sleep. We went along the old Vimy shelters and searched, over a mile away, until we were rewarded by finding a small stove and enough pipe to do. We carried it back to the hut and the rest turned out and helped us demolish a wooden shelter at the head of the camp. Then, in turn we kept the fire going and were able to sleep warmly. On parade we were told that a Christmas dinner was to be held, and Tommy and I were two of a party detailed to assist the preparations. We had to carry tables and benches from engineers' quarters, over a mile away, and set them up in a marquee. By the time we had made the last trip the dinner was under way. Only a company could be fed at a time and we had to wait our turn, as the others went first. We had been carrying tables since seven o'clock and we did not get into the dining tent until four in the afternoon. A lump of cold pudding, a mug of cold tea and a few biscuits were shoved at me, the same kind of dinner we had had in a leaky hut at Mount St. Eloi the previous year. "Where's the Christmas dinner?" blared Tommy. "What's the bloody joke?"

"That's all that's left," growled the cook. "What …"

Tommy drove his lump of cold duff at the fellow's head, and his mug of cold, greasy tea followed. I got him quieted enough to get him outside and almost all our platoon followed us. "Hi," yelled the cook from a safe vantage. "You guys can't beat it – you've got to stay and help wash up these dishes."

They had got enamel plates and mugs for the occasion and we were actually supposed to wash them, after doing all the work that was done that day, and not getting any dinner. It took all my persuasion to keep Tommy sane and "Old Bill" was ready to help him. We went up the valley to a Y.M.C.A. canteen and there got lukewarm cocoa and dry biscuits. We filled up on them, forced to do so, as we had no extra money, and "Old Bill" glared at the clerk as he eyed the tins of peaches on the shelves. We had asked for credit and of course it was not allowed. "I hope," he growled, "that one of them heavies comes over and blows the blinkin' 'Y' loose from its triangle."

Our next trip in was to Cite St. Theodore, a place of underground passages and concrete chambers. We were in a room that the Germans had made waterproof and almost shell proof. A good stove was in it and just outside in the passage there was a store of coal. Our mail came and brought us Christmas parcels and we had a splendid time. Tommy and I roamed up the street we were on and explored. Passages crossed the street, from cellar to cellar, and other tunnels opened from strong points. The Hun had used concrete lavishly. We found a place partially destroyed that contained German blankets, ground sheets and shrapnel helmets as well as two German rifles. A passage led from it and we went along it for a considerable distance, then up steps until we were blocked by wreckage that had fallen over the stairway. It was well we stopped. After we found openings through which we could look, we saw, about ten yards in front of us, four Germans. They were leaning against a wall, smoking and talking, as if they were waiting for someone. After a time two of them went away and then the other pair called out to someone we could not see. They were answered by a voice that was almost above us. A footway ran alongside the wreckage and another German was walking along it. Had we dislodged anything, spoken, had we been smoking, we must have been discovered. We stole back softly the way we had come and in our own quarters tried to formulate some plan whereby we could capture one of the Heinies and surprise the troops.

At dark we were called to do a ration party. It was raining and we tried a short cut coming back. It led us into a mud hole that was knee deep and we were sorry figures when we returned. The stove was red-hot in a short time. We made our beds and stripped all our wet clothing and hung it on wires we had strung. Shortly everything was steaming. The door opened and in came our officer. "Men," he squeaked, "the orders are that no man is to take off his boots, and have your rifle and equipment where you can get it at a moment's notice."

"Yes, sir," we chorused. He had looked at us through the steam from wet socks and trousers and he nodded and went away.

The 87th Battalion relieved us and we went back to Fosse 10. Tommy and I had not gone in our tunnel again and we left the sector without telling anyone of our discovery. From Fosse 10 we went to Noulles mines and were billeted in the town. The Hun shelled it the next day and killed a few of the civilians, one a little girl from the house where we were staying. I helped the mother pick her from the street. Her eyes were open, looking up, her hair thrown back from frightened, pinched features, a frail little elf, who had smiled at me and shyly called me "Canada."

That evening I was ordered to go with Eddie to Ferfay and report to the school there. Eddie had been a corporal and Davies told me that I would have to take a stripe. I warned him that I did not want one and told him about what had happened in Canada. The boys chaffed me as I took my pack and left them, but I had the last laugh on them. I found that there were other 42nd men at the school, men from the other battalions of the brigade, and we had a good time together, despite the fact that we were coralled by a 116th sergeant, who unfolded to our weary ears the mysteries of sighting, aiming, rapid fire, and triangles of errors. I chummed with Siddall, from one of our other companies, and Turner, a big South African who was with the 49th.

It was just before we finished our Course that I had the laugh on the boys. They had not been back to the front line, a fact which Tommy mourned, as he had wanted to kill a Hun, he said, on the Kaiser's birthday, and had had considerable drilling, and now "D" Company came to Ferfay. They were shined and cleaned so that I hardly recognized them and they drilled on the School parade ground in a way that made me proud that I belonged to them; they were shown as a model company. Our scouts went to Pernes and in competition there carried off all honours in sniping and observing. The 85th came to Rainbert, nearby, and I at once went to see them, for my brother had come to France. He had just arrived that night, had no rations, and was not issued any at the battalion.

I brought him back to Ferfay with me and took my blankets to madame
next door to our billet and she gave us a regular banquet of eggs and chips
and coffee and French bread; also an extra loaf for my brother. It was easy
to draw more blankets from the stores. "How long," asked my brother,
"does a battalion do in the front lines?"

"About six days," I said. "Sometimes more, sometimes less, never more
than seven or eight."

On March 6th we relieved the 116th Battalion, taking over a part of the
line on the left of Avion, near the embankment. Part of no man's "land" was
under water, flooded by the Hun, and wire had been thrown near the shore
so that anyone trying to wade across would get entangled. On the left flank
the line ran out to a listening post. Its garrison stayed in a cellar there, a
squalid little hole with a makeshift roof, and could not show itself in daylight as the place was in plain view of the big slag heap on the German side.
Six of us were posted out there. Two men were in a shallow crater blasted
in the chalky rim of the bank near where a bridge had existed. It had been
blown up by explosives and no one could cross to the other side.

Opposite us, continuing our line, was an imperial battalion. They had
no post at the canal bank, but used a flying patrol that came once every
two hours during the night. A heavy wire had been thrown to the other
bank and it was used as a signalling line. The Imperials tugged on it. If all
was quiet we tugged twice in reply, if we had heard or seen the Germans
near their part we pulled the wire three times. Barron had come back to
us and he and I were the first two on post. Sambro and Tommy were to
relieve us. We lay and gazed toward the Hun lines. It was not a cold night
and spring was in the air. On the way up we had smelled buds and green
things and had hated the front line again. It was hard to force to the background all fear of death at that most hopeful season of the year when men
care most for life.

Suddenly we heard the "flying patrol" coming. They were making plenty of noise and when they reached the bank they gave the signal wire a tug
that almost jerked Barron from our crater. "O-ky, Canada?" shrilled a
cockney voice. "I sye, o-ky."

"Shut your trap and get out of that or I'll 'o-ky' you," flared Barron, so
fiercely that the patrol did not come again that night.

It was dreadful in the daytime. The weather continued balmy and we
were cooped in a small space. The cellar was foul with slime from the canal

and stank dreadfully as the days got warmer. Big blue flies buzzed about. We were lousy and the air made our heads ache. The water in our bottles got stale and unfit to drink. We had no warm food, only bread and cheese and the tea we boiled at night. It took all of the corporal's cautioning to keep us under cover during the day.

During the third night we heard a German patrol. They came to the other side of the canal and we were able to make out two of them, but the corporal, Hoskins, would not let us shoot as it would give away our position. The Huns came within feet of our signal wire and every moment we expected to hear the Imperials coming, but they did not until the enemy had gone to their own lines. Six awful days we endured in that cellar, and six nights we enjoyed the cool air, every man going outside as soon as it was dark. Then we moved back to support. Hoskins had a few lines he used to recite about that post.

When the war is o'er
And I'm home once more
To the land I love the most,
When the sewers stink
I'll always think
Of the Isolation Post.

I cursed my luck
When that place I struck,
And I cursed the Kaiser's host
As I waded through
That bloody glue
To the Isolation Post.

I sat by the cesspool of disease
While the sun my back did roast,
With your cover the sky
And a wall three feet high,
The Isolation Post.

If ever I get the drop on Bill
I'll make him drink a toast

From a dead man's shoes,
Filled with slimy ooze
From the Isolation Post.

To one who's been and smelt and seen
This will seem no idle boast.
I've been to hell
For a six days' spell
At the Isolation Post.

The La Coulette brewery was the support quarters. It was a large place covered with sod reinforced by concrete. The Hun was supposed to be contemplating a big attack and orders came for us to hold ourselves in readiness for anything. Each man tensed accordingly and when there came an alarm we were outside in jig time. We lined a fire trench and waited there a long time, but nothing happened. Tempers were once more finely drawn. Then the Germans shelled the brewery and our batteries replied. The clamour throbbed and beat down to our underground retreat and quaking told of the near ones. Next day there was a shelling of the area just in our rear. We watched it for a long time. Every now and then there would come a great rushing noise followed by the roar of explosions, and from the dead, brick-strewn slopes there would shoot up a cloud of black and yellow fumes.

Instead of going back to billets we moved into the front line again, and the men groused wholeheartedly. An officer swam across the water to the German side and located one of their posts, returning unseen. The Hun shelled us spasmodically, as if he, too, had his wind up, and everyone was more or less jumpy. I was sent in daytime with a message to our support line and took a ramble around the brewery route before returning. Some impish impulse urged me to do so, and had I been questioned I would have had an awkward time, but it seemed as if it were fated that I should go as I did. A long-disused German gun pit drew my attention. An old sap had led to it and one could easily mistake his way and wander there.

As I went in to the emplacement I met an officer, and one glance told me that once more I had met with the peacock of Boulogne. He was different now, however, looked less than ever like a soldier, for fear was written large on his sallow visage. There had been a few salvos quite near where we were, but only the usual strafing. "Ah – my good fellow," he blurted. "Just where – what part of the line is this?"

It was easy to see that he was lost, completely bewildered and craven, and something seemed to give way within me, some control snapped. I was suddenly seeing as red as I had in Boulogne. "How about some snappy saluting?" I said sharply. "Isn't this as good a place as Boulogne?"

He stared at me, and mopped his face with a dainty handerkerchief. "Come – come, fellow," he said, trying to bluff, though his eyes were furtive. "I'm an officer and I want you to tell me where I am."

"You're almost up to where the soldiers are," I said, "and where none of your blasted monkey tricks will work. You were fine with a lovely lady hanging on your arm, how do you feel now?"

He drew back hastily and muttered that he would have me court-martialled and then snatched at his revolver. I had it from him in an instant, and I hurled it far over the trench side, then thrust him back into the emplacement. "If you were half a man I would give you what's due you," I raved on and then recovered myself. The head-splitting hours in that foul cellar, the tense atmosphere about the trenches, the heat, all had combined to make me forget what I was doing and I knew that I had made myself liable to serious accusation. I stopped my silly blustering, but talked very grimly and cooly for five minutes, telling him just what his kind were doing to hurt the army, and just what would happen to him at the front.

Instead of regaining his composure he seemed to get more frightened, staring at me in an odd manner, and when I showed him a trench to the rear he almost ran away. He had never asked my name or number and as I had on shorts I hoped that he had not noticed my badges. For several days I expected a summons, but none came. It was a most absurd thing for me to do, and I never saw a more spineless creature than that shaking, fear-stricken lieutenant. Tommy was the only one I told about him.

The men were savage when we did not leave the trenches when relieved, but stayed in reserve. Each night we worked, cleaning trenches and strengthening defenses, and then one morning there came sounds of a terrific bombardment on the Somme area. Rumours began to circulate and soon we forgot our grievances. The Hun was attacking, had broken through. We went about with questions on our lips, waiting orders, expecting almost any move. But nothing happened. We were told that the Canadians were to defend the Ridge at all costs, and we got to know that we were stretched across an immense frontage. Every available unit was being hurried to stem the German advance and reports came of reserve lines being constructed on Vimy and of Chinese labour battalions digging trenches farther in the rear. The air was tense with excitement and expectancy.

CHAPTER VI

The Longest Trip

There were constant patrols. Headquarters wanted information about the movements of the enemy and twice I was over to the German wire. The first time Tommy was with me and I had to keep close to him. Someone in our trench unthinkingly shot up a flare just as we got into no man's land, and for a moment we feared we might be discovered. We could see the black wall of the parapet we had left, the wire like frayed ribbons, two white faces under mushroom hats – the sentries – and then the darkness was more intense as the light went out. Tommy pushed against me and he was trembling. "I'm scared," he whispered.

"I feel shaky myself," I said, "but it's just the first feeling. Once we get out a few yards we'll be all right and there's plenty of cover for us."

We moved slowly and were an hour going the hundred yards, but he never halted, and when we returned to the trench told me that he had got hold of himself again, was glad he had gone. Anything unusual that night, a sudden strafing, or a failure to go on, and I believe he would have lost his nerve.

The next night I was out with a patrol from another platoon and we found a dead German several yards from the enemy wire. Apparently he had been on a lone reconnaisance and had been killed by a burst of machine gun fire. He had a machine pistol strapped to his chest, an unusual weapon, with a barrel about fifteen inches long. It fired over fifteen shots with one loading and would be as deadly as a Maxim at close quarters.

New men came to the company, a splendid draft, from the MacLean Highlanders. The first men I got acquainted with were Thompson and

Tulloch, two inseparables who came into our cellar and calmly took possession of the best corner – until gently shown the error of their ways. Tulloch was a cheerful chap and his main topic was his hope that he would soon get a "decent blighty." He assured us that the MacLean Kilties had been the finest bunch of men in khaki.

I was on one more patrol in that sector and the sergeant in charge had a very close call. It was still and warm and very dark, an ideal night for prowlers. We escaped treading into a pile of empty tins through the sergeant feeling one with his hand as he stooped to fasten a puttee, and as I had been out in the same spot the previous night and had not felt them nor disturbed them, I had suspicions. We got a stick and attached a wire to it, then went over to a shell hole and lay in it while we tugged the wire. The tins clattered together and instantly there came a perfect spray of machine bullets, thudding the ground, striking against the ruins behind us. The Hun, no doubt, thought he had made a fine killing. We lay still for over an hour and then heard men crawling towards the tins from the Hun side. I pitched a bomb in that direction and it burst just as it touched the ground. There was an awful scream, a death yell, and in a moment a shower of stick bombs came our way, but we escaped damage. If the sergeant had not felt the first tin with his hand both of us would have been riddled with bullets.

Over on one flank there was more line that was usually covered by a flying patrol. One of the officers and a private were crossing that way when they were seized by a party of Germans who had crept into our territory and lain in hiding. They were lifted bodily out of the trench and rushed toward the Hun lines, with revolvers to their heads to ensure quietness. In spite of this threat the officer managed to wrench free from his captors and to escape them altogether, getting back to his own lines. Thereafter we redoubled our caution in that part.

We were back again at the brewery and kept taut by occasional heavy shelling. After a working party just before dawn, during which we got soaked by sudden rain, rum was issued, and the sergeant in charge passed by "Old Bill" who had not gone out. "Old Bill" resented such an omission and said so with heat, such heat that caused him being brought before the captain for discipline. We were all too highly strung and there was more excuse for the veteran. He had Giger as his assistant and must have had his temper tried severely. After a prolonged session with red and white wines Giger had endeavored to show a kindly member of the military police that he should really be inflicted with an inferiority complex, and the net result had been clink as a counter-irritant to such an erroneous idea. After he emerged he was given in charge of "Old Bill," and faithfully performed his duties as long as he was under observation.

Tommy was interested in Giger's mentality and often talked with him, asking him curious questions. He discovered that the fellow's greatest fear was of being one of a trio to take "lights" from the same match. One of the three, he was certain, would be gathered unto his fathers without further preliminaries. Giger's pet saying while he was under the influence of the vin sisters was that he came from a tough land, where even the canary birds sang bass, and Tommy claimed that he heard him arguing with a beery A.S.C. driver about the Germans, declaring that the Junkers were those who demolished French houses.

From the brewery we went to the left front, the Lens area, and relieved a battalion of the Staffords. Many of them we talked with were the Londoners, cheery compounds of optimism and tenacity that made them incomparable front line holders. They chatted with us and informed us that "old Jerry" had invaded their trench and captured several prisoners, that he had not done it "on the level" but caught them when they were exhausted after a hard night's work. A party pressed by us carrying a blanket-covered form. "Who's that?" asked one "A new bloke wot forgot to duck his napper," came the quick answer. "Wouldn't it give you the camel's 'ump?"

We saw one carrying party crossing overland behind the trench and asked them who they were. "The King's Own 'Ymn of 'Aters," came the retort. "Wot's your mob?"

The German advance on the Somme had continued and there were many conflicting rumours. Nevertheless we sensed that the situation down there was critical and that we might be attacked at any time. Everyone was on his toes and we began to see more of the officers than at any time since I had joined the battalion. I was sent out with another man to go along the top of the railway embankment as far as possible and there keep watch on the German front and listen for sounds of a patrol. We kept between rails on the track and worked well over toward the enemy, then lay still. It was not very dark and we were in a very exposed position. I had found a place that had been hollowed slightly and gave cover, and after being there an hour was touched on the shoulder. "What is it?" I asked without looking around.

"What?" whispered the fellow. "I never said anything."

"Didn't you touch me?" I asked.

"No," he said. "I never moved."

In an instant I was crawling away. It had been months since I had felt a like touch but remembrance of it had never left me. Day and night I was keyed for messages from Steve; not for a single hour had I forgotten him. The man followed me in a startled way, and we went ahead several yards. No sooner were we settled again than a battery near Lieven fired, our own whizz bangs, and a salvo of shells passed just over the track – all but one. That one shell had not enough elevation. It struck the steel rail and detonated exactly where we had lain.

The man with me crouched lower. I could see him licking his lips, trembling. "Gosh," he breathed. "It was lucky you thought you heard something."

The weather had turned warm and in the morning we could hear the skylarks flooding the air with melody as they winged high and then dropped to earth again. Danedelions dotted every little patch of sod that remained in our area and the hard places grew dusty. The enemy tried to raid trenches over near Hill 70 and we saw our S.O.S. go up. The response of the artillery was magnificent and heartened us. It did not seem an instant until a barrage was falling on the German trenches and there was a defiant roar to the guns that made us tingle.

Sambro had a narrow escape while on post. One of the big ones came sailing over, the kind usually sent to back areas, and descended in front of him. Sambro was dazed when we reached him, and staring at a baby volcano just in front of his post. "I heard it coming and I couldn't move a step," he said. "There's something the matter with me."

He had not missed a turn in the line since coming to France and his health was not good. Our stay in the line without hot meals, and the lack of a bath, had its effects. He developed some skin disease and was covered with sores. The medical officer sent him down the line and we did not see him again for months. Others had the same trouble but many light cases were treated in the trenches, and that Queen of the Movies, the good old number nine, was often prominent. The need of a bath and change of clothes was, however, not ignored, and small parties were rushed back by light railway to the nearest soap-and-water establishment and there given an hour for ablutions. One place was a mine bath and French girls were the attendants. They were not embarrassed by our presence and hot suds took our attention.

We moved back to supports and a party was sent up to do wiring in a corner too difficult to approach on ordinary nights. But it was dark and raining and seemed the opportunity. We carried our stakes and wire with us and by the time we had navigated Cow Trench and reached our objective we were soaked and chilled. There the officer whispered hoarse instructions and found it necessary to stay very close to the trench exit. Three of us were detailed as covering party and we wandered out and out until we were sure we would soon step into the German trench. But the pouring, slashing rain made us indifferent. There was not the slightest shelter and it was one of those downpours that France often endured. We stood there together, rain running off our tin hats, down our necks, our legs, even our elbows. It was cold, too, and we did not want to move. Behind us the workers had an excellent chance to hurry for the deluge covered all small sounds. Tommy was beside me and I felt him stir slightly, and raised my head a trifle.

We did not move more than that, and we were shoulder to shoulder, leaning on our rifles. Two dim figures, Germans, passed in front of us so close that we could touch them, their feet squelching with water. They were panting as if they had come quickly and never noticed us. We did not start or move as they passed, but every moment seemed an eternity until one of the wiring party came and said that they had finished. Then we went to the trench and I kept close behind the third man until I could find out who he was. He had been pressed tight to Tommy on the other side. It was Sparky, a quiet, dark-eyed new man, one of the MacLean draft – and he had not flinched or spoken. They were good soldiers.

Next day he mentioned the matter to me and seemed very proud that he had seen a German. His talk made me think. So many men had come to France and had endured all weathers, all hardships, worked and died, without ever seeing an enemy or hearing one speak. Tommy had often referred to it, and I realized that many of the soldiers were curiously eager to see a live Hun. Some of them seemed to think they were likely to meet monsters like the characters in *Pilgrim's Progress*.

The sergeant-major came to our cellar and asked for volunteers for a raid. Tommy started up at once, then sank back as the murmur of voices increased. There were many questions and several of them jumped at the chance. We had many good men and the platoon was at full strength. Earle and Williams, Lockerbie and a Russian we called "Waterbottle," were all big men, cool-headed, active and courageous, a quartet ready for anything. Barron was also a good man, and Murray, a stocky 73rd lad, was his mate.

The raid was to be at the embankment and a fiery officer was to be in charge. He had not seen much action but seemed anxious to meet the Hun. I said nothing. The old bitterness I had brought to France had never left me entirely. Most "oldtimers" galled me. There was not one in the platoon who had seen as much continuous service as I had, had been on half the patrols, had seen as much of no man's land, and yet they swanked as the "old hands," and we were "umpty-umps," delayed in reaching France by the imbecility of those in authority, officials who were then scheming to force across the water those they had refused the opportunity. In addition, I had a queer temperament. I never talked about what I had seen or done, always kept in the background, and if asked questions by officers or non-coms some inexplicable contrariness of nature made me non-communicative, and I generally gave the impression that I was sullen and not ambitious. I knew that if I told an officer all the adventures I had had he would place me as an imaginative liar, and so I held to the other extreme and said nothing.

On the other hand we had several, chief among them the Newfoundlander, young Russell, who shouted out all they had seen or done, who made a great show of being hardy, Hun-eating lions, ready to bite bullets. Russell WAS a good soldier, had done a man's share all the time, and the others who talked and made a like show were also good, but the quartet I mentioned, and Sambro and Tommy and Barron and Murray were all their peers in any adventure "across the bags." The needed men were chosen and were sent back to the rear to rehearse their raid. They were to get a bath and have good meals for a few days. In a way I envied them; in another way I did not.

I would have liked to have shared their change from the line, we had now been in the trenches over a month, and to show Davies and Grafftey that I was not such an indifferent soldier, but I did not envy them their rushing into the German lines with a new officer at their head. I liked patrol work, loved crawling near the Hun wire, was not nervous when with good men, but I dreaded mob fighting, a dozen men against a score, with bayonets and trench knives the main weapons. In the dark of no man's land you had all the elements of surprise in your favour, it was your wits against the other fellow's, your cunning against his; in a raid it was a mad chance unless all things worked as planned, which was very seldom.

There had been several raids since we entered the line and none of them were a success. After the officer swam to the embankment a party was selected from fifteen and sixteen platoons and a raft was used to cross the water. A rope was attached to it and a number of men were ready to pull it back on our side as soon as the German post was raided. Something went wrong, I never knew what, and the raft was drawn back before they reached the other side. Another attempt was made near the embankment, but old Fritz was ready and inviting and the would-be raiders did not venture far. An "original" had come back to the company, they were rare specimens now, and he was credited with having unusual courage. He was to be one of the leading men in the attack.

Tommy and I went back to Lieven. There had been another rain and we were in search of a cellar or any cavity that had collected enough water to permit us to have a bath. We chose a part that seemed the most isolated from soldiers' paths, and the hollow reverberating sounds of our footsteps were caught up and echoed by the ruins. The street was blocked with debris and every living thing was absent with the exception of two black cats that stole about the wreckage as wild-eyed as evil spirits. In a small garden we found rambler roses in bloom and Tommy made a garland for his steel hat. We entered a very shaky ruin. Its walls still supported the roof and tiles clung crazily to it, but the interior was badly damaged. A shell or bomb explosion within a room had blown away partitions and a great hole gaped in the floor, revealing a cellar lined with bunks. We had candles with us and found that the place had been occupied by the Germans. Equipment and clothing were scattered about. Pockets had been turned inside out and a few letters were molding on the floor, thick paper covered with a Teutonic scrawl, discarded by hurried souvenir-hunters. A ghostly exhalation, that peculiar German odour, still lurked about the place.

We got back to the wrecked floor. It was dusk and the timbers creaked eerily beneath our tread. We hurried and they made more noise, as if the old house were a pallid ruin of imprisoned hopes, jibing the timorous and chuckling hideously as they fled. From a shell hole in a nearby wall came a glow of red as the sky behind was lit by gun flashes, and a sharp strafing began. The glows played on the walls of another ruin with a fascinating bizarre effect. The batteries were not a great distance behind us and we stayed a time and watched the light flicker, dance, vanish and whiten again. For over fifteen minutes the shelling kept on and then it quieted, and it seemed as if a waiting silence were over everything.

We went back to our cellar and Tommy and I were sent to company headquarters. It seemed that an attack was expected and we were to carry messages. There had been considerable shelling of the front line and the enemy seemed active. We were told to remain in an outer room of the cellar where the runners and a few signallers were gathered. A game of banker was in progress and Tommy, after watching it a time, asked me for a loan of five francs. I gave it to him and he lost it, and I gave him a second five. It was a lucky note. The play turned his way and did not change. Outside we could hear shells tearing all along Cow Trench, down by the cook's quarters, all along the sector, a general strafe. Our ears were attuned to every explosion, but we sat there in the candle light, looking at each other whenever a heavy one came especially near, and the play went on. When word came that we were to go out with the captain and see what damage had been done Tommy had over one hundred francs in his pocket.

We found trench sides smashed down, debris piled in different places, but no serious harm done, and the German guns had calmed. Sparky had had a narrow escape as a shell fragment had knocked his helmet from his head, but he was smiling steadily. He informed me that he had been on duty when it was not his turn, but that he had gone without complaint, hoping that his action would be afterward commended. Tommy grinned at me. Helping the other fellow, doing him a good turn, with the expectation that in the end you yourself will benefit the most, has been the cynosure of many faiths.

The days grew monotonous. It seemed years since we had even been back as far as the transport lines. Food grew tasteless and we could not eat. We had turned night into day so long that I could not sleep regular hours at all. When off duty in the daytime I would often wander around the trenches, watching the aeroplanes in combat or in acrobatic stunts as they dodged the shelling of the "Archies."

There was nothing we could do when not on working parties or on post. We had nothing to read but our letters and I had read French History until I loathed it, even Tommy knew my little guide book by heart. All the rumours that circulated were treated as plants needing careful nurture and none lost strength in their passage through our cellars. The MacLeans were told all the army yarns until the five favorites were common property. There was the one about the Ghurka and the German sentry. There had been the dark man's sudden appearance on the parapet, a lightning slash with his trusty blade, which must never be unsheathed without drawing blood. "Ah-ha," grunted the Heinie. "You're so smart you missed me."

"You shake your head," said the Ghurka laconically. Fritz did so, and it dropped to the trench floor.

Then there was the one about the prisoner. "Me no fighting man, me Minnieman." And the "dead men made into soap" story, and the "'forty-foot revolving' periscopes on the Hindenburg line." Then when the crowd was right, in the dead hours of the night, the story of the "angel of Mons" would go the rounds, and be believed, many times, by both teller and hearer.

The raid took place. It was postponed more or less, but at last the big night came and we were all watching and listening for results. Though more successful than the other attempts, it was a fizzle. Smoke bombs were used and under their screen the party pushed over, but tumbled into wire that had been put up the previous night, and after the scouts had reported. The Germans spotted their visitors and gave them harsh welcome, but rifle grenades were used and the raiders got into the enemy trench and chased the garrison, the fiery officer leading and the "original" with him. The officer was badly wounded and when his men tried to get him back the Germans had got in from the other side, and but for very plucky work by the "original" things might have gone more badly than they did. As it was they got their leader back to our lines and we met them in the trench, their faces blacked, armed to the teeth, winded and much excited. Next day there were many arguments about the unsuspected wire.

We went once more to hold the front line, this time in the sector about the "Minnie House." It was a ruin that had, beneath its cellar, a concrete hold that would have turned quite a large shell. It was a roomy place, large enough for a platoon to live in in comfort, and dry. I was warned for a patrol and went out with "Flighty," a sergeant of one of the other platoons. After we were a short distance beyond our wire he stared at the ruins about us and whispered that it was a very dangerous place and that we had not better go too far. I said, "You're in charge," and never offered a suggestion. We did not get ten yards further, but worked a little, left and right, still in sight of our wire, and there put in two hours. Later I heard the sergeant-major telling that "Flighty" had brought in a good report and that he had been very near the German posts.

Just before dawn Sparky came hurrying to me. An officer wanted me to come over to a post on the right. It was just breaking light. I went. Two of the new men were on post and were staring over the parapet. The officer was pacing back and forth. There had been some wiring to do, some work in a spot well out in front, and he had had charge of it. He had, of course, a covering party out, and to ensure his safety while he superintended the work, he had put them well out, near some trees of an old garden. The Hun had loosed a few rounds of machine gun ammunition just as the work was finished and, as the party hurried in, the officer had forgotten his covering crew. Now he had suddenly remembered them, but did not know exactly where they were, and it was almost day. He was in a state bordering on hysteria. He was new to the front, new to everything, and didn't want to get in wrong. Would I look for his men?

All this was said in the hearing of the sentries and Sparky. I asked who were out and was told that Mills was one, he was with us again, and Jones another. Jones was an "original" who had just returned, a big fellow, and one of the best chaps in the battalion. I went out. There was no time for crawling. The sun was nearly due. I left my steel hat and rifle, so as not to be hampered, and ran in a stooping position to trees that were nearest. There was no one there. I dodged over to the next ones. No one there. The third group were further out, but I hurried there, expecting every second a fusilade from the German trench. There were the boys, their rifles ready, wondering who was coming. They followed me without a word, but when we got to the trench there were very harsh and bitter ones. They had lain there five hours, waiting the order to come in, thinking something necessitated their staying there, and Mills spoke his mind freely. They thanked me warmly and I hustled out of the way. I did not want to hear the officer make his explanations.

The next night I went again on patrol, and was paired with the famous "original." We started out without a word. An enemy machine gun post had been bothersome and was to receive the attention of the Stokes if it could be located. My man was not friendly. He crawled without looking to see if I were following him and he did not ask me a question or give an order. We went out until we were among the ruins that I supposed housed the Maxim, and there we prowled over brick heaps and up ditches until I was sure we were in enemy territory. But not a Hun did we see or hear, and we returned slowly, listening long intervals. He made his report without saying anything to me and I went back to my dugout.

On the third night it was the turn of our platoon to do the patrol, and Davies very kindly offered to let another go in my place as I had been out two nights. I refused and only asked that Tommy go with me. Two or three men were all we used there, as the lines were not definite and the crawling had to be done around old buildings. We went out rapidly. I had only one intention and that was to go out further than we had gone the night before, and to stay until I located a German post. Tommy was willing. There was enough cover to protect us from any sudden machine gun fire and enough moon to let us see where we were going. We found a ditch that was not too wet and went up it a long distance. Not a German was to be seen or heard. I was dumbfounded. Something seemed wrong. We lay there and waited, listening, and had grown quite careless of our movements when three Germans suddenly appeared. They were walking along a path by a ruin near us and were as unconcerned as if in a back area. They walked by us and went on up the way we had come and into a post formed by an angle of walls, all that remained of a ruin. A machine gun was mounted there and we had not seen it as we crawled by. They soon fired a few rounds, and then were still. The moon grew brighter and Tommy and I lay there in the ditch, close together, staring at the ruin.

We dare not move. We were blocked by a high jumble of rubbish on one side that shadowed us, and to go the other way meant to cross their path in plain view. At long last, after we were cramped and stiff, the moon clouded, and we took a chance. We got to our feet and, keeping crouched, walked across the Hun path and into rough ground beyond. There we could crawl and use cover that would protect us from the gun. We got back safely to our trench and found that our officer was on duty, so reported to him and after much pointing showed him the location of the German gun. It was not over one hundred yards from where we stood. He promised to go to headquarters and report in full, and told us to go and have a drink of hot tea.

We went, and having the rest of the night off, tried to sleep, but could not; we were too excited over what we had seen. At last we went up to the trench again and to the officer's dugout, intending to inquire from him what the O. C. had said. The officer had a batman so furtive and small that we dubbed him "The Rat," and he had a brazier stationed at the foot of the stairway, cooking something on it. Just inside the gas blanket at the top of the steps someone had left the empty rum jug, and as we arrived a runner came plunging by us. He was known as "Doggy," a big, clumsy-footed youth who did not seem frightened of anything. He struck the rum jug and knocked it down the steps. It hounded through the air, striking the stairway but twice, and Doggy shouted, "Look out – rum jar."

Bang! The rum jar struck the brazier fairly and over it went, frying-pan and all, in a flurry of sizzling flame, smoke and fumes.

We stopped and looked at each other. What would the officer say? So we about-turned and waited in the trench until Doggy appeared. He was convulsed with laughter and maintained that when he reached the dugout both the Rat and his master were trying to get back of the iron cot at the rear. As we talked with him Earle came along the trench with water cans, old petrol tins, and asked me if I would go with him in search of "do-loo." The men were parched. Rations had been slim and it was said that the Rat had pinched the water supply in order to provide a bath for the lieutenant.

Earle and I walked and walked. The moon had gone and it was pitch dark. We had to feel our way around corners and it took us an hour to reach a water line the engineers had lain. There we filled our tins. It was just dawn and we could make out a Y.M.C.A. sign in the trench. It pointed to a cellar some distance away, but a passing soldier informed us that the place was closed, was never used in daytime and was under enemy observation. I had some money with me and had not seen a canteen for some time. Tinned fruit would be delicious, and chocolate ... I set my tins down and ran out over the hard ground, using the footpath. Earle followed and we reached the entrance to the cellar, but the door had been fastened. I picked up a plank that lay there and drove in the entrance, walking in over the wreckage. We selected all we could buy and I laid the money on the counter. The man in charge slept in a nearby dugout and we knew that he would reach the place as soon as anyone. Then we did a sprint to the trench, wended our way back to the "Minnie House," and breakfasted in style. Tommy was not well in the morning but he would not go sick. Once at Vimy he had had terrible cramps after three days of wading in slush and water, and had joined the sick parade. It was a time when the rations were short and no bully or hardtack available. All the new men circled the cook wagon like gulls and even sick men were hungry. The padre usually attended those morning sessions. He was a fluent speaker, a nice singer and really led a neat "church" service, but his place was with the officers and we all knew it. He made some remark about food, and Tommy cut loose in his usual fashion, and found himself hoisted out of the place without ever being questioned. From that time on he never reported sick no matter how he felt, and would have died in a dugout before complaining in the military way.

I got him excused from duty. None of us were in good health and the long strain was telling on the nerves of many. Men were jumpy, too watchful, too quick to take alarm. Twice outposts in the ruins had tried to shoot each other. Rumour came that we were to be relieved, but we simply hooted at it; we were past believing any rumour. But it was true. At last, after fifty-five days, we were withdrawn from the trenches and taken back beyond reach of machine guns.

It gave us curious feelings to be in the back areas again, to even see French people. We were billeted in a little village and there some of the boys went wild. They got wine and brandy and were hilariously drunk, shouting and marching around their billets. Others simply walked into the fields, along the hedges, and sat down and stared about them. It seemed wonderful to be back again where one could stand straight and walk about in daylight. After that one riotous night the boys sobered and were more like themselves. We marched again, on legs unused to such exercise, on cobbles we had not trod for a long time. Flowers were everywhere and all the world was flooded with glorious sunshine. We inhaled the breath of the fields and trees and there were spasms of singing. Emotions gripped us and one felt queerly choked. We passed places where the "outside" soldiers lived, and saw hut frontages adorned by flower-pots, white-washed stone circles and crests and doodads that did not seem to us in accord with war.

And then we came to St. Hilaire. It was a village of friendly people and there were shops and places where we could buy eggs and chips. We were billeted in barns, on clean straw, and after vigorous bathing and clean shirts felt more like living again. It was wonderful weather, sunny, warm, balmy. Poppies were like blood drops on banks of green, and the white-walled cottages seemed to enhance the verdure of the fields. Rations improved and parades were sensible. It was good to have survived the spring.

We slept in a ring around the building. "Old Bill" was near the door. Beside him were Walton and Morris, two husky lads who had come back to the battalion after being wounded at Vimy. Along one wall slept Harvey, a MacLean Highlander, a strong-built man; Rees, a young Welshman, with a sweet tenor voice; Thornton and myself. Along the end were Honer, another singer, suspected of having a "girl," at Ferfay; Ted, a little Liverpool lad, Tommy and Sparky. In the next barn were Earle, and Barron, and Murray, and Hughes, "Waterbottle," Williams and McPhee. Rats were very thick, the mud and straw walls of the buildings being honeycombed by their passages. Some of the boys tried to sleep with ground sheets over their heads, but were too warm. Our officer had gone from the line. He was indisposed. Four months up front was a long time for one of his kind. Tommy and I found out that he had never reported our location of the gun post; it was his turn to lead a raid.

Thornton slept with his mouth open and snored. I was roused by whiskers on my face one night and opened my eyes to see a huge rat scanning me gravely. He backed a trifle as I looked at him and pushed himself into the palm of my hand. Instantly I pitched him towards Thornton. There was an odd, choking gurgle, a strangling noise, a squeal. The rat had dived into Thornton's widespread mouth and Thornton had convulsively closed his teeth on the rodent's head. The rat's feet had clawed wildly on his chin and when Thornton released his mouthful the creature squealed as it sprang away and into the wall. Thornton sat up and spit for an hour afterwards and I rolled in mirth.

Honor was frightened of the rats. He sat up several times in the night and fought them with clubs he had brought in to his bed. We cut cheese into small fragments and slyly scattered them in the straw about his head. That night the rats came in gangs. Honor sat up with his clubs and a candle and held them off until one o'clock in the morning when he took his ground sheet and went outside. He finished the night under an apple tree.

We all began sleeping outside. The nights were deliciously cool and fragrant. Our cooks were down the street a distance, and when reveille blew we never roused. At the breakfast call we simply got up and reached for our mess-tins. Shortly there would be a parade that never failed to bring mirthful cackles from the peasants coming into the village with their dogs drawing two-wheeled carts. We went without our kilts, in shirts and boots, digging the sleep from our eyes, and then paraded back with steaming tea and porridge on which reposed strips of bacon.

I got acquainted with many of the new men. Some of them were good singers and entertainers and we had splendid evenings around the different farms. We got eggs and chips each night and I began to put on flesh again. Tommy was like himself once more. Christensen got books from some source and he and Sykes, who was our stretcher bearer, spent much time in reading. Eddie was the sergeant of thirteen platoon and we became accustomed to a new regimental the boys called "The Farmer." He had a slow way of speaking and walked as if following a plow. MacFarlane had been wounded.

Cockburn, who had been wounded at the same time as Laurie, returned to the battalion, and I got to know Haldane and Peeples, two big tall men who had come with the MacLean kilties. Then I got leave for a day and went over the country with a brigade signaller, a lad from my home town. Chinese labour battalions were everywhere, digging trenches, and we watched their curious way of shovelling. They used round shovels with very long handles and always had earth in the air, keeping the shovel going all the time and only taking a third as much gravel as we would lift. They carried their dixies of rice and tea level full, having them suspended from poles that sagged and allowed the dixie to swing, but they never spilled a drop, the carriers walking in a spring-kneed fashion. Some of them were enormous brutes, working in baggy trousers, naked from the waist. They had their own clothing and customs and were "bossed" by their own foremen, all being under British sergeants. We saw two of them scrapping, clawing and pulling at each other like school girls, and judged that one good white man could handle two or three of them. At night they had a band, each instrument having one string, and each drummer but one drumstick, and they played a weird music that was monotonous and doleful. They slept in ditches, lining the road for half a mile, or under bridges and would not lie in the open, fearing the German bombing planes.

Several times we heard the dread humming of the big Gothas and one night they came very near, dropping their loads between St. Hilaire and Bourecq, the next village. The Chinese ran all over the fields, jabbering and chattering, and were straggled for miles around before morning. Our lads found that they would buy bully and the cooks had a hard time keeping a supply on hand. Poker was the chief recreation after payday while crown-and-anchor men were always to be found. There was very little drinking, and not over three drunks came in all the time we were out on rest. Giger had had severe warnings. His latest "spill" had been the statement that he knew an archduke had started the war and that he had been killed for it.

On Sundays Earle and I walked to Lozingham, where we had billeted the previous summer. The 85th were there. I visited my brother and many other boys I knew, and always had our supper there. At night we walked back, nine kilometers, and did not mind the distance at all. The brigade signaller managed to arrange a day with one of the cars and we went away down south, passing a field where an inspection was in progress, men standing rigidly to attention before the scrutiny of an impressive group of brass hats, immaculate in ribbons and spurs and monocles. We saw more droves of Chinks, and Sengalese, strange, soft-eyed fellows with their hair done up in black buns, and there were Frenchman wearing red trousers and gay braid. At noon we got dinner with a Yank, a corporal, who had a brother in the fourth division. He was eager to talk about the war and luridly condemned his own people for not entering it sooner and for being so long in getting into action. He himself had been five months in camp and was fed-up with drilling.

There were rumours of field manoeuvres and trucks came and took us over the country. We were marched into long lines and imaginary positions, and had day-long picnics. Some of the officers took it seriously and bawled us out in harsh language, but the older ones were very calm and it did not break their hearts to see us lying on the soft gray banks and contemplating skylarks. Messages would be sent, and mixed into a mystery; we would go where we were not supposed to go; smoke bombs would be used at the wrong time.

Some of the manoeuvres were huge affairs, and one nice morning we were disturbed by furious voices and rose hastily to see the Corps commander and some of his staff. They did not seem pleased with the way we continually took cover and our officers covertly implored more action. At one point a village crossed our "battle ground" and we charged it heartily – at the wrong time – and rushed a Y.M.C.A. tent that was serving cocoa and biscuits to hungry soldiers. An enraged officer followed us in and wholesale murder was in his eye. He sent men out in various directions and followed some of them – while the first out returned by another way. At night we lay around the billets and related the incidents of the day and planned fresh frolic for the morrow. It was a wonderful vacation.

One afternoon Sparky and Tommy and I were "casualties" near a French house. After the company had gone we went in and talked with madame in the kitchen. She could speak English as well as we could her language and we got on famously together. She made coffee for us and fried eggs and was very kind. We wondered what made her so eager to help us and she said it was because she had "a Tommy."

We looked at Tommy and laughed as he blushed, but our grins faded when she went to the door of an inner room and led an apparently old man into view. The fellow's hair was white-streaked and he tottered as he walked. His eyes once seen could never be entirely forgotten. They were dreadful, blue orbs, distended, unwinking, and staring with a horror that startled us. "He is twenty-three," said madame, "and my only living son. There were two more but they are dead. This boy, Henri, was at Verdun. His mind is what you call at the halt – it cannot get past Verdun. He was wounded there, with dead men on him, and could not move. A day and a night he was like that and now, in his mind, he is still there."

We expected to hear her breathe maledictions on the Boche, as some of the French did, but she did not utter a word of hate. The poor creature she led would not remain where we were but slunk back into the darkened room. He would never, his mother said, go out into the fields or gardens, and his face was the waxen colour of death. For days after I could visualize his ghastly features and those awful staring eyes. We could see that he had been Tommy's twin in physique but it was difficult to believe that he had once the same red cheeks and impetuous, high-held chin.

The next few days brought rumours of big battles to be fought, and the company seemed to steady overnight.

CHAPTER VII

In a German Trench

We found a little estaminet between our village and Bourecq, a small house managed by a gaunt, bony-faced woman with eyesockets like a skull. A varied company used to gather there each night and spend money freely, but, like the widow's cruse, it never seemed to run dry of wine or coffee. It was there we met old "Peter."

We never knew him by any other name. He belonged to the R.C.R.'s and was a hard-bitten, fantastic old soldier used for odd duties. Tommy sympathized with him regarding his regiment's well-known liking for brasso and blanco, and was soon in his confidence. Peter wanted to win a medal. He had had nineteen months in the line without receiving the slightest recognition of his worth, and it grieved him.

"Some bleedin' pup comes over wot has money and goes in the line five minutes and has a Military Cross stuck on his chest," he wheezed. "Wot for, I awks yer? Nobody knows. Some chap'll come fresh and dandy from Blighty and be feelin' good as he gits in a big scrap. He pulls some blinkin' stunt and up goes a V.C. 'Course he's likely won the trinket, but I awks yer, wot would he be like if he'd had a year first in the muck. Jist like any of us, I tells yer, with his tail draggin' and only watchin' his own hide."

He had been crimed once for striking a sergeant. Up in the crater line at Vimy one night when it was raining in French style a messenger had said that the non-com wanted to see him. Peter asked if morning would not do, as he would be obliged to go overland to get to the sergeant's dugout, the sap having been blown in by Minnenwefers. No, it was urgent, so after Peter got through his turn on post he wallowed through the mire – and got caught by machine gun fire. For over half an hour he was forced to stay back of the trench, soaked, chilled, cramped, trying to lie flatter each time the gun fired. Then at last, after twice falling into water-filled craters, mud from hoofs to horns, dead beat, wet to the skin, fed up to the back teeth, he reached the sergeant's shelter where that three-striped authority had remained in dry comfort-and the non-com wished to know the number of his rifle.

"I soaked him a good one," said Peter. "Number of me blinkin' rifle! I hit him hard, I did."

He told us of another place they had been, some area on the Somme. They were hurried up after dark, before they had rations drawn, to repulse an expected German attack. It had rained a steady drizzle, and when they got to their place there was not a flare going up. They lay in a ditch, without definite orders, without food, without wire in front of them, waiting for an attack that never came, and just before daylight discovered that they were in the rear of the second defense line. "It were a terrible night," he said. "We couldn't move then, it were too late and we were perished with cold. When it's light we sees a trench we could have used, and up it comes a brigadier, with blood in his eye – the only time I seen one in the line – and a carload of brass hats in tow, and we gets it proper. It's a gime, a bleedin' gime, strite it is."

He was a find for us. We went there for several nights until we had heard all his tales, and his wish for a decoration was pathetic. "Barin' a bit of ribbon to wear for the old girl's sake," he said, "there's the ornament itself to have in yer parlour. If I don't get it mytes, I hopes I gits mine in no man's land, that's all."

And then we drew from him another queer idea. He considered that to be killed out in front, between the lines, the most fitting death a soldier could die. "Let the shells bury me," he grunted. "It's the plice for Peter, if I has to get me ticket."

I often thought of Peter afterwards. There was something that stirred one in his intensity of speech. That old derelict really had more of "the spirit of the trenches" than those specialists in safe places could possibly ferment, than any of the red tabs who ordered life and death as fancy moved them. There was something he could not express otherwise in his wish to fall, if he must, out in that Garden of Sleep between the wires, that Valhalla of the bravest of the brave, Nature's cemetery of the vanguard. And there was more than complaining in what he said about the winning

of medals. Was it not true that many decorations were won by conspicuous lads fresh from training camps, without a year of hard days of trench
routine, and shell fire and Death's flutter about them? Who knows how
strong their courage would have been then? And every man who fought at
the front knew that for every high honour awarded, hundreds were
deserved, that those given were the lucky ones seen by authority. Valiant
men in desperate battles performed prodigious feats of valour and
endurance, were killed and forgotten; others survived, with only a few
comrades knowing just what they had accomplished. Few men gained
Victoria Crosses without exhibiting extraordinary courage, *but* their
equals fought, unadorned, in every company on the western front.

A group of entertainers came to Bourecq and nearly everyone went to
see the show. It was some offering that included a cave scene, wherein an
imp gambolled about. We were to go to see it but Tommy's leave came
through and he was excited. "Me for a Piccadilly fairy instead of your
show," he chortled. "A nymph of 'de pave' is better than an imp in a cave.
Away with him."

Giger's leave came at the same time, and at a fitting time. It relieved
considerable anxiety on "Old Bill's" part. He had discovered Giger roam-
ing around an isolated farm of the poorer type. A melancholy female had
apparently attracted him. She was the attendant of two bony porkers and
a consumptive-looking cow, wore her frowsy hair in a loose knot, had
sores on her skin and was dressed mostly in soldiers' discards. Giger tried
to talk to her by sign language.

We told Tommy that he was responsible for his comrade and advised
Giger to stay by him. Giger grinned. Leave was going to be a red-letter
event in his life. "I kin talk German," he boasted. "One of them Yankees
learnt me."

We had seen him often in conversation with one of the MacLean Kilties, Coleman, a fair-haired boy from Montreal. "Let's hear you," we chorused, and Giger gave us his complete repertoire. "Donnerwetter," he
growled. "Herr O burst, Gutten tag. How's that?" We applauded.

The battalion moved to Bellacourt. It gave me queer feelings to be moving back to the front again. All of us had realized that we had not been
taken back and fed so well and trained for manoeuvres if there were not
some big attack in prospect. The company was in fine fettle, every man
bronzed and in perfect health – at least looking that way. But I knew that

there were many in the platoons who carried war-shattered nerves, nerve disabilities that were not suspected.

The weather had continued fine and the boys made fun and sang in their billets. One of the "originals," however, pulled a poor joke. He was in the pioneer section and he exhibited a wooden cross and said that orders had come to have the top bar lengthened, as the "umpty-umps" were coming now with box-car numbers. They had dubbed the MacLeans as "millionaires" because their battalion number had been "1030."

In the morning as we ate breakfast we had difficulty in getting our food without swallowing wasps. At any time in the summer that one opened a tin of jam or marmalade those black and yellow pests came circling around, but at Bellacourt they came in swarms. Russell fought them till he got stung. He and little Ted were enemies quite often, as they were jealous of each other. Rees, though not much bigger, would not have anything to do with them. He was a good-mannered lad and slightly reticent. Honor had entertained us in the night. He had been visiting friends and when he reached our billet it was midnight. He made his bed and lay down and there in the dark sang in the finest voice a hymn that brought thoughts that kept us all quiet. Not a man spoke or disturbed him, and when he had finished he slept.

O Love that will not let me go
I rest my weary soul on Thee.

Often afterward did I think of that strong tenor in the night in a French barn, swinging, swaying us, holding back every interruption.

… I yield my flickering torch to Thee.

How many would before the summer was gone?

The singing of the soldiers was something to ponder. Contrary to civilian ideas, they did not join lustily in the hymns of church parades. That part of his existence was woefully mis-managed. Something in every man, no matter what his record as a church-goer, resented the idea of having his religion forced on him. There was no greater stupidity shown, no more blind disregard of the soldier's intelligence and right to individualistic feeling, than compulsory church parades. They went because they had to go, and carried with them an instinctive defiance that no fine words of the padre could overcome. They would not and did not join in the singing. The padre himself and a few of his officers would usually struggle through "O God our help in ages past" and "Fight the good fight with all thy might." It seemed as if they did not think the soldier could possibly know any other hymns. But in the evenings, when there was opportunity, those same dumb-lipped men would go, voluntarily, to a Y.M.C.A. hut, and there fairly bring down the roof with singing that throbbed with fervour. Given their own freedom in the matter and religious services would have been enjoyed by the soldiers. As it was they went as the led horse to water.

In their billets when in the humour they would sing rollicking songs, sentimental ditties. "K-k-k-katy," "My Little Gray Home in the West," "When You Come Home, Dear," and "Hello My Dearie, I'm Lonesome for You." And "Mademoiselle from Armentieres," was always remembered, and the regimental march pasts were encores. "Oh, Jock, are ye glad ye enlisted; Oh, Jock is your belly full?" When near the "shino" boys the "forty-twas" would gently chant that rather vulgar old number about the R.C.R.'s sailing away and leaving things not as they ought to be, "... and when they get home there'll be ... to pay in the good old R.C.R.'s."

Yet those same singers, many a night in a cold, draughty billet, joined in hymns and sang then with all the feeling of any church choir. Padres, as a rule, were scorned, for only sincerity could live with the "other ranks," and they knew, whatever the showing, that he was not one of them. Our own padre was not disliked. Sometimes on the crater line he came at night with cigarettes and warm drinks and talked with a private, but he was apart from the men, and usually with, perhaps through circumstance, an officer whom the majority cordially hated.

We went from Bellacourt to support trenches at Neuville Vitasse, relieving the 27th Battalion. It was a quiet sector, and the weather continued warm. We lay in our bivvies and slept during the daytime. At night we went on working parties that were not hardships and of short duration. Then we sat on firesteps or on the grass outside the trench and watched the flares up ahead. I visited other companies and saw Siddall and Jimmy. Jimmy had a hard time at Passchendale and was very thin and nervous. He told me that Hill had been badly wounded and that the scouts never recognized him at all, with the exception of Brown who was as genial as ever. I saw the old chap myself and was introduced to Nauftts, a jolly, energetic fellow.

The MacLean men thought our trip a "Jake" war. Several of them had not come to the battalion until May, and among them were Batten, a nineteen-year-old boy from New York, and Johnny, another youngster. More new men joined us and one chap, Morris, took the bivvy next to mine that I had saved for Tommy. He was a tall, copper-haired chap with queer, dreamy eyes. At first I thought him very quiet but he came and sat with me in the morning and asked me countless questions, questions the ordinary men would never think of. "What did I think it felt like to be killed?" "Were we issued any dope that would ease pain in case we were hit?" He did not seem exactly right in his mind.

Tommy returned and was forced to share the bivvy. He roused me the last morning we were in the trench and I went out to see Morris lying in the shelter, rather badly battered, and to hear a strange story. Morris had asked Tommy endless questions as he had me, and Tommy had strung him a little about the Germans, saying they were not such bad heads and would use a man very kindly when he was taken prisoner. Morris had finally quieted and gone to sleep. Tommy said he had not slept an hour before he was awakened by a terrible grip on his throat. He could not cry out and was pinned so that he could not struggle very much. Morris was straddling him and seemed to have the strength of two men. He had a revolver which he pressed against Tommy's head and he hissed that if Tommy did not come with him he would shoot him. As the man seemed insane and as there was every chance of being rescued outside, Tommy readily agreed, but when they got into the trench there was not a man near. There were sentries by the gas alarms, but the night was dark and there were none near enough to summon. Morris kept the muzzle of the revolver against Tommy's spine and grated that he would kill him if he did not get over the trench parapet and go to the German lines.

The man meant every word he said, but he evidently had not taken in that we were only in support trenches. Tommy knew that his chance lay in not letting the fellow think differently until he could get to the front line. They got over the bags and went over the shell-pitted ground until back of the first trench. There Morris changed. He muttered to himself and peered at Tommy. They could hear men talking not far from where they stood, but his captor sensed that all was not as it should be, and he swung around, taking for an instant, the hard menace from Tommy's spine. It was enough. Tommy whipped over a beautiful right-hander that caught his man flush on the chin, sending him down like a log. Tommy disarmed him, and found the revolver empty!

It enraged him so to think that a brand-new man with an empty gun had so put the wind up him and run him around, that he suppressed his first impulse to call for help, and waited until Morris revived. Then, when he started to get up, he poked him another hard smash. Morris started to whimper and beg and Tommy yanked him up, though the other was the bigger man, and rushed him back the way they had come. He booted him into the trench and then gave him two more reminders of the reversed circumstances. Morris was entirely cowed. He crept into the bivvy like a whipped dog, but Tommy did not get in with him; he dare not go to sleep again beside him.

I talked to Morris and found that he had not known what he was doing. He even seemed different than when he had first talked to me. I questioned him further but could not get any assurance that he was all right. We did not report him, however, as Tommy did not want the story around the company, and we took turns in sleeping in my bivvy and watching our newcomer. I asked Batten about him, and he told me that on their way into the trenches a big shell had dropped beside Morris, knocking him off his feet and stunning him for several minutes. He had seemed queer when he recovered but in the excitement of new things to see Batten had forgotten him. We did not, however, but the man was more normal in daylight and seemed so contrite that we left him alone.

After a brief spell at Bellacourt again we returned and relieved the C.M.R.'s at Mercatel Switch. It was a very dark night when we took over and the relieved battalion moved out without giving us any definite information about our company front. I had hardly got established before a call came for me to report to the sergeant-major. No one knew how far away the Hun was, what the front was like, the wire, and I was to go out with the sergeant of fifteen platoon and explore.

We went slowly and carefully. Not a flare was going up and there was very little shooting. The second division had been on that front and had raided the Hun almost daily, and we figured that probably some unusual surprises were in store for us. We crept on and on. The ground was easy to travel, being mostly grass and weed patches, with only occasional shell craters. After a long time the sergeant grew impatient, and suggested that we go and get some of our own flares in order to see where we were. I agreed, but asked him to go just a few yards further before we turned. We got upright and walked, but I had not taken three steps before I descended through space – I had simply stepped off solid ground into a deep trench.

In daylight I scanned that part of the line and saw that that particular opening in the Hun wire through which I had gone was not four feet wide, and that all along the stretch in front of us there was not another gap. Pure chance had guided me. One loose wire was lying across the trench, seemingly left there as the barricade was finished; it was all new work. As I fell I struck the wire with my head and it rasped along my helmet, only one barb catching me just below the brow on the upper part of the eyelid. I struck heavily on the trench floor.

For an instant there was silence, then I heard a startled guttural query. I groped for my tin hat, found it and my rifle, and reached up to the sergeant. He had crouched on the parapet and he grasped my arm and yanked me up to him. We plunged back into no man's land for about twenty or thirty yards and into a deep shell hole. Phut! A streak of sparks and a flare sizzled aloft and shed its glow over everything. We huddled as low as possible. More flares went up. A machine gun opened fire and swept back and forth, its bullets snapping over our heads. Then stick bombs came looping through the air and exploded very near to us. There were several craters around that part and the Hun could only guess that one of them sheltered would-be raiders. Presently he quieted and we stole in. We had found where the German trench ran.

I thought that my eye had been damaged. I could not see and it was full of blood. Sykes looked at it and just put a loose bandage over it. The lid had dropped down and he was sure my eye was torn. Our shelters were along a sunken road and at the moment the Hun, no doubt alarmed by our visit, began shelling. It was not safe to go outside, but I could not wait. I wanted to know how badly my eye was injured. Earle was there and offered to take me across to the first aid station by an overland route. It would save time but was over exposed ground. It was a most unselfish thing for him to offer; he had finished his work for the night and had no need to take any more chances, but he insisted on going.

We had not got ten yards from my dugout when a salvo of shells came into the road just ahead of us. There were cries for a stretcher bearer and as we got there they were picking up poor little Johnny who was just making his second tour to the trenches, his first in the front line. He was dead before they could bandage him. We hurried on and when out on the exposed part shells came in a hurricane outburst. They fell ahead of us, behind us, all around us and we never stopped going. There was no adequate shelter and my eye was bleeding.

At last we jumped into the trench on the other side and were soon at the doctor's dugout. I was at once given an inoculation and then laid down on a cot while my eye was probed. It was painful but I did not mind when they discovered that the sight had not been injured at all. A few stitches put the lid back in place and then I was told to go to headquarters until morning. Outside the place I decided that I would go back with Earle. The shelling had died down and I could go around by the trench in the morning and see the doctor.

The sergeant-major humoured me. I was allowed to stay in my shelter instead of going back to transport lines until my eye healed. There was nothing I could do at either place and I liked being with the boys. Earle, Williams, Barron, "Waterbottle," and Lockerbie went out on a patrol and explored the wide area just to the right of our company front. It was discovered that the Germans had a post at a place called "Long Alley," and on the next night the party crept in close. "Waterbottle" and Williams got alongside and jumped into the sap, the others following. They attacked so suddenly and fiercely that not a prisoner was taken. Every sentry in reach was killed and the others fled. The patrol was not harmed at all and got back in safety. "Waterbottle" and Williams got Military Medals for their part in the attack.

A raid was planned on the usual scale. There were to be two parties, one to act as a covering crew. The "Secret Operation Orders" of that date, 17/7/18, stated that the intention was to "cut off enemy posts from the S.W., under cover of a barrage with a demonstration to attract enemies' attention to the N.W."

The covering party was to go out thirty minutes before zero hour and take up a position north of the attack, and to remain there until the raiders returned or until zero plus ten minutes. The signal was to be the opening of the barrage and smoke bombs were to be released. Two red flares were also shot on the northern side of the enemy line and six No. 27 rifle grenades discharged at the Hun posts. This was supposed to fool him as to where the real assault was taking place.

Like many another affair, all did not go smoothly. The covering party had the opportunities, the raiders did not. They had hardly got into position before a German patrol calmly strolled into view a few yards from them. It was a golden chance to bag prisoners *but* just a moment before the barrage opened, and the raiders were in readiness. A mixup of any kind might bring disaster, so they lay quiet and the Huns went on their way.

The barrage, red flares, grenades and all went perfectly and the party rushed out and over to their objective, but the birds had flown. The Germans sent up double red and green flares and golden sprays, and retaliation fell on our lines two minutes after zero hour. One of the raiding party was killed by a rifle shot, but the Hun sentry escaped capture. The net results were a loaf of black bread that Otto and Fritz had overlooked in their departure, and a small black dog – which was probably handed to the cooks.

We had an O-pip that our doughty friends, the engineers, had constructed and it was a beauty. I sat in it two days with a telescope to my good eye and watched two Germans working in their back area. I think they were burying their dead, as they seemed to be excavating that depth. They were both elderly men and worked slowly. Once in a while they would pause and shade their eyes and peer our way.

Word came that we were to be relieved by a battalion that had just come from Egypt, the King's Liverpool Regiment, and that we were to go to Wailly. My eye was much better and I had done a turn on listening post when they arrived. A new officer had just come to us, and I had had an interesting time with him. He was on duty in the trench for four hours, and was supposed to see that all the posts were all right. I offered to take him out to the listening post and he would not go. He did not make any excuses but talked plainly. He was a very nice fellow, well-bred, but a nerve wreck before reaching the front, and was simply scared stiff.

"I can't go over the parapet," he said. "It's all I can do to stay in the trench." Then a few shells came over, going quite a distance back, and he sat down on the trench floor, huddled there. I had seen three men fear-stricken but he was the first officer I saw collapse. At Passchendale a man had suddenly bolted when Gordon was killed. His nerves gave way. He had been ten months at the front and his chum had been killed the day before. He threw away his rifle and equipment and ran, plunging hip deep in mire, struggling free, plunging again, tearing, breathing and snorting like a runaway horse, until he was gone from view. He went back to Ypres unchecked, hid there in cellars and calmed enough to join us when we went out of the line. Then he went with us to Bourecq and gradually recovered himself. No one said anything to him and he was quite a man again, doing all the long trip without flunking. On the night that Tommy and I had gone to the company headquarters and won over one hundred francs at banker there had been heavy shelling near one of our posts and a sentry had suddenly bolted to the dugout and refused to leave it. He had been in France for several months and the long session of that spring had unnerved him. Hughes was his corporal and he did not report him, but was kind to him and had hot tea with him at midnight. After twenty-four hours the fellow regained his control and was all right. The third man quit at Vimy, but had been blown up by a "minnie" near La Salle Avenue and was partially shell-shocked.

I talked with the officer, fearing that the captain would come along the trench and find him, and after a time he sat up on a firestep beside me and there told me how he had enlisted because he felt he ought to, how he had been held back by different circumstances, and had been content so long as they were not of his own planning, and now that the ordeal had come he could not meet it. I never heard a more honest statement. He stayed his turn, however, and gradually conquered himself until he could go over the parapet, but it took more from him than for another man to go into bat-tle, and in a short time he was a physical wreck. No one could estimate the courage of that chap, what effort it cost him to stay under gun fire, and I believed more than ever that the bravest men in France were not those who did great deeds when officers were watching them, but the unnoticed individuals who never did anything more spectacular than their hours on sentry go or trench duty – when every sixty minutes held the agony of a torture rack.

The "Egyptians," as we called them, were even worse than we had feared. They knew nothing about trench fighting or the Germans, and an order came that a number of us were to stay with them until just before morning and show them the rounds. Tommy and Sparky and I were three of the men detailed and we had an exciting time. The officer in charge came to us and asked where he could keep his horse while the battalion was in the trenches. He actually thought that he could ride back and forth from headquarters under cover of darkness and so save himself considerable walking. Then he asked about rifle fire and the next we saw was several of his men going out with bits of rag and paper which they fixed in the wire. They were going to do the "five-rounds-rapid" stuff in the morning and he wanted some target for his men to use. We advised him to do his shooting some other time and explained just how proficient the Hun snipers were. We showed him the listening posts and I went out with two of his men and established them at one, explaining carefully the use of the signal wire. As I went in a bomb came hurtling at me from the post I had left. The sentry there had the signal wire to his wrist and yet he hurled a Mills grenade at me and only the fact that he did not know enough to pull the safety pin of the bomb saved me.

Tommy saw what happened. "Where's the officers?" he snorted. "Why didn't they stay and show these chaps the wrinkles? We'll be killed if we stay around here – I'm going."

He went, and I looked for Sparky. He, too, had flown and I followed quickly. As I went along the trench I asked for the others from the rest of the company. Not a man was there. All the Black Watch had hurried from that zone.

At Wailly there was talk of an inspection and as I had a troublesome tooth I reported for dental parade, thinking to escape a hot march and standing to attention before a row of brass hats. The dental headquarters were in the next village and I had quite a tramp over dusty roads. When I got there I was hardly in my chair before "Crash! Slam! Crash!" came three heavy explosions. The building rocked. Bricks fell, glass shattered, dust rose in clouds. There were yells in the street, calls for stretcher bearers. A trio of German bombing planes, flying very high, had unloosed their loads as they passed over the village. Several men in the street were killed or wounded and I forgot all about toothache. The dentist told me to come back the next day but I postponed the appointment. When I got back to Wailly I found that there had not been an inspection, and the laugh was on me. My brother came to see me and we went to an estaminet to meet some of the other chaps. A drunken A.S.C. man rode his horse right in the door and about the tables and wrecked much furniture. We hurried away from the place.

Outside we met a man of the first division who told us that they had captured a spy near Noulles mines. Spies were often the main topic in a billet and there were always cookhouse rumours about them. I had seen one captured but did not know what was happening until it was all over. Tommy and I had been on one of our visits to other battalions and were passing through a village on the way back when we saw a man up one of the concrete telephone poles. He had on an engineer's uniform and was working at the wires. Tommy knew a chap in some R.E. outfit and after we had gone by he turned and said he would ask the chap what company or battalion he belonged to. Before we reached him again a sergeant and another private were at the bottom of the pole and asking questions. The sergeant said "What do you belong to?" "The Royal Engineers," the fellow answered.

"Come down," said the sergeant. "I want to talk to you."

The fellow descended and at once the waiting pair gathered him in, making him walk between them. We stayed around for an hour to find out what was happening and were told that the man up the pole was a German spy, and that he had been tapping the wires for almost two weeks without being caught.

We told the First Division man about the "Egyptians" and in turn he told us about a spree his company had had with a fat major. They were in the ruins near St. Pierre and had come out of the line with a German prisoner, a young good-looking lad who was very scared. Some of the men had unearthed some French finery about the buildings and while waiting for an escort to take the German back to the cages they dressed him in the rigout, even to the bonnet. The young Hun got more alarmed than ever and when a fat major suddenly rounded a corner and met him the prisoner threw his arms around the officer's neck and wept on his rather expansive bosom. His captors were at first alarmed as to what might happen but they forgot their fears when the stout major patted "her" on the back and assured "her" that he would protect her from the rude soldiers.

We went to baths on our march back and then kept on going. Every man asked questions but an order was pasted in our paybooks. It read: "Keep your mouth shut," and finished with a warning not to talk to the French people or anyone about our movements. At one place where we stopped for a meal a sick parade was in progress. The men belonged to a labour battalion. Tommy and I strolled by and watched. The first man was a dreary-looking specimen. He was badly bowed in the legs and was pale of features. On his head was a drooping balaclava cap and he wore a blanket squaw fashion.

The corporal escorting him saluted the medical officer and we heard his voice through the open window. "'E syses 'e's dyin', sir." We could not catch the medical man's rejoinder.

Giger got drunk again and we discovered him in a French house singing to the inmates. He had one line and was repeating it with joyous vigor, though applause was lacking. "Allons infants dee la pattree," he chanted, "la joor de glory is arrivay." We could not bear to interrupt him.

And now we all knew that something big was looming on the horizon. Soldiers were on the move everywhere. The very air was tense. We went back through areas that the soldiers did not penetrate often and in one little village the French were much excited as they saw our kilts and the pipe band. We passed waving cornfields, little cottages with red roofs, old peasants driving big white Percherons with a single rein, poplar and willow trees along canal banks, placid waters, went endless kilometers on long straight roads lined by tall trees, with a crucifix at every crossway. On, on we went, no one knew whither, until at last we were at Amiens. It was a big city, but empty sounding as we went through streets on the outskirts. Tommy and I looked to see the cathedral, that our guide book said was the finest Gothic structure in existence. We stayed a time, as those in command were inquiring the way, in a barn-like building, and most of the boys marched about it in a mock procession. They were all excited, all thrilled with big expectancies. I did not want to think myself morbid and so did not say anything to Tommy about it, but all that journey I saw the old crowd in the cars as we went up to Passchendale; Melville, and the Professor and Mickey and Ira and Jennings; all that gallant band who had been together all the summer, singing, joking, frolicking, now and then quieting to wonder where their path might end.

Tulloch kept talking about getting a blighty, Thompson kept by him like a brother, saying little. Batten and Ted and Rees and Harvey were as youngsters, which they were. Russell blustered about in his usual fashion, now and then subdued by "Old Bill" or Barron or "Waterbottle." Thornton hummed in his happy way. Earle and Williams and Lockerbie and Murray were always together. Sykes had his books with him, and so did Christensen. Honor sang all the time. Sparky stuck with Mills and Jones. McPhee grinned at every one and the boys tumbled him about. Morris, the odd man, kept by himself; the other Morris and Walton were together. Eddie was a serious sergeant; he had got the Military Medal for his part in the raid at Long Alley. Hayward had come back to us. Cockburn was with Haldane and Peeples, telling them of Vimy. Our sergeant was an "original" who had been on jobs in back places, a very tall man we dubbed "Lofty." Our corporals were Hughes, good-natured as ever; "Ab," another oldtimer recently returned, and Geordie, a good-looking, quick-moving soldier back from Blighty for the third time, having been twice wounded. Smaillie was also with us after his long stay in England.

We left the city and marched out to a little village in the suburbs, a street of houses on a slope across the river. There was a small factory near the stream and the employees were all girls, a fact which did not deter the boys from having a luxurious swim in the sun-warmed water. At our billet an order was posted forbidding soldiers to take anything from the gardens. Rations had not kept up with us on our trek and we were unable to buy food in the little village. We waited till dark, and no bread and bully arrived. So Tommy and I went out and got a big kettle full of vegetables from a weed-grown garden. We cleaned them and put them on to boil. There was plenty of coal in the shed at the back of our cottage and the stove was a good one. We simply put out all lights and kept the door locked and no one came near us. After an anxious half hour our dinner was cooked and we ate our fill, then called in Sparky and Jones and Mills to help finish it.

In the morning two Yanks came among us. They had a camera and were taking pictures everywhere. They got us to pose for them outside the houses, singly, in groups, with our equipment on, every way. I gave them my address and they promised to send us a few of the snaps, but we never heard from them again. Then came a message that stunned us. The colonel had been killed!

He had been out the afternoon before to visit the line to which we were going and a shell had come suddenly and struck him down. There were colonels and colonels in the Corps. Some that the men swore at and some they swore by. I visited nearly every battalion in our division from time to time, and several in the second and fourth divisions and I never was in the company of any other "crowd" where love for their commander was as spontaneous and unanimous as in ours. We had bad eggs among us at times, all kinds of soldiers, but I never heard one of them say anything against the "old man." I never had conversation with him, but when at headquarters and on parade grounds it was easy to see that he was that which all officers were not – a perfect gentleman. He had no "command," his voice was not fitted for it, and yet could get snappier moves from the battalion than any other. His death was a calamity to us; we feared that we would not get another of his kind. I was called to go to fall in with a number of men who were to form the firing party. We cleaned and polished our equipment and looked our best.

We left our little village, St. Fuscien, on the 6th of August, marching off at dusk, and our route lay through Boves. It seemed as if every other battalion and battery, every branch of the service had also decided to move that night, and in the same direction. We did not make much more than one mile an hour. The road was practically blocked with traffic. Limbers and men were close-packed. Mules with transport, horses with field guns, tractors with heavy artillery, great lumbering, clanking tanks, followed each other in close succession. We were forced to ditches, in places to fields, and in and among the traffic saw messengers on motor cycles, even cars with loads of brass hats. Never had we seen such a jumble of traffic. If the German bombers had come overhead that night they would have made a ghastly killing.

It was nearly morning before we arrived in Gentelle Wood. Thousands of other soldiers were there, but all the wood was laid off in areas and each man stayed in his battalion square. Some of the men made shelters of branches and ground sheets, some tried to dig in. Tommy and I spread our beds on moss, lay down together and slept. Overhead the stars were twinkling. All around us was a hum, a murmur of voices and mild confusion. In the distance the tanks were still clanking and tractors were grinding. Farther away the guns were shelling in a spasmodic manner. Rumour had it that we were to join in an attack that would extend for twenty miles, that it was going to be a battle that would not be over until we had broken the Hun line. So we slept there together and dreamt of home.

The next day dawned bright and clear. Someone said it was Sunday and Giger wanted to know if there would be a church parade. Orders came for us to lie low, that there was to be no unnecessary movement. Tommy said that the army was improving. The fact that they did not fall us in and make us listen to the padre and officers sing "Fight the Good Fight," showed that intelligence was beginning to seep into headquarters. He had changed. The impulsive headlong boy who was continually in hot water had become a background cynic. Only once that summer had I had difficulty in curbing him. We were by a river where we could bathe each evening, and did. We also washed our shirts and socks and were cleaner than we had been any time previously. Yet headquarters did its stuff. We were forced to fall in and march about six miles over a hot, dusty road to baths, an old building where a huge pump was manipulated by one relay of men while the others stood inside in tubs and waited with bowed heads for seventeen drops of cold water. After these had trickled down the spine we were to get torn, wrinkled, buttonless shirts in place of our clean ones and after dressing go around and wring seventeen exquisite drops on the bent bodies waiting their turn. After this ritual was duly carried out, we marched back over the hot dusty road and when dismissed went straight to the river and washed away the sweat and dust and were clean again. Our shirts that we had scrubbed and mended and sewed buttons on were gone, but we mended the ones we had received in their places and expressed our emotions in choruses that would have moved an adjutant to tears. Tommy had almost gone wild. His issue had been a garment composed of two pieces. The front of the shirt was flimsy cotton, the back of material of which horse blankets are usually made. "Old Bill" told him it was for use in draughty buildings; all that was necessary was to keep your back to the opening. Tommy, fortunately, was able to "salvage" a shirt from one of the batmen.

The sergeants were busy all that day. They distributed Mills bombs, and bandoliers, and field dressings, and ground flares, everything but the shovels and sandbags we had got in the Salient. Then we had dinner. The day was clear and sunny. Every time an aeroplane wheeled overhead we cringed and looked up, but our airmen were on the job and no black-crossed hawks were sighted. Poker games were in progress. Other men wrote letters. Some sat together, chatting a little, mostly busy with their thoughts. Then, at dark, water bottles were filled and all was ready.

I was called by the sergeant-major and told that I must go to the assembly point, learn the route, and return and guide the company in. I left everything but my gas mask and went with the other scouts and guides. It was almost a mile to where we were moving, a deep trench south of the Amiens-Roye road. After finding the position "D" company would occupy I hurried back with a man from headquarters, and after getting into my harness joined the captain and led the way. It had turned bitterly cold and the men were impatient, but the great rustle of much movement all along the front soon stilled them. There was something in the night that seemed pregnant with sudden violence, as if at any time some smashing, crashing chaos might envelop all that area. Everyone grew silent, never complaining as we threaded in and out in snaky fashion to avoid other companies, and we were too amazed to say anything when we saw field guns being wheeled to postions just behind our trench. There were no pits for them or camouflage, and it showed just what the expectations were.

It was almost three o'clock when we were finally in our line, and I had been walking since eight in the evening. Some kind hero attached himself to my rations while I was on my first journey forward but I did not worry greatly; there would be plenty of chances to salvage for myself later. Zero hour had been set at 4.20 and every one grew tense. We knew that we were not going into the attack until three hours later, but were to leave our position, go down the slope in front and cross the river Luce. After that we would be in the fighting.

As I waited, standing on a firestep, watching the stars fade, Christensen came to me and held out his hand. "Good-bye, Bird," he said. "I'm going to find out to-day which of us is right."

He and I had argued about the hereafter, and I had tried hard to convince him everything, even to a blade of grass, cried out that there was a God who governed creation. But ... "What's got into you," I said. "You'll not get hit."

"I'll be killed," he said, smiling in a way that startled me. He didn't seem the least frightened, but was as matter-of-fact as if his leave had come through. "An hour ago," he said, "something came to me. It was as if every sound in the world was stilled at once, as if there was nothing more for me to hear, and I knew what it meant. I'm not the least bit afraid, and I'll be satisfied if it comes quick." It was useless to try to console him, he didn't want sympathy. Not one man who had mentioned the same thing to me had acted the same as he did. He almost seemed glad, and when I pointed out that, if he were right, there was some power beyond the visible that imparted information, he partially admitted it, and said that he was sorry he had not tried to learn something of religion, to become a Christian, but that he was not the kind to squeal at the last five minutes. Had the right kind of man been there to talk to him I know that in the last half hour he might have changed the Dane, but I could not do it, and I shook hands with him, as convinced as he that he would never see another day.

After he had gone, Tommy came and stood beside me, and it came. One instant we were speaking in low tones, watching a red flicker of artillery away on the right and the next heart beat the very earth seemed to quiver. One great sheet of flame seemed to leap along that twenty-mile front and the roar that made the trench tremble was so fused that we could not distinguish single explosions. It was a stupendous thing. We were shaken, stunned, bewildered. For a moment we could not make ourselves heard, then, gradually, the barrage became more broken, and by shouting we could make ourselves understood. Some one touched me on the shoulder. I turned and there stood Eddie, from thirteen platoon. He reached for my hand and his face was deathly white. I gave him a hearty grip and shouted, "Good luck, old timer."

He shook his head. "This is my last trip," he called. I made no reply. What could I say? We stood together, watching the flashes, and then he moved away, slowly, down to his men.

A short time later we filed down the slope to cross the river.

CHAPTER VIII

Parvillers

As we went towards the river black shrapnel began to burst overhead with snarling menace, and on the left there were sudden geysers of soil and smoke. The noise of the barrage prevented any conversation and each man was tingling so that he could hardly keep from shaking. It was interesting to watch the faces of the men. Some were pale and drawn as they thought of the perils ahead, some expressed horror, for certain individuals, like the Professor, lived every event twice. Others were simply anxious about their rifles and bombs.

There was a stone bridge crossing the river but it had been preserved for the use of heavy traffic, and we did not mind such an order. It was very probable that old Fritz knew the exact location of the bridge and could make crossings precarious. The engineers had gone forward and placed pontoon crossings of boats with bath mats spiked across them, rather fragile-looking structures, and we had to cross in single file. The long hours of tramping and going without sleep had been a strain and I had had nothing to eat. The others had had a hurried breakfast just before the barrage opened. When I got out on the swaying, dipping bath mats and saw the muddy river swirling just inches below me I was almost dizzy, and could not have hurried. But the Germans were now shelling all the stream and had wrecked the bridge to our left, used by another company, and every one was moving painfully slow. Shells rained on all the bridge area, but it was a marshy spot and partly under water so that the explosions did little more than shower us with black filth.

When we were finally across a thick mist had settled over everything and we could not see one hundred yards ahead. Word was passed along that the objective was a hill, Hill 104. We entered a wooded area and found a trench where we stayed for some time, as our jump-off was not until 8.20 a.m. One lone shell came quite near as we waited there and wounded the man who had lost his nerve at Passchendale. He had been very nervous all the while and when we saw he had a "blighty" we felt relieved. As the sun grew stronger and began to clear the mist we saw more trees ahead and soon were filing to them. It was a sparse fringe of wood, and a brick wall came a distance from the left. Some of the men rushed to its cover. The rest of us took shelter behind tree trunks. Wheee-bang. One shell came through the limbs of the trees where Tommy and I were standing and exploded about thirty yards behind us. We looked around and saw a man pitch to earth. It was Eddie. He had "got his ticket" before we saw a German – he had had a clear vision.

We all got near the trees. Just to the left of me I saw Ted cowering behind a big bole. He had his rifle butt on the ground and as he peered around to watch the ground in front he, in some manner, discharged the weapon. His arm was resting over the muzzle. He screamed in agony and we rushed to him to find that he had a fearful wound. There had been a muzzle cap on the Lee-Enfield and he had had it turned over in place. It had been blown through the flesh and muscles, leaving a gaping rent one could thrust his fingers in. We tied a tourniquet around his arm and twisted it with a stick, then bandaged the wound. He went white and sank to the ground just as we were signalled to advance.

We went up a long slope. Three Germans rose from the tall grass and shot at us before turning to run. Sparky dropped to his knees and sniped one of them very neatly, his first kill. He was exuberant and raced up the hill to look at his victim. Another of the trio fell before he reached the crest, potted by several bullets, but the third man vanished from view.

On top of the slope we looked down on a short length of grain that had been sown in that forward position. A deep ravine lay just beyond and we could see camouflage that told of gun emplacements. We were now in extended order and everyone was in great spirits. We were back of the first trench, had seen dead Germans sprawled there, very few of our own men among them, and the only Boche sighted were on the run. As I rushed along, anxious to reach the ravine, a German suddenly popped up in the grain a few feet ahead of me. He rose so suddenly that I shot without taking aim. Experience had taught me to carry my rifle under my right arm, steadied by my left, a finger on the trigger, and only a pressure was required to beat out the other fellow.

As the German dropped he gave a ghastly groan and then I saw that he was a wizened old chap with steel-rimmed spectacles and a scraggly beard. Probably an old character like Peter, and all he had wished was to surrender. He had no weapons of any kind. I looked down at him and saw that the bullet had entered his lungs. He tried to get up and I wanted to stop and help him, but Tommy urged me to keep on. We plunged down into the valley. Three guns were there with the canvas covers still over them. A dugout entrance was just in front of me and smoke was coming from the pipe at the side of the stairway. Over on the left, about fifty yards away I saw the fleeing gunners get neatly captured by men of another company. The leader of the men in gray was a fat officer with an Iron Cross dangling over his paunch. He lost it very quickly.

Our officer was vastly excited. It was his first time "over" and he had a brain wave. Why not wheel the guns around and strafe the enemy? He yelled at us to seize on the sheels and exert our strength, but I had none to waste. The long rush up the slopes had been a dragging task and I was ready to collapse unless I could get something to eat. Young Russell saw the dugout and ran to it, yelling his find. The others paid no attention to him and I went over. Possibly a Heinie was waiting below with a ready Luger, possibly a cook was down there with breakfast ready. I went down the steps. It was a splendid dugout, very elaborate. A clock was ticking on a shelf, two tumbled beds contained the finest linen; but what caught my eye was a jumbled heap of female finery and dainty slippers under the bed. Some lady had evidently just flown.

On the table between the beds were several letters, some unopened, a big parcel not opened, and a pile of German newspapers. I grabbed the parcel and at the same time glanced at the stove. A pan of eggs was still sizzling. Two were too crisp to consume but the others were suitable for me, and there were sausages, a few bottles of beer, and black bread on shelves. We sat down and ate and drank in great style, and Russell found the coffee pot on the floor – full of nice hot coffee. We gorged ourselves and then I slit the parcel open. It contained a few candles, a silk handkerchief, and a big cake covered with pink frosting. The address said it was from Berlin, so I cut the cake and handed Russell a healthy slice. He gobbled it down and I watched him anxiously while the clock ticked off the minutes. "Do you feel all right?" I asked. "Jake," he snorted. "Hand us another chunk."

I did, and then cut a huge slice for myself. We took the rest upstairs and found the officer fuming. Earle and Sparky and a few more loyal lads were straining their muscles as they tried to heave one of the guns around. "Come here, you two," the lieutenant yelled. "Give a hand." We ignored him and passed the cake. Russell told the boys how I had him test it and there was a wild hoot. Then we went on over the hill in front and the officer followed. Some of the boys said he marked the guns with chalk in order to prove our capture of them.

No sooner were we on the high ground than we met a party of Germans, prisoners coming back on the trot. There were over twenty of them and at the rear were three doctors who spoke English. One of them was in that helpless nightmare stupor that seems to fall on some of those taken prisoner, but his mates talked with us and seemed real decent fellows. They were more than willing to assist in looking after any wounded and assured us that we would now go far as there were no organized defenses for us to encounter. While Tommy and I talked with them the others had made a thorough search of the remaining prisoners and had acquired quite a haul of souvenirs in the shape of marks, two Iron Crosses, several watches, and fancy trinkets.

We went on over the slope until we were near Claude Wood and well beyond our objective. There was no fighting to mention but a shell dropped near and killed Cockburn and Christensen was hit in the arm by a piece of shrapnel. After he was bandaged I went over to him. "You see now that you were wrong," I said. "You're away for Blighty."

He simply grinned. "Bird," he said in his slow way. "By night I'll be a corpse. Remember what I tell you."

He went on over the hill out of sight and we went on toward the Wood and then extended and lay down on the soft grass. We could see Germans running everywhere on the horizon. Some were in the edge of the Wood hurriedly arranging machine guns, but the majority were fleeing on the other side, racing at top speed, without rifles or helmets. There was a village not far off, Beaucourt, and we could make out the Amiens-Roye Road. An aeroplane crashed down close beside us, startling every one as we had not heard its engine. The airman was a boy of twenty and both his legs had been almost severed with machine gun fire. We helped him to the ground and bandaged him as best we could. He seemed calm and only asked for a cigarette.

All at once there was a shout and we turned from watching the Huns scuttle about the Wood to see one of the finest spectacles, if not the finest, of the whole war. It is certain that very few were privileged to occupy such ringside seats as we had that day, and yet not be forced to take part or suffer from the contact. Over the slope came the cavalry, the Royal Canadian Dragoons, the Fort Garry Horse, the Strathconas, riding like mad, sabres flashing, lances glittering, all in perfect formation. They swept by us with a thundering beat of hoofs and drove at the Wood. Some passed to right and some to left of it. Following them came the whippets, small tanks with remarkable speed and with guns mounted on the top.

The mounted men dashed into the Wood, directly at the waiting gunners. Killing began as if on signal from some master director. The Maxims opened fire and men and horses rolled among the shrubbery or fell in the open. I saw an officer rise in his stirrups and strike a Hun across the neck with his sabre, so that the German's head lolled oddly. I saw a lancer pierce another gunner so that the weapon stuck out behind his shoulders. A trio of Huns were beaten to earth under the horses' hoofs as the cavalry rode straight at them. It was whirlwind fighting, so fast and furious that the machine guns did not take half the toll we expected. One crew alone survived the charge and a tank bore straight for them. They fired frantically and we saw a man on the tank slither to the ground, but the tank went on, and right over gun and crew, making the thrust so quickly that not a man escaped. After it had passed, we saw a body rolled on the sod, glistening white, completely stripped of clothing.

Those who had gone toward the village appeared to be in difficulties and we got more thrills. More pounding horses came into view, a battery of heavy guns. They rushed by us and over on the wide plateau swung about and into action with astounding speed. We saw the shells striking in the village, sending up great clouds of smoke and dust, and soon the cavalry pressed on.

After noon a long column of men came in sight, battalions of the Fourth Division going through to carry on the attack. I saw the 85th Battalion and hurried over to see my brother but he had gone by. Suddenly the fighting seemed far away. No shells were falling near us and no Germans except prisoners and dead men were in sight. The tanks had gone and the big ones were lumbering up, one laden with water and ammunition. We went on to Claude Wood and the dead Huns were searched for souvenirs. At dusk we had wandered far beyond and had found many things of interest. I had picked up a sabre, a long-bladed thing, that was very supple steel, and Tommy had got a very nice revolver, a German Luger.

We slept in the wood. Our cooks had come up and served a hot meal and the 49th had also come to the same area for the night. I saw Sergeant-major Davies and he told me that he had seen Eddie away back by the trees. Then he said. "Wasn't it funny about Christensen?"

"What?" I asked.

"He was alone, going through the same place, when a shell came and he was killed by shrapnel. He was away back there and one would have thought him safe for Blighty."

Tommy and I looked at each other, and said nothing.

We moved to Folles Village and there saw many signs of hurried German flight. All kinds of equipment and clothing lay about. A dressing station was nearby. Two dead Germans lay under blankets ready for burial. Other cots were just as the patients had been taken from them. Outside, packs and rifles and helmets and gas masks, piled in a passage way, were eloquent of heavy casualties. The weather continued dry and sultry and at evening the western sky was lovely, opalescent, radiant, a riot of colour. There were streamers of rose and onyx, flecks of pearl, lights of crimson and gold. We hated the smell of the building and occupied unique resting-places – wooden coffins that were stood against the rear end of the building. They were dry and fairly comfortable.

The next day we went on and halted at night by a field near the quarters occupied by the transport section. Tommy and I had our bed on a grassy bank near the road and I went over to the cobbled yard of the farmhouse where the transport men were staying. I had our water bottles and filled them at the pump there. When I had done so I strolled over to talk to a chap I knew who was smoking by a gate. Someone touched me on the arm and I swung around. It was light enough to see plainly as a harvest moon was overhead, and no one was there!

I left the man in the middle of my sentence, for I had become very sensitive to such touches. In a moment I was away from the yard and hurrying back to Tommy. Suddenly I heard a zoom-zoom-zoom above me –

Boche bombing planes – and before I had taken another stride a gash of scarlet flame spurted from the very gate at which I had been standing. More bombs crashed, and several were the kind the boys called the "spring" variety. They seemed to explode above the ground a few feet and spread death in a wide circle. Many horses were killed before the raid was over, thirty-six, a soldier said as we went forward to inquire. The man to whom I had been talking was horribly mangled. Two others had been killed and ten wounded.

We went to Parvillers. As we marched into the village and saw the square with its church still intact we thought that the war had become a grand picnic, but inside the hour our thoughts had changed. Salvos of shells came in among the buildings with diabolical accuracy. We ran for shelter, hurried around corners and headed for the old trenches of that area. We were to relieve a Borderer regiment but when we met their guides they seemed bewildered. They said the Hun was established in strength and that they had lost nearly three-quarters their strength in trying to drive him back. We grew impatient as the companies huddled about, too closely grouped, and nothing was done. Shells were coming very near. One dropped beside the officers as they conversed. Our colonel was talking to the colonel of the Borderers, and while he was not hurt the Borderer had his arm blown off and died before morning.

At length Williams and "Waterbottle" and I were called to the front and asked to find the way we should go. We managed to get the platoons into position shortly before daylight. We were in old grassed trenches, with concrete emplacements quite plentiful, and as we scanned the sector in the breaking light and saw wide tangles of rusting barbed wire in every direction, and dead Borderers strewn everywhere, we knew that we were to meet a grim proposition.

We slept a short while and then were roused. Williams and I were called again. He was to go to sixteen platoon and I to fifteen. Why we were to do so we could not find out, and the only satisfaction we got was that we would probably be needed before night. It was very hot, stifling hot in the old trench. The attack was not to take place until three, some said, but no one seemed to know definitely.

The platoon I was with filed slowly into an old trench that branched off the one we had first entered. There was a network of them everywhere, in all directions, and each platoon was to go a different route and try to meet as they got across the first area. We halted at a place where some of the dead Borderers were still lying, and waited there. There was not a breath of air. We sat, perspiring in the burning sun. It was still, uncannily still, except for the buzzing of flies about the corpses. They were turning black and there was a stench that made us want to get on with our work.

Then came word that there would not be any barrage. It seemed an odd thing to make a daylight attack without one but it was simply to be trench fighting, bombing and rushing. There would not be the usual deafening crescendo of drum fire to bewilder one, nor the whine and blast of five-nines to unsettle the nerves.

To my surprise I was told to remain in the rear of the platoon. Geordie was there, acting as company sergeant-major. We simply moved up the trench. Suddenly there came the clatter of machine gun fire. Rat-tat-tat-tat. It was everywhere. Bullets snapped and crackled over our heads and it seemed as if the guns were shooting from ahead, both sides, and the rear. We could not tell where the enemy was making his stand, or whether he was shooting at our lads or other platoons.

Suddenly, I saw a dead man lying in the trench. We walked past him. It was Haldane, the big MacLean Kiltie, a fine-built man, and he had been shot just below the heart as he rushed in as bayonet man. The bombers were going first, and the bayonet men followed up the throwing of grenades, while our Lewis gunners were ready for an opening. Again we passed a dead Canadian, and still no German was seen. Then I saw, in a long stretch, the captain, up with the leaders. He was with the platoon and had been in charge of the attack, so far ahead that we were sure he would be spotted and killed. We came to where a trench branched left. It was a high-banked affair and no one was in it. Where did it lead? Did it cross the trenches taken by the others? We went by it and came to a second turn, again to the left. A halt was made and word came that I was to take a man with me and go to explore the first trench for some distance, then send back a report.

As I hurried up the trench I saw that no one had been on it. The earth was not hardpacked and footprints showed. But I came to more turnings, three saps leading from the trench I followed, and I did not know which way to go first. I told the chap with me to go about fifty yards along the first sap, and then come back to me, while I watched the main trench. He had barely gone before I heard German voices almost beside me. I could not see a person but I sprang for cover. There was a V-shaped place that had evidently been an overland exit and I jumped into it and pulled a pin from a Mills bomb as I did so. The next instant three German officers appeared as if by magic. They came from the bowels of the earth, out of a dugout entrance I had not seen as it was almost obscured by overhanging weeds and grass. They were talking together, eagerly, excitedly, and never saw me as they started up the way I had been going. I released the lever, counted two, and tossed the bomb.

It exploded shoulder-high behind them, and they went down like jackstraws. I was ready with my rifle but there was no need. No others popped out of the dugout and the three in the trench lay still. I examined them. Two were dead, one with part of his head blown away, but the third man was still breathing. He was wounded about the neck and the spine so that he could not possibly live. I ran back to the sap where my helper had gone but he was not in sight. I went up the trench a distance to meet him, but did not see him, then came back and peered into the dugout. The wounded man had recovered consciousness and he looked at me and spoke in good English. "You are Canadians," he said.

I said "yes," curtly, and asked him how many more were in the dugout. He answered that there was not one, and that it was an underground place with a second opening. They had used it as a passage. He groaned then and twisted in agony. I stooped over him and took his Luger and also removed the weapons from the dead men. These I hid in the grass down the trench a distance and stuck a stick in the old parapet to mark the place.

My man did not return and I did not know what to do, so ran back and reported to the captain. He at once called for the "original" with whom I had gone on patrol, and told him to go with me and others up the trench I had been in, and to find a way to reach the other platoons on our left. The "others" were Peoples, Coleman, a Lewis gunner and his crew of three. When we got back to where the German officers lay I told the "original" how I had thrown the bomb, but he made no response. The wounded man looked up at me and asked me for a drink. I had no water left, none of us had, and the others did not want to wait. But the German had beckoned me to bend down and listen.

"In the dugout," he said, weakly, "there is a spring of water that is very good. Go down the steps and turn to your left about sixteen paces. You will find it."

He gasped the words out painfully and I told the men what he said. Coleman warned me that it was likely a trap. The "original" said nothing. He pushed on up the trench and the others followed slowly. I got a bomb ready and went through the hanging weeds and down the dugout stairs. I had no light, no candles, no matches, but I wanted to give that German a drink; I felt that killing from behind as I had done was a ghastly thing no matter what the rules of war.

I found the steps as he had said, turned left and went sixteen paces, put down my hand and touched cold water. I had often seen seepage in dugouts, but it was the only time I found a spring in an underground passage. I filled my water bottle and hurried up, and gave the German a drink. He had brown hair and brown eyes. One of the gunners and I bandaged him as best we could, but hurriedly, then moved him to a shady corner at the sap end. But it was fearfully warm; the sun blistered one. My head ached with the heat, and our steel helmets burned our necks if they touched the skin. Even our rifles were hot. And all about the area machine guns were crackling and bullets whining. There was a great deal of old wire strewn along the trench banks and there were continual ricochets from it.

We followed the party down the trench. It was a narrow cutting, and too straight to be rushed. But we did not meet any Germans and finally reached a very deep and wide trench that crossed our way and made a sharp "T." There we halted and the "original" seemed more nervous than the others. He asked Peeples and I to go to the left along the trench and explore for one hundred yards or so. He and the rest would cover our rear.

We went slowly. The trench sides were three feet higher than my head, and weeds and thistles and poppies grew on the banks. We could see webs of black, long-barbed wire beyond them. The trench floor was slimed in places and the wooden posts at corners were covered with moldy fringes. As we passed a third traverse I heard the sound of German voices and cautioned Peeples to keep ready while I climbed the trench side to see where the enemy was hiding. I had found a queer periscope resting on the firestep. Its frame was like ribs of an umbrella and it held an unusually large glass. I put it up and had just spotted a few pot helmets a considerable distance away when I heard an exclamation beside me. I turned and witnessed a tableau that is stored in my memory. Peeples was six feet three inches tall, and he had not shaved for several days. He held his bayonet ready and his kilt was high hitched above his great, bony knees. In his hand, pressed against the rifle barrel, was a Mills bomb. The German facing him was a young, white-faced fellow. He had stopped as if paralyzed, open-mouthed, cringing, and he was not armed.

Crack! Peeples, after sixty long seconds of gazing, pulled the trigger. He declared that he had not meant to, but his finger simply tightened. The muzzle was not six feet from the Hun and pointed at his stomach, and the poor chap groaned frightfully as he collapsed. I never heard a worse sound. The unexpected report and the groan startled Peeples so that he jumped about, losing the bomb, and ran headlong down the trench. I fell from my perch on the trench side, dived at the bomb – but the pin had not been pulled. No other Germans were in sight but I could now hear them jabbering just around the corner so I got the grenade ready and made a lovely throw into their bay. Then I hustled after Peeples.

He was telling the "original" all about it when I got to the trench corner, and was so excited that he hardly knew what he was saying. It was his first battle and his first kill. The "original" now suggested that Coleman and I go to the right and find where the Germans were. We went about one hundred yards and stopped at a traverse as we heard voices, then advanced very slowly. Perspiration was running down our faces. We had our tunics opened and our shirts rolled back. The "seam squirrels" were very busy and Coleman caught a very fine specimen and held him up to admire, saying that I could not match him. He was a very cool lad. There we were, away from the others, with the firing and sniping all around us, and voices ahead – and matching lice as if out at billets. I searched for one and secured a champion and was just holding him up when a party of Huns appeared about twenty yards away, coming around a traverse. I always had my rifle in position and it saved us. The Huns had their rifles up and the leader, a big man was taking aim as I simply slashed the trigger. The bullet caught his coal bucket helmet and struck the earth bank behind him in such a way as to scatter dust all over him and into the eyes of his mates. The German shot but his bullet struck the trench wall ahead of us, and as Coleman fired in turn he brought the big man down. I shot a second time, an easy kill, bringing down a short, fat goose-stepper. Then my rifle jammed. Coleman shot at a third German as he was running back and winged him in the arm. The man dropped his rifle and clutched the wound with his other hand and yelled wildly.

We hurried back to our post and told the "original" what had happened. He decided that we had better go back up the trench a distance so the Huns could not come at us from both sides. It was a wise move. We had not got back fifty yards up the narrow trench before Peeples, using his height, saw pot helmets bobbing along the trench toward where we had been. At the same time he saw five Germans get up on the bank and start overland, so as to cut off the corner and rush us where we were. He was so excited that he climbed out of our trench to meet them and we, not knowing what was happening, followed him. The Lewis men jumped back in the trench as soon as they saw the five gray men, but Coleman and I stayed a moment with Peeples. We fired at the Germans and they shot at us. The range was not over seventy-five yards and yet the first exchange had no results. We tried a second time, just as the "original," who had not left the trench, yelled for us to return, and both sides scored. Three of the Heinies "bit the dust," and both Peeples and Coleman were hit. We jumped down and found that Coleman had a bullet through the arm and that Peeples had one eye shot out, a horrible wound. We tied him up and Coleman led him down the trench, as he had lost sight of his other eye. I had heard a queer snapping noise but did not notice anything until one of the gunners pointed at my steel hat. Its rim was punctured on both sides.

The Germans pressed us. They stayed in the big, deep trench but they hurled potato masher bombs without stint, a regular barrage of them, while they sniped at us from all sides. We retreated until we had a good place to build a block and there put the gun in position. Then the "original" sent a man back to report to the captain and to ask for help. The captain himself returned with a small party, then sent a runner, my old friend, "Doggy," and I, to look up three saps and locate the man who had first come with me, and to find where the saps ended. We went up the first sap and found it ended at, and butted, a road. The man we were looking for was lying there, dead, his badges gone, his pockets ransacked. He had been shot by some sniper lying in wait as he looked over the road.

We went back and up the second sap and found a dugout entrance. Doggy had his pocket filled with bombs and he had a flashlight, so we went down to explore. There were several benches about the place, and an atmosphere that spoke of very recent occupation. It was a chamber of concrete walls and ceiling and very strongly built. In the centre was a table and on it were a big map and telephone, one of those funny, European "paper weight" kind. "Doggy" picked up the ear-piece and then grinned at me. German voices, harsh and heated, were clashing so that the wire almost curled. At the first lull Doggy put his mouth close to the speaking-tube and said slowly, "Get off the wire, you blasted squareheads. You've got the wrong number!"

The silence that followed was more eloquent than any reply could have been. We rushed back up the stairs and ran along looking for another dugout, but found none and reached the same road that headed the other sap. Doggy jumped up on it and ran up it a distance. I shouted to him to keep low but he waved to me to come and pointed out the end of the third sap. We jumped down into it to search for more underground places – and bumped headlong into three Germans. They had telephones and equipment and were without rifles, though each man had stick bombs and the leader had a Luger. He shot at Doggy from about a ten-foot range and missed him. Then that shaggy-headed, big-footed tumbler coolly reached back and seized my rifle. I had sense enough to let him have it and we made an exchange with a speed long practice could not have exceeded, I getting his revolver. Doggy hated pistols worse than poison, could not shoot straight with them, he had seen another runner get a wrist shattered through accidentally slipping the safety release off a Colt. From the time the Hun shot first until Doggy lunged at him would not be three counted seconds and his bayonet point spoiled the German's second try. Then Doggy was in on him, in an awkward but effectual fashion. He did not thrust in the orthodox manner but made a queer, overhead drive and the steel struck the Hun in the cheek, tearing flesh to the bone and ripping one nostril open. The German staggered back and dropped his pistol, trying to surrender but pawing at the air in a mad way. Blood gushed over his face and he breathed with a hard snuffle.

Doggy did not drive at him but found the trigger and shot the man. "You tried to plug me," he yelled, "there's yours."

While this was happening I had been shooting. I aimed at the second Hun who had dropped his load at his feet and snatched at the stick bombs hanging to his belt. He had one unhooked as the wounded man stumbled back against the trench side and he threw it high in order to avoid him. It exploded on the bank beside us, showering us with dust and chalky bits. I fired again as he threw a second, and the other German started to run.

Once more the potato masher burst on the bank. I shot a third time and the man went down just as Doggy dropped his adversary.

Wham! The trench was going around in circles and there was a tremendous roaring in my ears. That third Hun had hurled a stick bomb from his vantage point beyond and it had exploded between Doggy and I. Though I was the nearest to it I recovered the quickest. Doggy was slumped as if wounded and luckily for us the German tried to get away, dropping two more bombs in the trench as he ran. I recovered sufficiently to send a shot after him and by good luck drilled him fairly. He went down like a baseball player sliding to home plate.

Doggy was not hurt, only stunned. He shook himself and presently the ringing in our ears stopped. We looked at the second German and found that I had hit him every time. He had three bullets through him and all near the heart, yet had thrown three bombs after being hit the first time. We pushed the paraphernalia they had been carrying to one side and went into the dugout they had left. The entrance was not twenty feet from where we met them and we were sure that we had heard one of them speaking in the place on the next sap. There was nothing in the dugout except rations on the table and a few bottles of soda water. We opened two of them at once and Doggy tried to eat some black bread, but failed. We sat there on a bench and listened to the staccato shooting all around us. My hands were trembling a little and my clothes stuck to me. We were grimy with the dust that had plastered us from the bomb bursts and a small gravel stone had cut Doggy's cheek enough to make it bleed. It was cool down there and we sat long enough to empty a second bottle of the stuff. It helped our thirst but seemed to bloat one.

When we went up to the trench again Doggy ran back to the road at the end and stepped up on it in order to look around. He ducked down in a moment and beckoned to me. I got up beside him and saw about a dozen Germans filing hastily overland away ahead on one flank. They seemed to be in a maze of wire so that we knew they were near the trenches. As we looked a Lewis gun rattled from some point and two of the Huns pitched down at the first burst. The others promptly took cover, and then we saw a man rise up near where we had left the "original" and captain. He had an enormous rifle, and a second man scrambled out of a trench and helped him carry it. It was an "anti-tank" gun, the first I had seen, and I fired at the carriers until they dropped it and ran. Doggy declared I hit one man but I was not sure. As I watched to see them re-appear I felt a light tap on the shoulder. I wheeled instantly. No one was there! "Come," I shouted, and jumped into the trench.

Doggy thought I had seen something and dived after me. As he did a Maxim opened fire from somewhere ahead and clipped weeds like a scythe in the very place where we had been crouched. We had been seen and would have been filled with bullets had I not had that touch in time.

When we reported there was not much shooting. It was nearly dusk and the firing had stopped, making the sector a weird place. Everyone was watching in all directions as we did not know where we were, where the other platoons were, or where the Germans might pop into view from some underground place. Two more dugouts had been found on the trench where I had killed the officers and they were connected by a passage.

Doggy and I were to go with the sergeant-major and captain and find how the rest of the company was established for the night. I saw a thirteen platoon man, big Dave, an ex-member of the Edinburgh police force, escorting nine Germans down a trench we reached on the left, and at once went up the way he had come. We found 42nd men in three different directions and all seemed well. There did not seem anything for me to do as Doggy was sent with a message and so I wandered up one trench until I met Tommy. He was seated on planks at a bashed-in dugout entrance binding up the hurts of a man from one of the other companies. Beside him were dried pools of blood and stained cotton wads and when I looked around the bay I saw a dead Hun lying there, a chap with both arms bandaged.

Tommy was excited. We were glad to see each other and after comparing notes I was sure that he had had the more hectic afternoon. He said that "Waterbottle" and Earle and Lockerbie and Barron had made the greatest team he had seen in action. They had got far in advance as they cleared the trenches and an officer of the 44th Battalion had followed along, cheering them, advising them.

"Old Waterbottle was worth four ordinary men," said Tommy. "Him and Lockerbie rushed old Heinie so fast he couldn't get set anywhere. They kept right on his heels and Earle and Barron were there to take their turn. Waterbottle twice caught stick bombs, snatched them as they came at him, and threw them back. He hit a Heinie with a Mills bomb and knocked him down. Potato mashers went off all around them. He and Lockerbie ran right at about half a dozen Germans who were slinging bombs as fast as they could pull the strings and neither man was hit. Once I saw a potato masher burst beside Waterbottle and he only jumped and yelled. He and Lockerbie were terrors with the bayonet and that's how Lockerbie got killed."

"Killed?" I said.

"Yes," said Tommy. "He tried to get in on four Heinies who were waiting around the bay, rushed them with the steel and they shot him full of holes. Then a big Hun ran along the bank of the trench and threw an egg bomb at Barron so hard that it broke his shoulder bone – and yet the bomb never exploded. Earle and Waterbottle went on. Thornton got his, up on a firing step trying to fight two Heinie guns at once. He put one chap out of business, we found him afterwards, and then he got a dozen bullets in the head."

I went up the trench with Tommy. Dead Germans were around every traverse, some killed by bombs, some by bayonets, some by bullets. "Old Bill" and Hayward had been stationed to watch at a branching sap and a trio of Huns had appeared with an antitank gun. The Germans had expected the tanks in our attack. We found three of those "elephant guns" in and near the trenches, and there were many more seen. When the three faced "Old Bill" he let out a yell and charged them and he and Hayward shot one fellow. The rest beat it.

Then there had been a block to be rushed and in the excitement Morris, the new man, got ahead and into the Huns. He was terribly wounded before the rest of the boys got to him but the Germans were routed. They fixed him up as best they could, bandaging his wounds, and went on up the trench. A second block faced them but before they could attack it a party of Huns came overland and attacked from the rear. They rushed back by Morris and managed to escape the sandwich, then scattered the flanking party, killing most of them. It was an hour, however, before they fought through and cleared the trench where Morris had lain. He was not there but they found him further up the trench. He was lying on a length of bath mat, and his badges, even his tunic buttons were gone. The Germans had tried to carry him away with them, but our boys had pressed them too closely. He told the fellows that the Heinies had had six men killed there at the block and had carried them all back before they retired, and that they had threatened him, Morris, with their bayonets as they left him. But an officer had saved him, driving his men away. He was very white then and had asked Tommy when they could take him to an ambulance. Tommy had made him some promise and gotten away. He knew that Morris would never leave the trench alive. He died at dusk.

Beyond a low road the clearing party had sighted the same wide, deep trench that we had found up our way. But a machine gun had been placed on the bank of the deep trench, facing the long part of the "T" and they knew it would be suicide to try to rush the place. Fourteen platoon, however, had another new officer. Since McIntyre had been killed at Passchendale new officers had been the platoon's epidemic. This particular one had had no experience in France but a great deal of tactical work on parade grounds and in lecture halls. He promptly ordered the men forward. One quick rush would cow the Huns. The party hung back, staring at him, and pointing out the position of the gun. "Pooh!" he snorted. "I'm ordering you to rush it."

Earle and Waterbottle had been fighting continually for five hours and were in no mood for such an order. The officer had not been near them at all the critical points, only the 44th major keeping the work organized, and Earle faced around and very plainly told the man that he was a fool and that they *were not* going up the trench-unless he chose to lead them. The officer grasped his revolver. "Go," he shouted, "or I'll ..."

He got no further, as he was looking into the small dark barrel of a Lee-Enfield, and was hearing several very cool voices telling him that just one more little move would be the last he would make on this earth. He choked, sputtered, went white, but put back his revolver. His mouth opened and shut but no words came. The men ignored him and began to plan as to how to take the machine gun post. In his excitement the officer stepped too far ahead of where they were standing. He was barely in view at the end of a sixty-yard stretch, yet the Maxim sent a blast of bullets and one pierced his neck. He bled like a stuck pig, yet after he was bandaged and helped away down the trench was so enraged that he sought out the captain and reported Earle and his band of brigands. His effort was entirely wasted; the captain knew his men.

As soon as the officer was out of the way Earle and Waterbottle planned to rush the Hun from overland by two parties. Earle got out on the left and sent over a rifle grenade and then began sniping from a shell hole. The

Huns at once gave him all their attention. They simply cut the earth to powder with machine gun bullets and hurled stick bombs in showers. All the while big Waterbottle was creeping through foot-high thistles on the right. When within a few yards of the cross trench, he rose up, rushed like a great moose, leaping the trench, and was in on the terrified Huns yelling like a berserk killer. He speared the man at the gun before he could swing the weapon and all the crew and bomb throwers surrendered.

They had gone on then until they reached a second road where they had established for the night. Tommy said that he believed Waterbottle and his three with him had accounted for over fifty Germans, killed and captured. There were all kinds of rumours as I made my way around the maze of trenches. It seemed that in spite of the fact that over four miles of the network had been captured we had not cleared the Hun from the sector, and there was to be more work in the morning. Meanwhile we were to get ready to repulse night attacks. I heard that Boland had been killed, fighting his Lewis gun to the last, and that there were several boys wounded. As I went back to get around to my "original's" post someone called to me faintly. A wounded man was lying on the trench floor. It was Siddall, with whom I had chummed at Ferfay.

He was badly wounded, too hurt to live, and I saw it as I knelt beside him. He looked at me a moment before he spoke and then he whispered. "Tell me straight – have I got mine?"

It was a hard question, but I answered him as I would have wanted anyone to answer me in a like position. "Yes, I think you have," I said. "Is there anything I can do?"

He smiled. "Just a drink of water, that's all," he said. "I'm glad you told me. I can get myself ready now."

I hadn't a drop left in my bottle and so I went back to the place where the three officers lay and into the dugout where the cold water was to be found. I filled two bottles there, his and mine, and brought them back to where he lay. It was all the pay I wished to hear him murmur his thanks and then he begged that I sit beside him for a while until he went "to sleep." It was strange to sit there in the dusk, sit without speaking, and wait till he quieted. I gave him water several times and then after a long silence – even the distant guns seemed stilled – I looked at him and he was rigid.

As I got up I remembered the Lugers I had taken and hidden in the morning and I made my way around to the trench and found them. A voice startled me. The German I had bandaged had not died. He was still conscious though he had lain there all those hours in the hot sun, and he wanted a drink. I gave it to him, and after he thanked me he said that he did not hold any grudge against anyone; that we were all fighting for our different flags, and might the best side win. At the foot of our trench I found several men of the different platoons. Some of them had acted as stretcher bearers and some had escorted prisoners to the rear. A wounded German lay in the next bay. He was to be carried back as soon as a stretcher came, and he was moaning softly. Batten was with the men and I talked with him a time and then we lay back in the trench in a reclining position and slept. At least we tried to, but I could not stop seeing all that happened that day passing in kaleidoscopical procession. When I did doze Batten roused me. "Just listen to that noise, will you," he muttered. "I can't sleep on account of him. What'll I do?"

I had not noticed the sound, but the German seemed delirious and was calling continually some word that sounded like "water – water."

"Go around and put him to sleep," I said, jokingly, and dozed again.

A rough foot wakened me. "Who stuck that Heinie?" demanded Sykes.

I got up in amazement and followed him. A bayonet was driven into the German to the hilt, the rifle leaned over to one side resting against the trench wall. It was a sickening thing. "I can't tell you," I said. "I never saw anyone go near him."

Sykes made a fuss. He hated such work, and I went back to my place. Batten had his boyish face upturned and was sleeping like a child.

CHAPTER IX

Jigsaw Wood

Before dawn we were astir. Most of us had only slept an hour or two and were feeling draggy, but there was work to be done. There were two posts on the road to be cleared and I was called to the trench block the "original" had established. An officer from another company was there and he was going to lead an attack up the trench. It was the same narrow, straight way we had retreated from the previous afternoon and I knew it would be sheer suicide to venture up it. I went to the sergeant-major and told him so, but he said I might be mistaken. The face of the officer was enough for me. I saw him shake hands with the captain and lead by the block. The "original" fell in behind him. I was third, a new man fourth, and then there was a gap before the rest of the party followed. It was well that gap existed. As soon as the officer stepped around the bend the machine gun fired, so suddenly, that we all went down as by a blast. The lieutenant took most of the bullets, was instantly killed. The "original" was shot through the neck. I flopped backward and bowled the new man off his feet as bullets whistled over us. The rest had not come close and none were hit. I had turned as I fell and the whole bottom part of my mess-tin, which was strapped to my haversack at the back, was shot away.

We went back and it was decided that there were better ways to manage Heinie. A flanking party caught him by surprise and he was soon put out of action. Shortly afterward we were in possession of all that ground. Another officer had been wished on us, one from the other platoons. He had been to France before and was supposed to be a dare-devil. Murray had chased a Heinie who was carrying a small machine gun, a queer weapon almost as light as a rifle. The fellow ducked into a sap leading to a latrine and was shot as he tried to scramble overland. He and the gun both fell back into the latrine pit.

The officer arrived and wanted to examine the gun. At the same time Tommy and I were sent out across the road at the head of the trenches to a forward post where we could watch and listen. It was about twenty yards in front of the trench and after having a drink of tea we were sent out again and told to keep moving on a half circle. The posts were so spread that every man was needed. Shells came over, gas shells, and Sykes and some others who were eating in a concrete underground became sick and had to get into the open.

Just before midnight we heard a German patrol quite near and shot at them. They shot back at us and then crawled to hiding. We did not know where they had gone and as we tried to locate them by listening our officer came up the trench with the gun he had resurrected. It stank dreadfully, but he had been having several issues of rum – possibly intended for the troops – and did not mind. Not satisfied with tinkering with the thing he came to our part of the front and began hammering at it in an effort to fire it. Tommy was so enraged that he took a German egg bomb from his pocket and threw it at him. The bomb exploded just a few feet from the officer and sent him scuttling down the trench, and Tommy said he wished it had gone nearer.

All the rest of that night the Germans prowled about. A party of them came down a sap towards the post Earle was on and called out in English, "Are you the Pats?"

One of the new men shouted back "no we're the 'forty-twas'," before Earle could stop him.

There was silence for a moment and then two stick bombs came sailing towards them. Earle and another jumped over the trench bank and ran nearer with Mills bombs which they threw. Next morning a dead Heinie was lying in the sap. The moon was very bright and bombing planes were over. We could hear the crashes of their "eggs" back in the village and even in the support trenches. We held the safest position. All the next morning we waited for a relief and about four o'clock in the afternoon we began to be withdrawn. I had had nothing to eat since morning and sat on a firestep boiling a mess-tin of tea. In order to keep awake I cleaned my rifle. I oiled the parts and had the magazine lying on the bank beside me. As I extinguished the tommy cooker I heard sudden guttural voices. The next

instant a German stepped around the bay and confronted me. I had a
stomach-sinking tension of nerves, but acted as if on wires. One swift
motion threw the rifle up and I released the safety and pulled the trigger
before my arms had straightened. There was only a dull click. The magazine and its contents were lying on the firestep. My knees weakened. I
never was more frightened, but the face of the Hun was that of a man
under torture. He had no means of knowing that the rifle was not loaded
and I had acted so quickly that he could not dodge. We stood a few heart
beats, staring at each other, then I noticed that he was unarmed. Instantly
I swung the rifle club-fashion and would have used it had not a rough
voice inquired "What the — is wrong here?"

I looked beyond my chap and saw other Germans huddled against the
trench wall, peering at me. Pushing by them was their escort, a husky
"forty-niner," and he grinned from ear to ear as he looked at the German
and my ready rifle. I told him what had happened. When he had gone I
went to company headquarters on an errand and was sent from there as a
guide for a platoon of the 13th Battalion which was relieving us. When I
got them in place I again reported to the headquarters post. They were at
the entrance to one of the concrete shelters, the cooks and signallers and
runners and batmen, all seated around with their loads ready. The trench
was very deep and wide and the banks were like small cliffs above us. As
we waited for the captain I once more heard the German language and
again had a touch of heart failure. The Huns were not in the trench but
were approaching overland and it seemed impossible that any up there
should be prisoners. In an instant we were all ready for action but once
more it was a false alarm. A "forty-niner" had merely lost his way and was
wandering around with four Germans in tow.

When we went back to the village a body was lying out near the end of
the trenches. I raised the ground sheet that covered the face. It was Doggy
– good old, big-footed Doggy – all through with fighting.

We billeted in rough quarters, some ruined buildings, but could have
slept on spikes. An hour after we were laid down and enjoying slumber
that even a bombing plane did not disturb, a new man, up with a new officer as batman, came plunging in where Tommy and I lay, shouting, "Germans – on the road!"

I woke, but not enough to realize what he was saying. In some vague
way I knew I should move, but seemed incapable of action. Tommy was

the only hero. He had been sleeping soundly but he sprang up and seized his rifle and rushed out ready to do or die. He saw the Germans – a file of prisoners marching along in the moonlight. Wham! It was a cruel blow, and the batman went down heavily, but Tommy was highly-strung, had been wakened out of a sleep that was sorely needed. He settled down again, but the rest of the night was filled with sudden wakenings. We would start up, bathed in perspiration despite the slight chill of the air, again facing the Huns, again watching a potato masher come sailing for us. Each hour some man cried out and ground his teeth and muttered curses.

We moved next day to Hamon Wood. It was a glorious spot. Tommy and I had a bivvy on a slope that was shadowed by great trees. Sambro came back to the battalion and was beside us. We went to the River Luce and washed away all the sweat and grime of our fighting and marching and then lay around in the cool green wood, resting and sleeping. The new officer called me to his place and lectured me because I did not have a kilt. I wore shorts, my old trues cut off above the knees, my battered steel hat, a very ragged shirt and was brown as a berry. "You," he said, "are a very poor specimen of a soldier."

After I escaped him I saw him in conversation with the company quarter-master but no new kilt reached me. I heard that the 85th Battalion was over near Caix Wood and when the brigade signaller came and visited me that evening I asked him to go with me to see them. We walked nine kilometers to find them. My brother was there, in good spirits, had come through the fighting without a scratch. Stanley was there also, had got his wish – his passage back to France – and he was looking forward to another big scrap in which he might take part. We sat around and talked with the boys until ten o'clock then started on our way back. Half-way home we became very hungry. It had been a long hike and we had not had a hearty supper. A Y.M.C.A. tent loomed through the night, but evidently it had been closed for some time. We saw a lone soldier near and he told us that the "Y" had just moved there that day and had not been set up. As he left us we made the discovery that neither of us had any money.

We looked around, at the stars overhead. It was a long way back to camp, and if we only had some chocolate, a box of biscuit. "Are you game?" I asked, and he nodded. In a moment we had unfastened the tent flaps and were crawling inside.

I went to the left, feeling my way for the place was pocket-black. He went to the right. A moment we crawled, then there was a startled exclamation, a gasp, a struggle. It became furious, feet threshing the earth, striking boxes. I found a match and lighted it. The signaller and a "Y" man were entangled in deadly grips and rolling on the grassy floor. The "Y" man had been sleeping there just inside the tent, without covering, and had been awakened by the palm of a hand planted firmly in his face as the signals man crept forward. Instantly the sleeper had thrown up his arms and grappled with the intruder. Wakened out of a sound sleep, in a country where all had become change and route, he did not know who might be invading his tent.

When I could stop laughing long enough to light a candle and get them separated, the "Y" man took it all in good part. I told him frankly our intentions and he not only made us tea in his own private teapot but gave us a good feed and filled our pockets. He was a prince of a fellow and laughed heartily with us as we left, saying that he had had his biggest thrill since arriving in France.

The "big guns" came to see us but the inspections were easy. There was not much cry about polish and the speech that Clemenceau made was interesting. Generals were plentiful, Haig, Rawlinson and Lipsett, and we had a nice sing-song afterwards, there among the cool trees. The weather continued wonderful, sunshiny and clear, with bombing planes at night. None reached our bivouac and we marched away towards Arras.

We marched nearly all one night, as I had seen the battalion going up to Ypres, drifting along with only the shuffle of heavy boots, the creak of equipment, our steps echoing as we went through sleeping villages. The moon was full and everything bathed in white light. It was calm and cool and far better than the heat of the day, but the hours had their influence; we thought of the boys that were not with us, Christensen, and Eddie, and Lockerbie, Boland, Cockburn, Thornton and Doggy, big Haldane and strange, slow-speaking Morris. I thought of Siddal wanting me to sit beside him until he "went to sleep," of the touch I had had when sniping with Doggy. Sambro marched beside me and now and then asked questions about the boys. He was glad to be back and I was glad he had come.

We were in "Y" Camp at Duisans and there heard rumours of another great push. The Canadians were to attack Monchy and all that hilly, wooded country beyond. It was to be another big push, and there would be more missing faces. New men joined us, a rather poor lot, and we were not as friendly with them as we should have been. Then we went to Arras, that fine old city where all French history has its ghosts. It was there that Julius Caesar had his headquarters for a time, where at the time of the Revolution the guillotine in the square lopped heads like turnips are cut in the fields at autumn, a city with underground caverns that would hold divisions, with its Grande Place full of barbed wire and grass growing between the cobbles. We went through the streets at night and stopped at ruins on the outskirts, taking refuge in connected cellars as a rather severe strafing crossed our path. It was about three in the morning when we arrived there, and the rumours said we were to go into action at half past four. We sat there in the cellar, talking, eating, smoking. Hughes sat in front of me, Murray alongside me, Hayward next him. Across from us were Earle and Harvey and two new men. It was only a small place and "Old Bill" was near Earle. They had purchased some tinned salmon and as the old fellow was going into the scrap with us they were planning to keep together.

All at once I looked up and Steve was standing beside me. He did not say a word but looked around the cellar, then at me, and nodded toward the stairway. I placed my mess-tin on the stone where I was sitting and followed him across the steps.

"Don't go up," Hughes said. "There's a lot of stuff coming pretty close, and orders are to keep under cover."

"I'll just be a minute," I said, and never stopped. Steve was just ahead of me, as plain to my eyes as any of the others, and I was eager, keen. Would he speak to me?

As we stepped out of the entrance to the road a salvo of shells crashed into a field just in front and, like the smoke and mist that drifted away from them, Steve faded away from view. I stood peering, watching where I had seen him last and – crash! A terrific explosion in the cellar!

I plunged down. The place was pitch-dark. There were fumes of explosives, groans. I called out. No one answered. Then I struck a light, and stood, horrified.

The place was a shambles. Hughes was leaning against the wall where he sat, blood pouring from a great hole in his head. In the corner behind him Harvey was slumped, his head bowed low while another stream of blood poured from him. Two men lay on the floor. One had a gash on his forehead and was stunned. The other watched, moved, got up and bolted like a singed cat. I never saw him again – he had been shell-shocked before he saw a trench.

Hayward staggered towards me and said his back was on fire. I tore off his clothing and found that from his shoulders down was bathed in blood. He was pitted with shrapnel. An entrance had been cut through to the cellar of the next house. I had not noticed it before but now there were voices and scared faces looked through at us. A number of stretcher bearers, Imperial chaps, and ambulance men were there. I called to them to come and lend a hand but they were shivering with fright. The shelling overhead, and the cellar explosion, had frightened them badly. We swathed Hayward in bandages and helped him away, and then I saw that "Old Bill" was busy with Earle. Earle was hit in both thighs, in the body, in one arm, and another piece had entered above one eye and destroyed it. He was terribly wounded. Murray was beside him, his arms and wrists covered with blood. A new man had been loading his rifle and had discharged it in some manner, the bullet striking a bag of bombs in the middle of the cellar.

After we got the wounded bandaged we called to the Imperials to remove Earle. But they hung back. He was a big man and the cellar passage was narrow – and the shelling outside continued. "Old Bill" and Tommy and I seized our rifles and we prodded those lads to action in a manner they had not encountered before. Up we went to the roadway, a queer procession, and we saw to it that they carried him to an ambulance before they stopped. He was conscious twice on the way down to the Base, just long enough to hear a doctor say he could not possibly live, woke the third time in England, and finally recovered. But he never came to France again.

We left the cellars. My mess-tin had been crumpled out of shape by a bomb end, and I took one of the others left by the casualties and we divided their rations. We went up into trenches on the slope and made our way slowly. It was half past four in the afternoon, instead of morning, before the battalion got into action, and then our Company remained in the rear, in reserve. We could hear machine guns and bombs ahead, but moved rapidly to our objective and the only evidence of fighting we had was the dead Germans and 42nd men we passed.

Just before dark we were in a trench on an open slope. No officer had been near us and we were told to remain where we were for the night. One of the new men in the platoon behind us started to clean his rifle. It was discharged as he fumbled with it and the bullet shattered the leg of big Dave, the ex-policeman. He was carried away on a stretcher. The night was cool. About one in the morning I heard a low voice calling. "Otto – Otto."

It came from grass and weeds a distance in front of our trench. I roused Tommy and he and I went out. We found a wounded German, a blonde chap, badly hurt. He had been bandaged and left there. We carried him to the trench and were kind to him. At first he had been very frightened and had mumbled pitifully. When he saw that we wanted to help him he smiled. We got Sykes to attend to him and had him carried away to the rear.

Just before dawn I got up from the trench where I was lying and looked around. We had no one in charge of our section. Poor Hughes was gone, and Ab had been left at the transports – the "originals" were never taken in twice in succession in the big scraps – and Geordie was acting sergeant-major. Only Lofty remained and he was with another platoon for the moment, it having lost its sergeant. As I looked I saw heads appear above the thick grass. They came toward our trench, a long row of them, and then I saw bayonets. For the moment I was bewildered. How had the Hun got to the rear?

They came nearer, much nearer, and still I stood looking at them, unable to comprehend their movements or not knowing what to do. The men about me were still sleeping. "Who are you?" I called. I had suddenly seen that the helmets were "washbasins" and not "coal hods."

An officer in advance aimed a pistol at me. "Who are you?" he shot back.

"Forty-twas," I said. "Are you practicing some stunt?"

He almost wilted. Just behind him his men were all ready to throw bombs. They were of another brigade in our division and were to carry on the attack. Somehow orders were mixed and wrong directions given and had I not yelled when I did we would have been attacked. They had spotted me and thought that I was a Heinie sentry.

After they had passed on, walking upright and swearing among themselves, I roused Tommy and told him what had happened. It was well that the front ranks had passed on. The idea of being killed by his own kind as he rested did not appeal to him. That night we moved along to the ninth brigade area and after some waiting and uncertainty relieved the 58th Battalion. We were in trenches and there were rumours flying as thick as usual. It was said that the ninth brigade men had tried to take Jigsaw Wood and had been driven back after getting a foothold, and that we were to try to capture the place the next day. There is nothing worse than trying to oust a foe that has already repulsed an attack. They have the confidence while the attackers have not.

Towards morning Sparky came to me. His voice was unsteady. "Bill," he said. "I've heard you chaps talk about fellows knowing when they're going to get it. How – what gives them the idea?"

"I don't know, Sparky," I said. "I guess they fancy it themselves. I wouldn't put much stock in it."

I spoke much bolder than I thought, but it was of no use. "I never had a dream or saw or heard anything, and nothing's happened to make me think the way I do," he said. "But it's just slid into my mind that I'm going to be killed to-day."

"Nonsense," I said. "We might be relieved without leaving these trenches. You just push that stuff out of your mind and you'll be all right."

"Don't think I'm scared," he returned, as if I had not spoken. "That's the funny part. I've been scared bad most of the time, but now that I'm for it I don't mind near as much, and if I get a chance at all I'm going to do something worth while."

Word came that we were to attack, and without a barrage; the lines were too complicated to allow artillery support. Some of the boys looked shaky but the most of them were cool. Here and there I saw lips moving, and I believe that more mothers' prayers were remembered in those jumping-off trenches than anywhere else on earth. I was not the least bit nervous myself. It was not that I had courage, but the fact that I could go over with a curious inexplicable feeling that my body was functioning quite apart from me. I saw myself doing strange things and seemed powerless to prevent or assist that which happened.

We left the trench, simply getting out of it without hurry and extended in groups and hurried to where rifle pits had been dug on the hillside. A machine gun fired and there was considerable sniping but not nearly the reception we had expected. Down the slope in front of us we saw a roof slanting outward, that of a little shelter, and two Germans were just outside it. I rushed toward them and Tommy and Sparky followed. The Germans ducked from view, showed themselves on the other side, and then five of them appeared and two had rifles. They fired at us. Sparky was running like a racer. I saw his body leap in the air, hurl itself, and then he was on the sod and rolling over and over. There was a look of horror and surprise in his eyes. His hands were clenched and his body jerked oddly. I asked him if he were hurt. He did not reply but caught at his middle as if suffering from cramps. His arms and legs made a few queer, stiff motions – and he was dead.

I fired at the Germans and Tommy or I winged one. The others yelled "Kamerad" and waited till we got up to them. It was a signallers' shelter and they were all bright young fellows. They saw Sparky lying where he had huddled and I saw fear in their eyes as we approached, but we pointed back toward our trench and told them to hustle. They went in a hurry, gladly, but two of them looked behind every few steps. I went into the shelter and pocketed a map that was there as well as a photo that was stuck on the wall. It was a snapshot of the shelter and three of the men in the picture were among our prisoners.

We crossed the hollow at the foot of the slope and started up the opposite side. It was a much longer slope and grain was blowing and rustling in a soft wind. On the left we saw mounds that indicated a trench and then the Wood began. We were apparently to go up on the right of it. The sniping continued but there was very little machine gun fire. When we reached the next stop, a series of shell holes, Batten was next to us in place with McPhee and big Barney, the Lewis gunner. Suddenly, as we halted there, he looked up and said, "What does it feel like to be hit?"

"You'll know when you get one," said McPhee.

"But would I know if I were?" he insisted.

"Certainly you would," McPhee retorted.

"Well, I never felt anything hit me," he said, "but I can't feel from my waist down. I've lost the use of my legs and I'm queer all over."

We looked at him. He was sitting there, quite pale, and with questioning large in his eyes. Suddenly, without another word, he tipped forward, dead. A moment before he had been speaking in normal tones, asking questions. We pulled him over and found that a bullet had gone through his heart. He had died as he spoke the last time.

Sambro came over and joined me and we rushed up the hill to a small hole. Suddenly a few shells dropped about us, throwing earth sky high. There were only about a dozen of them and no one was hit. Over near the Wood we saw a runner go towards a dark entrance we knew to be a dugout. He stopped there in an instant, then ran over toward the trench. Presently an officer, one of the company commanders, walked that way with his batman. They went to the entrance and we counted eighteen Germans who came out of that dark hole with their hands above their heads.

The machine gun began barking again and we saw the platoon with the "wise guy" officer, he who had salvaged the latrine machine gun, at their head. He was leading his men toward a German trench at the beginning of the Wood. We saw several pot helmets appear and duck down again. Williams was over there, next the officer. A German captain stood up at the end of the trench and pointed his pistol at our officer and fired rapidly. Our man went down, wounded. Williams yelled and charged with his bayonet. The German fired at him three times, and sent a bullet into Williams' thigh, then put up his hands.

"You – squarehead," we heard Williams yell. "You needn't put them up now." He drove his bayonet into the captain with such force that both of them went into the trench among the Germans. But all the rest had surrendered. Hansen, one of our other Lewis gunners, had got to the edge of the Wood without being stopped, and he had a line on the trench, could have killed every man in it, so they did the "kamerad" act.

Fifteen platoon went into the Wood as soon as the prisoners were hustled away. A dozen of us kept well out and worked toward the field of grain. A Maxim opened fierce fire from in front, its bullets whistled through the wheat. Jones and Mills had joined Sambro and Sykes and we made a rush that carried us to the crest of the grain field. To go further meant to show ourselves. As we lay there we heard the platoon on our left fighting with bombs in the Wood. Then, all at once, came a perfect downpour of rain, a shower that soaked us as we lay. We did not mind it the least. It was cooling, refreshing. The rain stopped as suddenly as it began and we rushed a distance before flopping again. While upright, Jones had spotted the gunners, and he fired at them. The Germans fled, but we did not know it until they were almost gone from sight. We got up and followed them.

"Let's keep them going," yelled Tommy. He had come up from behind and joined us. Tulloch and Thompson followed him. We hurried on at a jog trot, then I saw a great spread of camouflage – and Germans!

Not one hundred yards from us was a pile of wickerwork cases. Beside them we made out a dark vent that was blocked by white faces. Germans!

All watching us. We were in an open field without a bit of cover. Was it a trap? "Come on," I yelled, and put my bayonet level in front of me and charged in a manner that would have tickled the "canaries" at the "Bull Rings."

We ran straight at the faces and as we neared them the Germans suddenly swarmed out of their underground place with their hands aloft. It was the emplacement of a big naval gun, a monster, with its pit the size of a house. All was concealed by a grass-carpet of camouflage spread across the cavity. A major headed the men and I ran at him and searched him. He eyed me sharply but made no move to protest as I took a beautiful gold watch and a pearl-handled Luger from his pockets. Then I plunged into the pit. Two machine guns were mounted by the entrance and if the crew had decided to fight they could easily have cut us down. Back of the big gun was a heap of hasty discards, Lugers, binoculars, those round cloth red-and-gray caps they wore, and a pile of newspapers. I had picked up a bomb bucket and I filled it with pistols and field glasses, then rushed up the entrance and told the boys that there were plenty of souvenirs about. They had searched all the prisoners and Tommy had found one chap wearing a revolver under his tunic. There were thirty-five in the crew and as I looked at them, one chap nodded to one side, indicating that he would like to see me there. I could not understand his signs but had my finger on my rifle trigger and let him come over to me. He at once began talking French so rapidly that I could not understand him at all, but some of the Germans did, and we had to shout at them and menace them in order to keep them back. I caught the word "spy" and at once hustled my lad back towards our second line who were coming towards us. I never saw the lad again or verified any of the rumours I heard but Tommy said that the man was a French spy who had been with the gun crew as a member and that he had maps of all that area concealed on him.

We rushed on again. Lofty caught up to us while we were handing over the prisoners to an escort. He saw my bag of souvenirs, and growled his displeasure, then asked me for the pistols I displayed. I told him that there were lots more souvenirs ahead and those who went first would get them, but he did not seem anxious to lead the way. It had been rumoured around the platoon that I had sold my lot I got at Parvillers for two hundred francs, and I had, to airmen who seemed so anxious to buy that I regretted I had not raised my price.

All at once the fighting in the Wood seemed to quieten and we hurried as fast as possible over the field back of the emplacement. We could just see, in the distance, that two lines of trenches crossed our way. Suddenly a machine gun fired at us. Two men, one a lance-corporal, from sixteen platoon, suddenly went down, shot through the legs. We did not stop but kept on, hoping to have the Huns surrender as the others had done. I looked around and saw most of those who had caught up with us slowing down. The sight of our easy capture had incited them to join us, but machine gun bullets made the proposition look different. A fat Lewis gunner went down, shot through the leg, and then a fourth man dropped, wounded the same way. We kept on. Not a man had been killed.

Sykes had got a revolver and had it in his hand. He was running alongside of me, and Jones and Mills were close behind us. Just back of them, in a straggling line, were Tulloch and Thompson and Sambro. As we neared the first trench the machine gun stopped shooting at us and we saw the gunners getting their weapon back to the second defenses. Away on the left another Maxim was shooting from a mound, a built-up emplacement, but the bullets did not come our way. An officer jumped up from the trench and shot at us with his pistol, emptied it and never touched us. We shot back at him as we ran, but apparently he was not hit and he ran toward the second trench. Just before he reached it Jones fired. He pitched headlong to earth and we supposed him dead.

We got into the trench, a long shallow affair with numerous low-roofed shelters. I dived into the one where the officer had been and found his kit, taking from it an Iron Cross and his "housewife," coloured thread and needles and folding scissors, as well as a dictionary of German and English. We moved along the trench to the left, Jones had taken the lead and was after the machine gunner who was still shooting at our lads near the Wood. Sykes and Tommy and I were looking in all the shelters for souvenirs. In every place there were packs and gas masks and greatcoats and blankets. Suddenly the Germans began sniping at us from the second trench, which was about one hundred yards away. We shot back at them but it got to be dangerous to show our heads. Jones worked over to the left and got in position to snipe at the gunners in their emplacement. One man left it and ran almost to the second trench before he fell. The other chap started out and ducked back again. The rest of the company were rushing in during the lull and Thompson was wounded as he looked over the trench bank. Hansen, the Lewis gunner, and Lofty came tumbling in. Meanwhile a few men were coming from the Wood and it was necessary to prevent the machine gun from getting into action. Jones rushed along the trench and although the snipers shot at him they missed him. We saw the gunner bolt and then Sykes and Mills and I hurried after Jones. We came to a covered-in part and both Mills and I went under it on our hands and knees. Sykes waited a moment, then leaped outside and ran around and jumped in the trench again on the far side of the covered part. I had just emerged there and he fell at my feet. I heard a queer, bubbling sound and dropped beside him. His jugular had been cut by a sniper's bullet. He was dead before Mills got through the tunnel.

With the machine gun out of action, men came with a rush. One big shelter in the centre of the trench was a sort of headquarters, and there Geordie and Flighty rested. Tulloch went into it with another man just as a barrage opened. The Hun strafed us with whizz bangs and there were many bursts very near the trench. We spread out as much as possible and Sambro and I occupied one bivvy. There came a cry for stretcher-bearers and word came that Lofty had been wounded badly in the stomach. Shortly after we saw his stretcher being pushed out at the back and then he was carried away. I could see that "Old Bill" was one of his carriers.

Wham! There came a very sharp explosion, very close. We saw smoke and dust in a cloud. The big shelter had been blown in, a shell exploding on its roof. We rushed to the wreckage and found one man dead; Tulloch with a leg shredded; Flighty wounded and Geordie with his third Blighty, a very painful wound. We got him on a stretcher and Sambro and I helped lift him out. Then came a call for me and I was ordered to take a man with me and go back to meet our relieving battalion and guide a company to our position.

Sambro offered to go with me, and as men were needed in the trench we helped carry Geordie as we went. A new man was teamed at one end with Sambro and I had a German prisoner as my partner. It was a long journey back over the field we had covered in the afternoon and had got dark. We reached the trench we had left in the morning and went through a part the R.C.R.'s had captured. There we stopped to rest and I saw several dead Canadians nearby. Something urged me to go over and look at them, and there lay old Peter, his rifle still gripped in his hands, his body smashed by shrapnel. Near him were two men I knew well from my home town.

We went on and Geordie suffered much pain. At length we reached battalion headquarters and there found a party of prisoners squatted about a dugout entrance. Tulloch arrived on a stretcher just as we left to meet our relieving company.

It was almost dawn by the time we had gone back once more over the same route and completed the relief. Again we walked down the slope and into the hollow where Batten lay in his crater. On again by old Peter, killed in fighting out in front, as he wished. Then we reached the big dugout again. Flighty was lying there on a stretcher and Geordie was still there. I went to see Tulloch – and he was dead! Sambro and I had given him a cigarette and talked with him as we had left on the way up, and he was talking about his "jake blighty." He didn't mind losing one leg, he said.

Morning came and we kept on down toward Arras. It seemed a long, long way and the men began falling out. Sambro sat down to rest but I kept on and on and at last staggered into the barracks we were to use, almost asleep on my feet. Ab was there to meet the stragglers and he grinned at me sheepishly. I had never been left out of any scrap but I knew I would hate to wait there and meet the survivors.

We slept all the rest of that day and all that night. Next morning I went out to the "Y" canteen and sold one pistol and a pair of field glasses, getting one hundred and fifty francs. I now felt rich and as the rations were poor and we had not had parcels for a time, resolved that I would get a good feed for all our crew. I fell in line in a queue and when I reached the counter asked for a dozen tins of cherries and the same of peaches. The clerk looked at me pityingly. "Don't you know," he said, "that you can only have one of anything."

"But why?" I asked. There seemed to be an endless supply on the shelves and in piled cases at the rear.

"Because we never know how much the officers will want," he said irritably.

I got "one of each" and went outside. Tommy was waiting for me and I told him my luck. He went wild, would have charged the counter. "Officers!" he raved. "The ratters feed on the best in the land, double what we get, and all prepared for them, and rum to go with it, and not doing one quarter the work we do. Bah – batmen to wait on them, keeping that many less to do the work in the trenches, meaning we've got to take that many more chances, do more hours on duty. And now we've got money we can't buy anything because the dears might want a little extra to entertain guests or French Janes. Officers only – I'll ..."

It was difficult to quiet him. Tommy was getting worn and tired. It seemed years since we had come to France and he had seen so many of our lads maimed and broken or left on the fields and in trenches. As I got him to go away without trying to do damage we saw a batman come from the rear of the building. He was carrying a case of tinned cherries. I knew him and at once stopped him and asked questions. He grinned at us and seemed glad to show just how clever he and his kind were. "Sure, I can get all I want," he said. "This lot's for a feed a bunch of us are having. We just get an order signed, tell our officer we need the stuff, then go and get it. We'll use half the lot ourselves."

I looked at the blank chits he carried, and when we went back we got paper and made up a few. Then we watched the canteen until the clerk was relieved by another and went to him with an order for a case of tinned fruit. We got it without a question being asked, and went again for biscuits and chocolate, even getting a box of Marguerite cigars, a kind that were "Old Bill's" favorites. Back at the barracks that night we had a glorious time, and then I was told to go and look at battalion orders. They stated that I had been made a lance-corporal. Davies had never asked me what I wished regarding the matter, had simply put the promotion through. Three times I had refused it, and I intended to do so again, but Tommy argued that if I did not take the "dog's leg" some of the new men might get it, and make things rotten for the few of the old gang that remained.

The bombing planes were busy and the Hun also shelled the city. We went to the station and looked about it. The next day we were moved just outside to a cemetery area. Sambro and I had a bed together in a grassy hollow, not bothering to dig in and make a shelter, and in the night several big shells fell very close to us. We did not leave our place, however, and in the morning saw several graves that had been torn wide, leaving shattered caskets and skeletons in the glare of the morning sun. Near us was a man with a long black beard and with some decoration on his black frock coat. He looked as if he had not been buried more than a week and was in a sitting-up position, thrown that way by a shell explosion.

Again we moved up front, a long hike, Sambro and Tommy and I together, chatting about those we had left behind; Tulloch with his blighty talk; Sykes with his books; poor Corporal Hughes, killed in a cellar accidentally, after all he had survived; and then were silent as we wondered who were the next to go, what we would face next time. War seemed a different thing now, no six days in and six days out of the trenches, no six-hour shifts on posts, but "over the top" work, charging Hun machine guns, killing around trench bays with bomb and bayonet, and we had got so accustomed to German prisoners and wounded that they no longer seemed something alien and apart. I had seen Sambro and a dark-haired Heinie sitting together on a trench bank, smoking, had seen Tommy give the last water in his bottle to a wounded man in gray. And I was conscious of a change in myself. I felt old, indescribably weary at times, dull, listless; indifferent to anything but thoughts of Steve.

Cave returned to the battalion. I seldom visited headquarters, but I knew he had been away a long time and now he wore a Sam Browne and was an officer. He greeted me as kindly as ever. I saw Naufts. Sedgewick was with him but he did not recognize me. Seeing him made me think of Jimmy and I looked him up. He was taciturn, gloomy, smoking by himself; did not care what the battalion did or where they went.

We went into the cellar of a Chateau and from there did several carrying parties. I was sent on patrols and worked along ground where the only line I was sure of was our own posts. There were no trenches fenced with wire to guide one, and sunken roads gave cover to both friend and foe. We were in good quarters and the building over us had not been damaged to any extent. Back a distance there was a pond and the wreckage of a German training school. Beyond it lay a one-street village, badly battered by shell fire. Tommy and I decided to visit it.

We made our way over in the mist of a showery morning and reached the place without difficulty. We had no blankets and had slept cold for a few nights, as it was September and a chill was in the air. The first few houses were so wrecked that there was nothing to get. The Huns had entered with axes and smashed every stick of furniture, even to the pictures on the walls, had driven their tools into the walls, crashed doors from hinges, broken all the windows. It was simply a scene of wanton, hellish destruction.

The priest's house was not so badly wrecked, and an inner chamber was almost intact. We stripped the bed of fine sheets and pillows and a beautiful eiderdown puff. I went into the cellar and found nothing, but as I turned to come up noticed a cupboard stood in one corner. It did not seem to belong to the cellar and we examined it thoroughly but it was empty. Then Tommy tugged it away from the wall to look behind – and there was a square opening in the masonry!

We lighted a candle and peered in. It was a small circular place, with shelves ringed around it, and on the shelves were hundreds of bottles. We took them to the light and discovered that they were the finest wines that France produced, and some of them were quite aged. We gathered a dozen of them into our sheets and stole from the place. Not half an hour later the Hun dropped shells all along the street we had travelled.

Back in the cellar we slept warmly and comfortable but our bottled treat was misused. Several of the boys got so jovial over the wine that we had to take the rest from them, and the sergeant-major was a perplexed man. He could not figure the source of supply.

CHAPTER X

The Student

The last night I was on patrol we had an exchange of shots with the Germans who were some distance from us in the dark. There was considerable shelling and gas was used, several of our men getting caught before they suspected it. Before morning we had fifteen cases lying around the building, being cared for by a medical officer.

When we moved back I was again used as a guide and we had to move sharply as the Hun dropped a few salvos near the chateau grounds. After a long, hard march we reached a huge cave near Vis en Artois and went down steps in the dark. Away down in the bowels of the earth we saw the big passages and chambers, seemingly endless. It was a damp and depressing place but we slept soundly. I was wakened by a runner and told that I was to go with a working party to *repair roads* – and go at once.

It was not seven o'clock in the morning and we had not reached the cave until just before midnight. A working party! I got up, and as I pulled on my boots was somewhat startled to see a place in the chalk where an explosive had been placed. It was not connected by wiring. The men were all grousing and swearing. There had been no hot tea for them and they were hungry. We saw engineers about, looking at the many places where explosives had been placed, and they told us that a lighting plant was in seemingly perfect order. One man had been on the point of starting it when it was discovered that a single revolution of the engine would detonate explosives that would wreck the cave. Besides that trap they found that one of the rail ropes down the stairway was connected with a mine that would blow up the passage. Had any man grasped the rope as we went down we would have been blown to atoms.

We got outside in the chilly air. No one was about and the cooks were not in sight. We were paraded by a very neat and trim officer, just over from Blighty, and marched away to a road near the village. There we found picks and shovels left by a party of engineers and were told to fill in holes and fix up the road. It was not in a bad condition, had not been wrecked and there was no traffic on it at all. To make matters worse, we saw a labour battalion encamped a short distance from us and as we went to work their reveille was blown. They tumbled out of their tents and went to their cook wagon where they were served a breakfast we had not known in a month, plenty of bacon, and porridge and big slices of bread with jam and cheese.

Tommy hurled his pick to the bank. "Arrest me or anything you like," he snorted. "There's a labour mob just turning out now, after quitting at five yesterday. We've marched half the night in a rain, are still wet and cold, have had no hot tea or breakfast-and look at them blighters. We're worse than dogs. Anybody in the army is used better than the men who do the fighting. I'll not do another stroke this morning."

I walked away and left him and at the end of the party found the officer industriously showing a man how to fill a six-inch hole. Then I looked over the bank and saw a "Y" marquee. I went back to Tommy and his crowd and told them to go and get some tea or cocoa and biscuits or anything they wished, and gave them a sheaf of francs. They went instantly. I walked back the other way and saw the officer hurry by in search of the missing ones. He had not spoken to me except to snap some order. I told the crowd he had made work where the rest had gone and they soon vanished. I looked around and saw the officer *running* in circles, and followed the men to the big tent.

It was well-stocked and soon we were seated around enjoying ourselves. We had a clear twenty minutes before the Sam Browne found us. He was raging and ordered us all outside "instantly." We wandered out and he led us back to the road. He was dancing and fuming. Over the way the labour battalion was enjoying its breakfast with a leisure we had seldom witnessed. "Corporal," he barked at me. "We'll get into serious trouble if we don't get on with this work."

"I think, sir," I returned, "that you're more likely to get into trouble if you try to do it."

The men had filed to their picks and shovels, but a filling of hot tea and biscuits and tinned fruit and sardines did not help them be lively. They were sleepy, too sleepy to move. One by one they sank on the grassy road bank and relaxed into slumber. The officer roused them, yelled at them, but more were sleeping than at work. He ran to me and ordered me to take their names. He was going to crime the entire party. Tommy was especially defiant and had told him to go "chase his tail."

I looked the officer in the eye and told him in very plain and straightforward language just what was what. "Somebody in charge has slipped a cog," I said. "These men should not be roused to-day except for meals like those labour men are getting, and they, not us, should be booted out here at seven to get to work. I'm with the men, whatever they do."

He gasped and reached for a note book. His fingers trembled. "You realize, of course," he sputtered, "that this means court martial."

"I don't care what it means," I snapped.

"Give me your name and number," he shouted.

Then he went to the cave, leaving us to straggle where we liked. We found good places in the driest spots, well away from the road where we had thrown down our tools, and there slept all the day until nearly dusk.

When I returned to the cave I was at once ordered to go to the captain. The officer was there and I heard horrible charges of disobedience, insulting an officer, neglect of duty, a dozen of them. When it was finished the captain allowed the others to go, then he talked kindly, explaining that he regretted the way the boys had been used, and asked that we overlook it and soldier as "D" company always did. There was not another mention of my crimes. The next day the new officer was transferred to another company.

Cherisy was near us and a splendid canteen was there. I heard the 85th were in the area and were patronizing it, and looked for my brother, intending to give him the pearl-handled Luger. I did not see him, but met men of his company who told me that Stanley had been killed in the fighting at Drury and that he was buried at Cherisy. I was stunned by such news. As I walked back to the cave I saw a German airman come darting from the clouds and open fire on one of our sausage balloons. It exploded in a great burst of fire and smoke that hid his plane, enveloped it, but he emerged apparently not damaged, and flew away. When I reached the place where the debris had fallen I saw men there who arranged the balloon as a trap. The men in the basket were dummies and special explosive had been used, but failed to hurt the Hun. Lieutenant Cave asked that I go with some men from the companies to practice shooting on a short range. I went and amused myself by doing some good work. He got very interested and talked in a kind manner, asking me how I had fared in the company. I did not tell him of any of my experiences.

A small crowd was at the entrance to our cavern when I reached it and they were carrying away someone on a stretcher. It was the body of the sour cook. He had been friendly with me during all the summer, but kept his usual manner toward the newcomers to the company. Very reserved, making no close friends, reading little, apparently brooding, a sullen person, I wondered what history lay behind his attitude. I felt certain that something in his life had made him bitter and wished that I had got to know him. He had been killed by the only shell that came near our quarters; even his death seemed an irony of fate.

We moved back to Dainville and I had opportunity to go to the trenches we had occupied on the sunken road and see the place where I had fallen on the wire and cut my eyelid. It was strange that I was not captured that night. One Hun post had been within thirty feet of where I tumbled, and must surely have been occupied. Tommy and I went out to Long Alley and saw where Waterbottle and his crew had killed the German sentries.

Rumours flew thick again. Another draft came and filled our ranks and I was made a corporal. We moved towards Cambrai and heard great stories of the Canal we were to cross. Tommy was not himself. There were days when he could not eat, and he was cynical and bitter in his conversation. Everyone, however, was more optimistic of the ending of the war. Surely we could keep the Hun on the retreat.

We marched part of one night and arrived at a place of old trenches. There were a few dugouts about and we explored two. The investigation induced a unanimous preference for the open. Dead Germans were in them. Eight bodies lay about the floor, all bandaged men who had died while waiting further attention. On one bunk, seated so that his back was against the wall, was an elderly fellow with a bushy beard, probably a flare man. Sims, a coarse fellow who had come with the last draft, but who had been in France before, leaned toward him and beckoned to a young lad also newly-joined. "Come here," he said. "This old chap isn't really dead. He's just making believe."

The lad looked uneasy and we could see that he was very nervous. "I'm going out of this place," he said.

"But look," said Sims. "Watch his face. Say, old man, if you're not dead, just open your eyes."

The German's eyes sagged open, staring!

There was a fearful scream. The watching youth plunged up the stairway, yelling, mouthing hysteria. They caught him outside and tried to soothe him, and could not, and in an hour he was away down the line, still gibbering. Sims had placed his hand in a friendly fashion on the dead man's shoulder and had slyly worked his finger into the bushy beard. He tugged it and the skin of the cheeks pulled down so as to reveal the eyes. It was a ghastly thing to do and we booted Sims up the steps and away from our company.

Tommy and I saw the ruins of a village nearby and went over to it to find a place to spend the day. We were to move again the next night and go into battle. One of the new men was wandering that way and we spoke to him. His rejoinder made me ask him to come with us. He had a quiet, easy voice that suggested culture and accomplishment. Tommy looked around quickly. "Who are you?" he asked, in his abrupt fashion.

"I'm the Student," came the answer. "I've got a name, Linder, but all the draft I came with called me 'the Student.'"

"Why?" blurted Tommy.

"I suppose it was partly because I've been to college and partly because I read when there is opportunity."

We reached the village and saw a flow of traffic that exuded portent of what the next few days would bring. There were columns of marching men, and lorries packed with soldiers; ammunition columns, side cars, and field batteries; field kitchens and more lorries, some loaded with plank and barbed wire. Two tractors ground past dragging big guns. Moonlight hovered over all, making dark alleys of narrow side streets and black voids of gutted doorways and windows. A shattered church was revealed in grim silhouette.

The first place we inspected was nauseating. There were smells that repelled us, the smell of broken, mouldy house plaster, of rotting wallpaper, of filth and debris a foot deep on the kitchen floor, and the reek of green slime in the cellar. Leaving it, we went on and found three ruins with blankets over the windows and the interiors fitted with bunks. Men were there, men from the line, dirty, unshaven, listless creatures who had just arrived from the trenches. There were odours again, the smell of mud and toil and unwashed weariness, the odour of the life they were living and the death that lurked about all wrecked places. Three men passed us without a glance, their faces set, white masks, in which only eyes moved; they had water bottles hung about them and were going in search of a pump or well before they slept.

Beyond the third ruin a stretcher leaned against the wall. The Student's flashlight revealed dark stains on its canvas, and then the beams flickered to a huddled figure on the ground. It was covered with a rubber sheet and a muddy steel helmet was on one corner to prevent the slight breeze from raising it. We could not find a place that was suitable and so went over in the field until we had found a soft hollow and there spread our bed and slept together.

It was noon when I awoke and the Student was sitting up beside me, smoking. He had fine, well-cut features, fair hair and eyes as soft as a girl's. Tommy was still sleeping and I could not help noticing how browned and hard and crease-lined his face had become; even in repose it seemed bitter, saddened. Beside him the Student looked as fresh and unsophisticated as a child just washed.

"Look," he said softly, and pointed.

I raised up. Just a few yards from us an old trench zigzagged its way across the chalky slope, probably the front line of the year before. The parapets were crumbling, the sandbags rotting so that they had burst in many places and oozed their contents. In front the black-rusted wire was half-hidden by tall weeds and thistles, and just where the Student pointed, in a hollow, shredded remains of a uniform clung to the barbs and held to view a grinning skull that seemed to mock us. "That," said the Student, "seems very fitting in this country."

"It is – now," I admitted, "but it should not be."

"No?" he answered, quizzically. "They pointed you out to me as a grizzled oldtimer. I expected to hear you discourse on the glory of fighting for King and Country."

"If you read you'll get that in the piffle of the war correspondents," I said. "They tell you how happy we are to die in battle, how hard it is to restrain us in the big attacks."

He smiled, and seemed more whimsical than before. "Don't you uphold the tartan and traditions of the famous Black Watch?" he mocked. "Doesn't the sound of the bagpipes set your blood on fire?"

"I like to hear them when we're coming back from the trenches," I said confidently. The Student could say things without hurting one's feelings or rousing his temper. "We think we can't drag one foot after another and then they come and after the first squeal we're stepping on air and swing into camp like new men."

"I know that," he said, and sobered.

"What I like best," I went on, "is the bugle blowing Last Post, or a trumpeter sounding an evening call. Something that is softening, restful."

The Student looked at me, then at Tommy. "Let's go for a walk," he said. "I've not met many I can talk with in the last few weeks."

"I haven't for months," I said. The fact had struck me. Not since the Professor had been with us, and Melville and little Mickey, had I talked and thought of things that did not belong to warfare and the trenches, and I told the Student so as we strolled in the sunlight. Up ahead the guns were clamouring with a new din and on the road many ambulances were coming and going.

I told him how inquisitive I had been when I arrived in France, yet bitter against the old men, and how our little band had talked long hours, of the 7th Battalion man I met in hospital, of Stewart, the stretcher bearer, in the moonlight by the old bridge; then I told myself as well as him that Passchendale had deadened all my senses, changed me, dulled me, that the long trip in the spring had maintained the stupor, a sort of unconscious acceptance of life as I met it. We talked about the men we had seen in the night, the battalion just out of the fighting, and I told him how lucky he had been to come to our "crowd," and to our company in particular, explaining that our officers were humane in their management and did not sap the stamina of the men with fool drilling and spit-and-polish spectacles for gilded staffs, and that our captain was better than ordinary.

As we talked I heard a sudden whining roar and threw myself into the old trench. He jumped down beside me in a flustered way. Whamm! A mighty explosion that seemed to rock the ground. Clods showered about us. A cloud of fine dust drifted by mingled with acrid fumes. Some men of the resting battalion had been near the place where the shell landed, lousing their shirts. We got up slowly and heard a quiet moan, almost without complaint of pain, but quavering with infinite weariness.

We reached the fellow as his mates knelt over him. He was a small man, almost puny, and still clung to the grimy garment he had been searching.

Blood welled from a great wound in his chest and it was useless to try to bind it. He was dead before they could bandage him.

The Student was very white. He did not speak until we were away from the spot and then he said tensely.

"Fancy it, that poor little lad going through hell up front and escaping it, then to be killed back here. Do you think that God ever intended such things as that?"

"That's too big a question for me," I said, "but one I'd like to have answered because it's been with me for a long time. I used to like a verse I remember, by Noyes:

In the light of the silent stars that shine on the struggling sea,
In the weary cry of the wind and the whisper of flower and tree,
Under the breath of laughter, deep in the tide of tears,
I hear the Loom of the Weaver that weaves the web of years.

"But I can't believe that man is not responsible for this, I don't mean the Kaiser and all that stuff, but Man, those who are the head of Empires and States. I don't think that God wanted it at all."

"Then why did you come to give a hand if you think it's all wrong?" he asked.

"That," I shot back, "is another question I can't answer."

Tommy had been wakened by the shell. He had gone to the well, easily seen in daylight, and got water enough for us all to have a good wash, but he was surly. "Have a look at the guys in the lines back of the village," he growled. "Transport chaps, fat, happy beggars who don't know what war is. Why couldn't that shell have gone in among them?"

We strolled over that way, after we had eaten, to appease him. A number of drivers were there, churning chains in sandbags to make them glitter. They were complacent fellows, chatting and smoking, contented looking, with comfortable waist lines.

"When this mess is over, if it ever is," Tommy went on, "those well-fed bucks will get all the glory. We'll be a bunch of cripples, mental, and physical, tucked away in some institution, remembered at Christmas or some such times. They'll be the heroes the kiddies will look up to, and they'll tell tall tales of what they did in the Great War, them and the brass hats."

The Student glanced at me. "Tommy," I said, "is bitter towards all who wear red tabs and ribbons."

"I am," he snapped. "I hate ducking into ditches to let some pot-bellied old mucker shoot by in a cushioned car, and I hate this blah-blah they shoot us before they think we'll be killed, brass hats telling us what a name *we've* made and how nobly *we'll* carry on, and then some silly ass waving his arm and shouting for three cheers for General Dugout or Awayback. What ... by the sweet breath of old Queen Anne – look over there."

We looked. It was a French home that had escaped damage with the exception of losing one corner of its roof, and was now an officers' mess. They were having lunch. A table was spread with a white cloth. On it were real dishes, a bowl of roses, tall bottles with expensive labels. The officers were in slacks, clean clothed and their batmen hovered about arranging seats for them.

It was too much for us to watch. We went out front and saw the men lined up for their meal. They carried dirty mess-tins and were issued with a ladle-full of greasy mulligan in the tin tops, and weak-looking tea. They sat around the ruins and ate wherever they could squat, without speaking, hurriedly, as if they hated the business. Some emptied part of their issue on the ground and scrubbed their mess-tins with bits of sandbags as they shambled off to where they slept.

"Is that fair?" grated Tommy. "There are the boys who've done the work, who've held the trenches, who've met old Heinie and beat him back. Those la-dee-das having servants hand them their wines were probably in the dugouts, and when they did a couple of hours up in the line they had so much rum that they had to have their batmen with them. Roses on the table! Man, dear man, I could ..." He almost sobbed, and I gripped his arm. "They'd hearten anyone more than barrels of rum," he choked.

I looked at the Student. "Tommy sounds bitter," I said, "but he doesn't mean it all. There are mighty good officers as well as men, and you can't blame them for having as good as they can get. Tommy's been out here a long time, and ..."

The Student nodded. "I understand," he said in his quiet way, and Tommy calmed at once.

We went on and looked around the ruins. It had once been a pretty village, with a little brook running through the back gardens, and with big, shady trees on the by-lanes. "I like France," said the Student, "at least the

France that Hugo has described, and I saw his places as we came up here, quaint villages with the lime-washed cottage walls shining through the trees, blue shutters to match the whiteness, and elms and hedges all around as background, with the church near the centre like a hen watching over her brood. We stopped off near one of those places and I walked over the fields. The sky was bluer than blue, and there were buttercups and red clover in bloom as if it were the first of summer. At the brook I found old stone steps, mossed over, and kiddies were there playing in a pool. I could have stayed there for years, and I'd like to come here after the war and look around," he said.

"I wouldn't," said Tommy. "There'll be too many white crosses."

We turned about at the end of the place and saw an old French couple pottering about a garden. They were living in a cellar and when the Student talked to them they told him proudly that they were in luck. Their piano had miraculously escaped destruction. We looked into the rooms above their cellar. Nearly all had been destroyed and part of the kitchen had been blown to powder, but in the inner room the furniture remained intact. Only the plaster had fallen from the walls. And in a corner was a piano.

It was covered by a sheet of mottled canvas, a strip of camouflage the man had salvaged. The Student pulled it aside and sat down on the bench as if he had, without effort, forgotten us. He began to play and Tommy and I found seats. In one surging, sweeping wave I was carried back – back – away from all that surrounded us, away from war and blood and guns and killing, drifting peacefully and without exertion over vast depths and spaces, moving gently, softly, soothingly. Loads seemed lifted from me, weariness magically removed, and all the world was lulled. How long he played we did not know; we were enthralled, entranced, only aware of floods of alluring rhythm, exquisite melody. Then, suddenly, he stopped playing, and jerked the canvas back into place. We did not speak. As the music ceased it seemed as if something sinister, throttling, had swooped down and was all about us. The Student led the way outside and we walked back to the place where we had slept. Sambro came to us and passed cigarettes. I looked at his drawn, bony features, his black, curly hair; he seemed years and years older than he was.

Men were gossiping as we went forward that night. An old hand just up from a Base job said that the war would be over next year. The German transport was giving out, and that was why we were pushing him back so far, and the Yanks were really fighting. They had long been a joke that left bad taste and were now seldom mentioned. For two-and-a-half years they had watched old England and France fighting the greatest war machine ever organized, and then had stepped in to lend a hand. A year later they had not done anything to help, and we forgot them; when remembered they were derided.

We stopped in a field where gas hung heavy and saw dead men along the way. At one point a wrecked limber was overturned and I saw a British warm pinned under a wheel. The driver was dead, lying near. He had had the jacket beside him as the day was warm. I took it and prized it for the air was damp and chilly. The Student asked me curiously if I did not think I might incur bad luck by taking a dead man's possessions, and I laughed at him, and went to a fat German who lay with his head back and almost under him. I rifled his pockets and found a few marks and some obscene postcards. "If there is such a thing as luck," I said, "I can't chance mine, for I've broken every rule the ordinary soldier respects. I'll take the third light off a match any time and I never knock on wood."

Then I told him how so often I seemed to stand mentally outside myself and wonder at my actions, and of the way Steve came to me. He was intensely interested and we became close friends. In the morning we filed along a high embankment in a driving rain. Dead men of the Fourth Division were strewed along the way, the majority members of the 72nd and 85th Battalions. The Hun shelled us continually and there were a few casualties. We huddled by a cutting for hours and then when it was dark went up a sunken road and past a village. Gas clung to the low places and some men put on their masks. We reached a grain field and were told to rest as comfortably as possible, that we were to attack as soon as it was light.

The grain was wet and the ground muddy. We scooped little hollows and curled in them and tried to sleep. I could not, but sat with the Student, and thought of all the vanished faces I had watched before other battles. He was in my section and I had seven others, Miller, a lanky lad who had been wounded at Vimy, Walton and Morris, Sambro and the old hand from the Base, and two new men of the last draft.

Our officer was a good man, an ex-sergeant from the 73rd, and I was glad he was with us. Davies was with him, the first time in a long period that I had seen him at a jumping-off position. Dawn brought a light mist and we remained in hiding. Not one of us knew the area ahead but were told that a railway embankment and Hun lumber yard were on lower ground.

At last the sun broke through in the east, a thin line as if made by a red pencil. The mist curled up, lifting like a gauzy drop curtain and revealed the slope as we rose and formed open formation. There were lumber piles near the railway, and a number of mounds or shelters. I saw the Germans scurry to different places, but what held my gaze was row upon row of long-barbed wire across our path.

I was at the head of my section. Machine guns opened on us as well as shell fire and I turned up the collar of the British warm and started at a jog. The officer and Davies rushed to the centre of the first wave, shouting something about the wire. Before we had gone ten yards they were both down, wounded. A section from thirteen platoon was even with us. There was the shrill screech of a shell and I saw, in the fraction of a second, the figure of a man in the air, lifted bodily by the explosion. There were cries and yells for help as we rushed on.

Someone behind me shouted. Machine gun bullets were snapping my ears, there seemed an awful din. I swung around and saw Miller on the ground, trying to rise. "Keep down," I yelled. "Don't make yourself a target. You'll be all right."

He had half-raised again even as I called, and I saw him go down a second time, struck by another bullet. Straight ahead I saw a party of Germans frantically setting up a machine gun tripod and I raced at them with all speed. I never knew when I reached the wire and went over it. I had seen a mound that would shelter us and I had watched the Hun with the gun. Four of us reached the mound, Sambro and Tommy and the Student and I, and we opened fire as we plunged to earth. There came a wild whoop from alongside us and I saw Waterbottle, a great wild man in kilts, drive over the wire and at the Huns. They scuttled like rabbits, leaving half their number on the ground, victims of our shooting. Waterbottle dropped beside us and we opened fire on the nearest group by the railway embankment. Behind us and to the right I saw more men behind a mound, with Smaillie in charge. A dozen others were still struggling among the barbs and wooden stakes. Over on the left was a third group, with McPhee and his Lewis gun in their midst. No others seemed to have survived. On the left flank we saw another company charge at the lumber

piles and saw a number of our men shot down like ninepins. Then all disappeared among the heaps in a wild flurry of fighting.

We routed the Hun post with our shooting but a party of them had
worked to our right and enfiladed us, wounding Walton and Morris and
the old hand from the Base. The two new men rose up in a bewildered way
and were both killed. Sambro looked to the left of the mound and found
there an entrance to an underground chamber and in a moment we were
in it. It was a flare store, and only a big shell could dislodge us. From our
shelter we waved to McPhee and he opened fire with his Lewis gun and
cleared our attackers, killing the most of them. Then Smaillie's crew came
to us and on the way found another pit that contained a number of big
shells. Just in front of it there had been a gun emplacement. All that afternoon we exchanged shots with Germans by the right of the embankment
and the Lewis gun kept answering Maxims. Darkness found us in the
same position, with considerable shelling in progress.

I went out and found young Rees and another man in position between
us and the other company. The lad had all kinds of pluck. As we came back
someone called to us in the dark. It was Russell. He had been recommended for his work at Jigsaw Wood and was acting as a runner, and had
lost his nerve completely. He had messages to carry and could not find his
way. I had other work to do, and did not make offer to help him. He had
always shouted his worth about the company and many far better lads had
never been recognized. Young Rees, however, went with him, guiding him
around, and at the worst places went with the messages alone. He was out
most of the night with him.

In the morning we got word that we were to attack again. The Hun had
retired across the track to a position on a sunken road, and his batteries
were shelling us. There had been many casualties. Tommy's face set and he
never spoke. "All right," I said to the corporal who came. "We'll go as soon
as we get the signal."

McPhee and his crew got ready with us. Away we went. The machine
gun fire opened promptly but only a new man and McPhee were hit.
His second man grabbed the gun and we swung on. Looking back I saw
that Smaillie and his crew had not joined us. Several big shells were
dropping very near their dugout and they hesitated. As I looked back I
saw a great spurt of black earth and debris, some sheets of iron in the
air. A shell had gone in the entrance of their refuge and had exploded

inside, blowing the roof sky high. There were only fragments of Smaillie and his crew.

We had not reached a bank that was to give us cover before our own batteries opened a barrage on the sunken road. It was very well-aimed and soon the Huns were running in all directions. We sniped a dozen of them from where we lay and then were motioned on by an officer of the R.C.R.'s. When we stopped again we were at the crest of a long slope. Beyond lay a village and we could see the outskirts of Cambrai. The brigade had had fearful casualties. A few R.C.R.'s were with us and said that the survivors of their company would not make one platoon, and that not an officer was left. I saw a place where a man had started digging before going to carry a message, and thought I would take it. Hardly had I stepped down and started digging than I had a touch on the shoulder. No one was near me. I leaped from the hole but there was no cover around and so I stood undecided. The R.C.R. next to me looked up and asked if I were leaving where I had started. I said "Yes," and he jumped down and seized the shovel.

Blump! He fell backward heavily as his legs caught on the edge of the cavity. A single bullet, probably a stray, had caught him just above the heart. As soon as we had dragged him back out of the way I stepped into the place where he had been digging and worked as fast as I could. Bullets whined around us but not another man was hit until we were dug in, when a shell splinter wounded the R.C.R. non-com.

That night we held our line, ready to meet an attack at any time, and heard that the Pats had lost almost all their officers and half their men. In the morning we could see the Germans working hard at emplacements between us and the village on our left. Our Lewis guns fired at them and an answering fire wounded both Hansen and Ab, who was now a sergeant and who had been in charge of the trench. The R.C.R. officer had been wounded in the night and we were without anyone of higher rank than a corporal on the right of our line. Then headquarters men came pushing up and we saw our colonel, a big, soldierly man, watching both flanks with field glasses. A battalion came swarming over the sunken road in the rear, two battalions, Second Division men, and swept across our trench and over to the right. The Hun was charged so swiftly, despite casualties, that he had not time to retreat and all the garrison we had watched surrendered. In a few moments they were busy digging a new trench for their conquerors. On the left First Division men went over and into the village. We saw them engaged in fierce hand-to-hand fighting and then stragglers began to fall back toward us. Our colonel left the trench, revolver in hand, and went forward to meet them. It was an inspiring thing to see him, disregarding all bullets that sang and crackled around, all the stray shells that crashed near.

He stopped the retreating men with harsh orders, halted them and reformed them, then he came our way and our remnant of "D" Company got out of the trench and we went over in an attack for the third time in three days. The village was carried again and the First Division men established their posts. Then we dug in in a link to the Second Division line and were shelled and sniped at all the afternoon. When it was dark we got out of our holes in which we had hidden and patrolled the gaps. A rumour came that at last we were to be relieved, but no one in authority carried the message. At last a runner came to me and said that an officer had been lost. He was another new man, and had been sent up to take command of our line.

We could not find him. A German patrol was driven back with the usual bombing and shooting – I was now too weary to note details – and then Waterbottle and Tommy and I made a systematic search. We failed to unearth our man. Back a distance from us was a tank that had been stranded there in the autumn of '17. We looked in it and found only a few bones, and now I suggested that we see if there were anyone *under* it. Waterbottle scouted the idea as he had called around it, but we went and explored and found a small hole just large enough to admit a man. We shouted down and no one answered, but Waterbottle used a match and saw boots. We held another covered light – and there was the officer and his batman, crouched in a three-foot space, white-faced, too scared to answer our calls.

Waterbottle was not a talkative character but he used unmistakable English for a few minutes and Tommy seconded every emotion. The batman was yanked forth by the heels and the officer crept after him. He was shaking badly and in spite of our trouble I was sorry for him. He had not the physique a soldier needed and he was new to the front; no one had told him anything definite and he had simply stumbled his way in over dead Germans and Canadians. I told him he had charge of the relief and we rounded our men, taking another hour to do so, then wended back over the long slopes we had fought over. It was daylight when we reached shelters near Bourlon Wood. Before I was asleep an officer sought me out, a man newly arrived, had said that on his way up he saw a wounded 85th man, my brother, who had asked him to tell me that he was headed for Blighty. He had severe wounds in his knee and light hurts in the arm and head. Then the lieutenant told me that he was proud to be with such men and asked if I knew that our battalion had lost seventeen officers in two days.

For a week we lay about and rested. Never had I been so worn and Tommy was wan and had no appetite. We lay in our shelters only emerging to get our tea and rations. A new sergeant, promoted from another platoon, tried to get us on a parade; the officer wanted a little drill and rifle inspections. We ignored them and were not disturbed by other orders. I walked over the fields by myself, thinking. So many old friends had been killed – how much longer could I go on? Jimmy had fallen at last; Nauffts at headquarters, and Sedgewick, had gone with him. Scarce an "old man" remained. In all "D" Company there was not a man who had not missed more time than I since the Somme. The battalion had been three days in the Vimy fighting while I was away with mumps. I got back to them as they went up after the attack and had not missed anything since. My leave had been given while the battalion rested at Bourecq.

Conscripts had reached the front and we heard that the First Division stragglers were such material and that the old men of the battalion had been heartbroken. A few came to us. We did not abuse them or use them differently than other new men. They were of average build and intelligence and should make soldiers. We moved to Queant finally and there we heard that Russell was to receive a second decoration for bravery. Tommy cursed for an hour and almost went to the captain in protest but I quieted him. Men like Earle and Barron and Murray and Lockerbie, and Tommy himself, had never received any consideration. It was a tragic farce sometimes, the awarding of medal ribbons.

We were shocked one morning to hear that General Lipsett had been killed. We had often seen him; he seemed nearer to us than other brass hats, was often in the trenches, and I had never heard a man speak against him. His funeral was most impressive, a special firing party from his old battalion, the celebrated Little Black Devils, attending. We saw the Prince of Wales for the first time, a clean-looking, boyish sort of fellow.

All through the Cambrai fighting the Student had held his place in the platoon. He was not a blood-thirsty fighter, but he kept pace with those next him and never flinched or took cover before they did. When he helped bandage a boy who was bleeding to death, and when he had to help drag dead Germans from a post we wanted to use, I saw him go white and tremble, but he never shirked in either case. He had grit that spells control.

The battalion joined in the general pursuit of the fleeing "goose steppers" and we marched through villages with inhabitants almost delirious. They shouted at us and the children ran alongside yelling "Bon Canadaw." Here and there we saw things that whitened the faces of the new men and made Tommy's jaws set grimmer. At one place an old peasant beckoned to us to watch him. He hurried to an outbuilding and worked with a long-handled rake until he pulled from under the floor the badly-hacked body of a German officer. The Frenchman stamped on the battered face with his boots until we spoke sharply to him and walked away. Again we saw a more pitiful sight, escaped prisoners, who had lain hidden for two days in a Wood. It was hard to recognize them as British soldiers. They were walking skeletons, with matted hair and beards, rags on their feet in lieu of boots, their tattered clothing crawling with vermin. Haggard, weak-voiced, piteous, it made one see red as he thought of those well-fed, well-housed, comfortable German prisoners seen about the farms in northern parts of England.

We saw refugees with great, sweat-dried Percherons drawing farm carts heaped with mattresses and furniture, with lean cows tethered to the rear, and old men following with barrows and push carts piled with other possessions, nearly everyone dressed in his or her Sunday best, usually black, and very tired, foot sore and pathetic. Some hissed their hatred in vitriolic language, some were dull and would not talk, poor creatures too beaten by life's ironies for even the joy of deliverance. At one place a pig was eating a dead horse by the roadside and was driven away with shrill cries as women attacked the carcass with knives and stripped every shred of meat for their own consumption. We gave most of our rations to children, and to mothers in whose eyes one read the story of the long paralysis of the Hun. One night as we were going past the outskirts of a village a Red Cross sergeant called me to a building, a door-less stable that had sheltered a few of the fugitives. Shells were dropping near, the village had been strafed all the afternoon, and all the rest had fled and left him with a woman who lay on blankets in one corner.

"Help me, corporal," he said. "I'm alone for the time but my men will soon be here with an ambulance. This woman has been deserted by everybody and is going to have a child."

He had only a lantern he had salvaged and a pair of sheets taken from a farmhouse. The house was a wreck as a shell had hit it but the stove was still in order and I made a fire in it to heat water. I worked there with the sergeant, a man with three years at a medical college, until the ambulance came and took away the mother and baby, both, the sergeant said, doing far better than he had expected.

The company was at the other end of the village when I reached them and I found Tommy and Sambra and Kennedy and the Student in a house with a fire going. "There's all kinds of stuff in the garden," said Sambro, "if only we don't have to do picket or anything we'll have a feed."

We filled a big black kettle with vegetables and water and set it on the stove. Overhead, beans were tied in bunches, drying. We shelled them and put them in the pot, then clamped on the cover. A bed was in the second room and after hanging blankets over the windows and barring the doors we all lay crossways the mattress and went to sleep. I was wakened by the Student. The room was filled with steam and smells. We lighted a candle and found that the beans had swelled and overflowed on the hot stove. We got the covers cleared by sweeping all to the floor and found that our dinner was soft enough to eat. A half-tin of margarine was dumped into the boiled peas and carrots and potatoes and all was jammed into a batter. We served it on mess-tin tops and plates and enjoyed the meal as much as a hotel dinner. Then came a report that set all the company swearing. A Dane who came with the MacLean men had been given the Victoria Cross for work at Parvillers!

We knew he was a "Blue-blood," that his letters bore a family crest, that he was wealthy, and in France solely on adventure, but we did not think he would have his aims so gratified. He was a good soldier, courageous and willing, but had not the experience nor half the ability of men like Waterbottle, Earle or Williams. The men of his own platoon seemed most surprised. Tommy grinned at everyone and said the war was keeping its reputation.

The next day we reached the fringe of the Raismes Forest and entered it in close pursuit of Huns we had twice sighted. It was cold and damp, a late October night, and the Student and I talked a long time in a brush shelter.

CHAPTER XI

Raismes Forest

The Student talked about an officer. "He's a decent chap," he said. "He's clean and intelligent, and probably has applied himself conscientiously to his business of killing the Hun, but I felt sorry for him when we were lined up out at billets and he was examining our iron rations and field dressings. Gregory, that tall, blonde, easy-moving fellow smiled at him when he came along. He was inches taller than the officer, so much more *man* beside him, and when the officer tried to make some pleasantry Gregory made such a swift rejoinder that he was nonplussed. He flushed and stammered and took refuge behind sharp orders. Every man in the platoon could see that Gregory should have been wearing the Sam Browne. I believe he could handle a company without effort."

The Student had made correct observation. Gregory was a graduate of Edinburgh University, and of good birth, yet he stayed in the ranks, easygoing, quizzical, observing, as if he really enjoyed seeing the futility of assumed rank. He had a splendid carriage, the confidence of the men, and would have made an ideal leader, yet I never heard him speak either scathingly or pityingly of those who ordered his existence and were, usually, much his inferior.

"What does it matter anyway?" said the Student, as we huddled together. "This whole ghastly business is futile in the extreme, and that's what makes it so illimitably cruel. It doesn't matter who wins, the underdogs will remain in their places, the top ones will be at the top, and after a few years there'll be more wars, just as senseless. Our leaders know it, all history is full of lessons on its futility, yet we go on."

"... and – we – go – on."

I remembered poor little Mickey gasping, with his last breath, his protest of such a rule. So I told the Student about him, of the white tunic that had meant purity, the red one as a token of the spilling of blood, and how Mickey cried out that he had never worn them, never wanted to, so why should he be drawn in the maw of the insatiable, monstrous machine of war.

Two figures came out of the dripping darkness and crouched beside us, Tommy, shivering, bitter-voiced, and Giger, who was again with the company.

"Not a drop of rum for us on a night like this," said Tommy, "and yesterday a bunch of transport drivers were so drunk they couldn't keep on the road. They have all they want all the time, and so much bread that they peddle it to the estaminets for beer."

He was in his usual mood and the Student seemed to sympathize with him. They talked of the cycles in history that seemed to chain mankind. Every period had its wars, now one nation, now another, getting its life blood drained without hope of betterment. Why did our statesmen, other statesmen, allow such things? Why was there war?

"If they'd only take them that made it, and wanted it, and give them bayonets and put them in trenches, in mud and rain, and say, 'There you are, have your fill. Kill the other chap, and we'll get rations to you day after to-morrow,' how much war would there be?" rasped Tommy. "It's not them that fight, the ones who start it, they're always safe and have plenty, it's the poor devils who never know what it's all about and can't see for flags waving or hear anything but drums and patriotic speeches. They join up, or the big boys in the safe places make laws and force them out in front of the guns and see them blown to shambles. I wish that every person responsible, on both sides, could be dragged by the heels around Passchendale and then shelled by high velocity guns till they died of sheer fright."

Giger got so excited that he could not stay quiet. He had filled out, grown stout, and was a walking testimony to the nutritive value of bully, bacon and army biscuits. "I'd like to smash the Kaiser," he grunted. "I'd like to stick him with my bayonet, and listen, I'm not going to take no prisoners. Every Fritz I get near is going to get his."

No one checked him and he grew more confident. "I got back to the platoon," he boasted. "Binks, him that went down sick, give me a charm.

He took it off a Heinie, it's a wrist ring of hair, and Binks said it was sure good luck. The Heinie was killed by a shell after Binks took it from him, but Binks put it on and went all through the scrap at Parvillers and at Jigsaw Wood and was never touched. We got the Germans runnin' now and I got this charm, so I come back to get a crack at some of them. I ain't never killed one yet and I'd hate to go back to Canada and have to say that."

There was a sincerity in his speech that made me shiver. It was Tommy who stopped his tongue. "Shut up," he ordered. "You're no better than the Heinies yourself. Who wants to kill people?"

Then he turned to us and raved about the unfairness of the way the army was handled. "They sent two more guys to the rest camp," he grated. "Both of them come to us last spring, after we'd been with the battalion more than a year. Yet we stayed in for everything and that pair goes to the seashore."

"But they're no good in the line, Tommy," I said, "and you know it."

"Which doesn't alter things one iota. It's the rotten injustice that gets me." Tommy was wound up. "They can send a certain number of men out on rest, so they pick out chaps that need officers over them all the time, and they keep the men who've been two years in this mess, never mind how much they need to relax. They know that when a bunch of us old fellows are in front it doesn't make any odds where the officers are. And look at the whole blasted game – about five men *back* of every one that's up front, five men who don't know what it is to face machine guns, getting the same pay as us and ten times the privileges, and all the glory. Hell …"

"It used to be," said the Student, "that the fighters did the fighting and the rest stayed on the land. Now it's the amateurs that fight, and the professional soldiers are in the rear at headquarters or Base jobs."

"I'd like a job tendin' them squareheads in the cages," said Giger. "I'd make them step. They wouldn't go round with their heads up if I was over them."

"Will you shut up," snapped Tommy. "You make me sick."

"Where's the padre?" asked the Student. "Before I came over I fancied that they were always with the soldiers, helping the wounded ones and having little services every chance they got."

"Don't," said Tommy, "start that argument. I was a member of the Methodist Church when I enlisted. Now I don't know or care about anything connected with it. Preachers and padres are not any better than brass hats. They're out of touch with the men, and they've lost their hold."

"Don't you believe in God?" asked the Student.

"I do" said Tommy gravely and reverently. "If I didn't I'd quit everything. But I'm going to have my own belief in my own way. It's all going to be between Him and me, and no preacher is going to have anything to do with it. They tell you it's wrong to hate another man, wrong to kill a man, and that's a commandment, and yet they get up in pulpits and out on church parades and tell you that we're fighting for the Lord and talk as if the Germans were devils, and that it's all right to kill them. Bah – padres, I'm sick of them. They say just what the brass hats want them to say, there's not a sincere man among them. If there was he'd be out between the lines trying to stop both sides from killing each other."

"He'd get killed himself," said Giger. "Them Heinies'd shoot anybody."

We pushed Giger outside and he went, muttering to himself, to shiver elsewhere.

"I don't believe," said Tommy, "that God is on either side of this war, but I believe that He's with the poor chaps like little Mickey – on both sides. If there's a hell the big bugs will surely get there."

I got tired of hearing his bitterness and gradually he quieted. At dawn we were stiff with cold and ate cold rations, then started down a road in the forest. It had once been a grand old Wood where French nobles had great bear hunts, but now it was a place where sudden death lurked among the bushes. We saw Germans about ten o'clock, two of them near the road. The captain had just come up to speak to us when they rose and fired down the clearing. He moved as rapidly as we did. For the next hour we tried our best stalking methods but did not glimpse our quarry.

All that day we went through the wet Wood and watched on every side. It was an experience we would not forget. Not a sound could be heard, save low voices when two men came together. We had a long extended line that kept well in advance of the main party, and we had to work forward as if every thicket held an enemy. The Germans were retreating and had plenty of time to shoot and get away, all the advantages being with them. Night found us at a wood-cutter's cabin and there we bivouacked, a few sentries remaining on duty some distance in front so as to prevent a surprise attack.

The Student and I slept together again and I told him about the 7th Battalion man's theory that we are greater than we realize and Spike's belief that we take our memories and affections with us when we go on. "I don't like to think that," said the Student. "If that's so we'll always have visions with us that we abhor. Do you want to keep your memory of this war?"

His question startled me. I had not thought of it before, and I could not answer. I told him of the German wriggling, sliding, on my bayonet at Passchendale, of the sniping I had done at Vimy, the three Germans I had killed with a bomb from behind; I didn't want to remember such things. Then I told him of the officer asking for a drink, and how I had got it for him, of Siddall wanting me to stay while he went "to sleep," of the German I had surprised in the old sap in front of Avion, and had let go; there were so many things I wanted to remember.

"I'll never know," I said. "This chaos has wrecked all my senses of value. Do you?"

"No," he said quickly, sharply. "I hate it all, it's so utterly insane."

He made me think of the Professor and I told him of the talks we had on our way to the Salient, and of Freddy's premonitions.

"If I thought," he said, "that it's true we can't escape a cyclometry form of existence I'd find some quiet brookside or nook among the hills and live there on berries and nuts and simply watch the clouds and sunrise and sunset. What's the use of building or learning new things if we are carried mercilessly into another era of destruction. Far better to just sit and watch the birds and squirrels."

The conversation was too melancholy for me, and so I switched to a lighter vein and told him there was humour even in the trenches. He looked at me despairingly, and I told him of little Joe, our Cockney runner, who had been shot through both legs at Passchendale and had lain two days beside a group of dead Germans. When we found him he pointed at the nearest corpse, a bloated figure, and whispered. "Turn 'im over, will yer mytes? 'E as an 'orrible fice."

The Student did not relax his glumness and I told him of the new officer that came to us at Lieven. He was taking two of his draft to a post in some ruined buildings on the outskirts of Lens, and got mixed in his turnings. No one was in sight. All the wreckage looked alike, and there were no trenches, yet he knew that the post must be nearby, perhaps in one of the ruins. So he led the way around one of them and called in at openings on each side to know if there were any of "D" Company there. As he got no response his voice grew bolder. After a complete circuit of the building, a rather long one, he got more mixed and made the same circle, calling as before. His heroes plodded behind him without comment, until he started the third round. Then the man in the rear complained.

"Shut up, Bill," said his mate. "This here's Joshua and we're on a seven-day tramp around Jericho."

The sun shone the next afternoon and our spirits grew lighter. I walked with Sambro in the morning, finding him always the same. In the afternoon the Student came with me again and as we prowled through the underbrush, or halted at some point to wait for the line to grow even, he told me that he had a girl in Canada whom he was going to marry as soon as he returned. "I'd never have enlisted if it wasn't for her," he said. "She never said anything outright but I knew she thought I ought to go – women will never understand what a futile mess this is."

"I think they do," I said. "Perhaps better than we."

"Well," he said, "I wouldn't mind if I knew for sure I'd get back all right, but if this war's going to last another winter I'll go crazy."

"You won't," I said. "You'll just carry on like the rest of us. One never knows how much he can stand until he has to. After you've been here a year you'll get so you just go on and on and on, as if you were on a great long slide and couldn't stop if you wanted to. We all get that way."

Ahead of us we saw a clearing and a small farm. A little cottage stood on a knoll with a shed close by. There was a fence about the place and a few apple trees near the house. We hurried toward them when I saw Steve step from the cottage door and hold up his hand. I stood, spell-bound, a moment, unable to move. It was clear and bright and I could see the very buttons on his tunic, the way his belt was loosely hooked. Never had I had such a clear picture of him and I was sure he would speak.

The Student walked by me right towards him. I watched to see if he would notice the soldier that wore trues instead of kilts, and then – too late – I realized the danger.

"Come back," I shouted, in such a voice that the Student turned, but even as he did it seemed as if Steve had simply changed into a tall German who aimed a rifle.

Crack! A sharp report and the Student fell without speaking, crumbling in a heap. I fired from the hip without raising my rifle but the sniper had ducked back into the cottage. Jones and Mills and Tommy and I ran back into the trees and started to surround the place so that he could not escape but he got through a window at the rear and ran for cover. It was useless. The range was not sixty yards and he went down under our first fire.

I hurried back to the Student. He was plucking feebly at one of his tunic pockets and I unfastened it for him. In it, protected by his paybook, was a photo of a lovely girl. I held it so he could look at it and saw his lips move in thanks. He gazed at the picture until his eyes dimmed, then smiled as though he thought the face so near his would understand, and the smile stayed when we left him.

Tommy looked at the dead German, and at the house. "What earthly use was it for that Heinie to pull such a stunt?" he demanded. "He hadn't any chance to get away afterwards and what good did it do him to kill poor Linder?"

"There's one more dead on each side," answered Jones, who was looking at the two still forms, "and that means we're so much nearer the end of the war."

I looked at him. Jones was a big, placid-appearing man, but there was a tinge of bitterness in his tone. "When there has been enough of us killed the folks at home will begin to protest and this whole business will collapse," he said as we moved on. "Then each side will blame the other and them that's left will go back and carry on."

A short distance ahead we saw a road that curved among the trees. On the left there was a pile of short logs that had been recently cut. Seated on them was a German soldier, a rather slight man, his grotesque steel helmet looking like a shell. We were treading on moss and old leaves, and the dampness had softened everything so that we made no sound. The German never heard us. Someone pushed by me, breathing with short, eager intakes. It was Giger. He was creeping up behind the unsuspecting Hun like a great, blood-thirsty tiger.

The fellow never saw him until he was at the end of the logs, and then he surrendered at once, shooting his arms into the air and whining "Kamerad."

Giger walked up to him softly, easily, watching, until he was around the heap, then he tensed and thrust with all his strength, driving his bayonet with all the brutal savagery of a killer. It was a ghastly, merciless thing, and I shuddered. Tommy stood, white-faced, and looked around for an officer. Giger grinned back at us. "How's that?" he called. "I …"

A second German shot up from some hiding place at the far end of the logs. He had not his bayonet but the woodman's axe that had been left there, and before Giger could jump from danger or withdraw his bayonet he was cut down by a fearful blow on the neck and shoulder. Then the German ran like a deer – and no one fired a shot at him.

There was nothing we could do for Giger. Everything had happened so quickly, so strangely, that we had simply been inert witnesses. His eyes sought his wrist, and I saw the hair ring on it, the "charm" Binks had given him. He died with startled incredulity in his gaze.

When we reached the end of the forest it was night, just dusk, and Tommy and I were in the lead. A new officer was with us, and was another good one, a very silent man, but without frills or foolishness. I had my binoculars with me and scanned the village at the top of a slope leading from the Wood edge. Only French people were in sight. I looked along the trees to the left and saw two Germans standing beside lone trees. At first glance I had thought them labourers, as they were talking and not watching the Forest.

Barron had returned to us and he was with the officer. A few yards out in the open was a brick building that might be used as a shelter. They moved out to inspect it. I called to them and pointed out the Germans, but after a look at them they shouted that they were Frenchmen, and went on toward the building. When almost to it the Germans saw them, and at once started running up the slope toward the village. They were quite a distance away and had a chance. Barron started shooting at them and at each shot the runners increased their pace. Tommy and I had our first good laugh in several weeks.

As darkness came we filed from the Wood and into the building. We placed two groups of men in hollows at the foot of the slope, having them as posts to prevent any possible surprise. Barron was a corporal and for the first half of the night visited them each hour. Then it was my turn and I strolled out and located both parties and talked with them. I had hardly reached the building when crack-crack-crack, machine gun bullets knocked tiles down on us and pattered on the bricks. Our Lewis gun outside loosed a pan and instantly there came a crackling of rifles. It sounded as though the Hun were in force and closing in on us. Our sentries came plunging in.

They had routed their first assailants, who had come along a road towards them, but they had been almost caught by fire from a second gun, and had been forced to retire. We waited a time, and were ready with bombs in case they came close, but nothing happened. Then two of us ventured outside with the officer and found the way clear into the Wood. We stole out as silent as Indians and reached cover in time to hear our visitors shooting more tiles off the rafters. Our Lewis gun rattled its defiance from the rear of a big stump and there was silence at once. The Hun did not fire another shot, evidently thinking that reinforcements had arrived. In daylight we advanced into the village but found that, as usual, the enemy had flown.

At night it was raining again, a cold drizzle. We had not sighted Huns in the afternoon and were quite near another village. Orders came that we were to line a hedge and dig in for the night. Sambro and Tommy and Kennedy and I were disgusted. Just ahead were houses that would provide shelter and beds. Why not go to them? We waited until all was quiet and then crept away and into the murk. We went to the third house, arriving from the rear, hoping we would not alarm the folks so as to let the sentries back at the hedge know who we were. I tried the door and it opened easily. A clock was ticking in the room but no one answered my soft call. We struck a match and saw that the place was empty, vacated, and in an inner room found a big bed. We hung blankets over the windows before striking a light and in a short time had stripped our boots and kilts and were under sheets, lying crossways the mattress which we had dragged to the floor.

We slept warm and comfortably but I woke with a start. Something seemed wrong, though the others were not stirring. I rose up in my bare feet and padded to the window to take down the blanket. Something held me back, made me peep out one corner, and for a moment I held my breath.

On the street, not ten feet from me, two Germans were standing, resting from carrying a dixie of soup or tea. One had his back to me, the other's face was towards me but he was looking up at an aeroplane, otherwise he must have noticed me at the window. I slipped back to the door but found that I could not lock it, tip-toed in again and wakened the boys. We dressed more quickly than we had ever dressed before and then took stock. We only had two bombs with us, we could not tell how many Germans there were, and whether or not our men had retired. For some time we stood by the door, listening. Several times we heard harsh guttural voices and heavy feet on the cobbles, and then a man came along close to the houses. He entered the next home to ours and we heard him tramping about in a way that told us the building was empty. When he came out he walked toward the very door at which we were standing. He had his hand on the latch and his foot on the step when someone called to him. I had my rifle barrel level with his heart and my finger on the trigger. Had the door moved inward a few inches he would had died very suddenly, but he hesitated, then answered grumpily and went back down the street.

We all drew a long breath. I was bathed in perspiration. For long minutes we stood there, looking at each other, listening, then the suspense grew too great. "I'm going out that back door," I said, "and make a run for it. I can't stick here like this."

The others agreed heartily. We opened the door and peered out, ready to shoot. Not a German was in sight. We ducked out and in between buildings, watching the next house. No one was in it. Tommy looked down the street. At the far end a squad of men in gray were hurrying away from the village. We turned and grinned at each other, then sobered. A party of our men had just come to the first house and were exploring cautiously. When they saw us they stared, open-mouthed.

"We nearly bagged a couple of Heinies," I said carelessly, "but the beggars got away."

The officer did not say anything. He watched us for a time and then seemed to forget the incident. Before night we heard rumours of a C.M.R. party being captured in bed as we had been, and also of a Trench Mortar limber driving into the German lines with a corporal and his gun on board.

We were in a village again at nightfall and Sambro and I were ordered to take position in a field as an outpost. It was drizzling again, and cold, and we were sure no Germans were near, so decided to take another chance – to the rear this time. We waited until nearly ten o'clock and then went back to a cottage somewhat apart from the others. A queer old crone was there. She was a shrivelled old woman with a huge blue birthmark on her left cheek that gave her a peculiarly witch-like appearance, and her half-wit son lolled on a chair in one corner.

The old woman gave us bowls of coffee that cheered us immensely and made us very sleepy. We told her we wanted to sleep there the rest of the night and she nodded assent and pointed to "beds," rolls of straw that were against the wall. They were simply rolled out flat and used as mattresses by the poor. We rolled out one each and lay down, leaving our rifles and equipment by the door. In a few moments we were sound asleep as the room was warm.

I was wakened by an old hag clearing her throat, and was very much awake as I glanced around. Other refugees had come in after we were asleep and had rolled out beds like ours. Seven old women were sleeping along the room and the eighth was on the other side of Sambro. She had scanty gray hair and the features of a vulture. A single dirty blanket constituted her bed and she was sitting up and scratching industriously, her claws making a noise similar to the use of sandpaper. Her principal garment was a soldier's shirt.

Fortunately I had lain down at the end of the room so as to be as far as possible from the stove. I got my boots on and then lay back, after nudging Sambro. He opened his eyes – and was facing the crone. There was a long moment of heavy silence and then I received a poke in the ribs.

"Bill," said Sambro huskily. "Let's drag out of here."

We did, strolling up and down a wet field path until it was light. Then we went back to the house and found our party broken up, all the old women had flown. We got more hot coffee and then the old blue-cheeked witch asked us to look in her cellar. We went down with her to humour her. It had been fitted with four good beds and furniture, but on the floor was the body of a German officer, with the head chopped from the shoulders.

It was a sickening sight and we hurried out. "I did it," cackled the old woman, "I and my son, with a big axe. He was drunk, the foul bull."

We passed through Valenciennes soon after it was ridded of the enemy and everywhere were hailed with joy. The new men thought they were having a wonderful time, that the war was a great adventure. On we went to Quivrechem, and there I heard a soldier tell that he had seen a German major killed in the street by infuriated women. He had been captured by the Fourth Division and was being escorted through the village where he had been a Commandant. It seemed that he had ruled harshly, being an arrogant, bull-headed type who elbowed old women from his path and kicked dogs and children. When he was seen a howl went up from the watching villagers and they closed in on him and his escort, screaming their hate. The soldiers, not knowing just what was wrong, slipped into the crowd. Instantly the German was seized. He went down in a melee of clubs, trying to strike, to fight, shouting in an agonized voice for his late enemies to rescue him, but they, understanding the situation, did not interfere, and the formless pulp that was dragged from the Square was hideous to see.

Thelien, and then we dragged wearily into Jemappes. It was Saturday night and we were footsore and very hungry. Sambro and Jones and I were together. All the afternoon we had heard shelling and it seemed as if we were nearing the fighting again. Rumours had come that an armistice would be signed, that the war was nearly over, and had caused rough comment; bitter, cynical speeches from the older men, eager speculation by the newly-joined. Jones was not impressed at all. "I've heard all that dope before," he said. "It's just another false hope. You can hear the guns, can't you? Does that say war's over? No, Heinie has gone back and will go further yet, to save his transport system, and then he'll dig in, likely has trenches all ready now, and we'll be there for the winter."

"If we're that near Germany," I said, "our airmen ought to reach Berlin with their bombs."

"They won't do it," said Sambro. "We never do things until we've lost all we can stand. We let him use gas first and never come back at him until he had his gas masks ready. Then he had to bomb women and children and get to London itself before the old brass hats would send our planes over at him. Now they're letting him starve his prisoners to death, boot them to death, anything, while they fatten ours and tend them like babies."

"Sure," said Tommy from the file behind. "It's the poor 'other ranks' that gets it in the neck over in Germany. The officers he takes prisoners are looked after all right, so it doesn't matter what they do to the other poor beggars."

Tommy was beginning to get on my nerves, or perhaps the war had tightened them and made me mind him more. And now as we went into Jemappes I hated the thought that we were going into the fighting again. If only I could go back to England and see that kind-faced old man who envied me "my day." He could have it and welcome; I loathed "my day." I'd have to get a change, a rest, somewhere, for I was weakening, and so was Tommy. Twice in Raismes Forest I had been close to Germans, young lads, frightened-looking fellows, and could easily have shot them, and instead just let them know I was there. And then I had caught Tommy doing the same thing, hot-headed, fire-eating old Tommy, watching a Hun waddle from sight and only firing a shot in the trees above him to give him speed. He had turned, then, and seen that I knew, and he had reddened and went on without explanation. I didn't know what he longed for, but I wanted to be back in the dusk listening to the crooning of that little waterfall, to hear the murmur of children's voices, with the knowledge that after a time I would go to sleep on clean linen in the clean, big-timbered bedroom in the "Black Boar." It would all be healing, wonderful, only I wouldn't want to see the people going into the little church to pray for "victory." It seemed sacrilege to me.

No rations had "come up" when we fell out in the street and scattered to find places in which to rest overnight, and so Sambro and Tommy and Jones and I wandered around until we found an old couple in a kitchen who could let us have some hot coffee and fried potatoes and bread. We sat there and ate like wolves and the old Belgian kept chattering in his tongue, trying to tell us what some Hun shells had done in his town. Sambro mentioned the "war over" rumours and Jones cut him off sharply. "We'd heard all that guff when Heinie pulled back off the Somme," he said. "The war isn't over and I won't believe it's over till we're on our way back home." It was only then that I understood Jones. His words were only to camouflage the fierce hope that had gripped him. He had been thirty-five months in France, and half that time up at the front. "I feel sometimes," he had told me, "as if I didn't know anything else but war, as if I had been born here. It's hard for me to remember anything at home."

I thought of his words as we sat at the Belgian table. Home seemed a thing remote, something we had once known. It was to me but a hazy picture, vague, indistinct, something like childhood, passed out of our reckoning; I could not grasp the fact that it still existed. Mills came in. He had seen our lighted windows and he brought his brother with him. The brother had been in France since '14, with a veterinary bunch, and had transferred to us. We shared our good luck with them, and they brought fresh rumours. A runner from brigade had told them that the war was almost over, that he had heard his officer say so.

Jones almost grew violent; he ordered them to stop such nonsense, and cursed all runners and their rumours. We finished our meal in an awkward silence and went outside. One of our headquarter's corporals came along the street. "Boy," he said, "have you heard the news?"

We looked at him sullenly. "The battalion's going to stay here to-morrow and rest up, and on Monday morning the armistice is going to be signed – and everything's finished."

He spoke so enthusiastically, so sincerely, that we were forced to believe him. The Mills brothers shook hands. Tommy and Sambro did the same. I looked at Jones, but he had turned on his heels and was walking away. We followed him and found a house where we could stay. We made our beds in an empty room, and slept on the floor.

Church bells roused me in the morning and I dressed hurriedly; all the others had gone out. It was a beautiful Sabbath. The sun had flooded a yard at the rear of our billet and there I discovered Jones seated on the door step with two little girls on his knees, trying to talk Flemish to them. Tommy and Sambro were lounged comfortably against a wall, smoking. Mills and his brother were out at the front of the house. "There's your breakfast on that window sill," said Tommy, pointing. "You think now that the war's over you can lie in in the mornings like a gentleman."

He was grinning, sour Tommy was grinning again. "Boy," he continued, "I'm thinking of buying this place and settling here. Then when the tourists come I'll tell them that this is just where I was when it finished and I'm waiting till they start up again." He sobered then. "I'll bet," he added, "that there will be another war inside of twenty years. There was the Civil War and the Spanish War, and the Japs and Russians, and the Boer War, and now this mess. There'll always be wars just as long as the sheep are ready to jump around when the big fellows give the word. You'd better go on shares with me, Jones, and stay here. We won't have to come overseas when she starts again. They'll have their submarines a lot better then and there'll be twice the chance of getting sunk."

"I wouldn't want to stay here," said Jones. "I'll go up in the Salient, in one of those wrecks up there, with sandbag walls and corrugated iron roof, rats running free, a manure heap in the front yard, a gas alarm by the door, and all I'll read will be the speeches of the Brass Hats in the *Daily Mail*, telling how they won the war."

"You darned old pessimist," said Sambro. "You make me ..."

"Bird!" It was the harsh voice of the sergeant who was temporarily in charge of our platoon, and there was something in his tone that made me get to my feet. "Get your section ready at once – battle order. Leave all your other stuff in your billets. We'll get it after."

Mills had come in the yard. The cigarette in his fingers dropped to the flagged walk and showered sparks. His face was set and white. "What's up?" I heard myself ask the question, and had not known I wanted to speak.

"Mons." The sergeant's voice was a snarl. "Get your men ready."

"But – wait, sergeant." Mills had thrust off his daze. "We're not going into a scrap, are we? The war's over to-morrow, I got it straight. There'll be no fighting now, will there? What are we to do?"

"You're going to do just what you're told to do," came the rough answer. The sergeant's face was pale and set. The harshness in his voice was unusual. "You don't know anything about the war being over. That's all from the horse lines. Go on, get ready."

Jones put the little girls off his knee, then coaxed one for a kiss, and she gave it to him shyly. "That's my luck," he smiled. "See you later, mademoiselle." The little girl laughed at him.

When the platoon formed up every man was irritable. They swore over trivial matters, they hitched and changed position, they looked at their watches. One or two were cursing, with frightful emphasis, the ones responsible for the new orders.

I said nothing but looked away on the left where I could see a few long-range crumps leaving black smoke trails. The war was going on the same; we had been fools to think anything different. We fell in and marched down the road and after a distance entered a field.

The Hun began to shell with shrapnel and gas. No one was hurt as nothing came very near and we crossed a deep ditch by using a stretcher as a bridge. An hour later we were in a brewery. A shell, or the soldiers, had started one vat leaking and there were many jests as some of the lad's sampled the beverage. But the shells that came near sounded very alarming within the building and several H.E.'s came very near the entrance. Jones filled his mess-tin with the beer and raised to his lips. "Here's to the day when we go home," he said as he drank.

Mills swore at him. The lad was tense and white and his brother kept close to him. We left the place and went on, the platoons separating, and finally the advance was by sections. We were near a road embankment advancing toward houses when we saw our officer and the sergeant with a few men of their section scramble over the road to the other side where more shelter could be obtained. We hurried forward to where they had crossed intending to do the same. Jones and the two Mills brothers were with me, and "Old Bill" and Johnson, who had returned to the battalion. Tommy and Sambro and Kennedy were over on our right, working in under cover of rough ground.

Just as we rose to go up the embankment a German machine gun opened fire, sweeping the road with a perfect hail of bullets making it impossible to cross, and at the same time shells began to fall in the stretch of open ground between us and the nearest houses. They were quite near and bits of earth fell about us and shrapnel whined and sang. A small out-building was just a few yards from us and we hurried to it but found the door fastened. A plank lay there and Jones and I picked it up and rammed the entrance. An old barrel on its side was by the door, and there was nothing else of importance in the shed. Jones sat on the barrel as I said we would wait for a lull in the firing of either machine gun or battery. The Mills brothers were at the rear of the building. Johnson was outside, just in front of me. "Old Bill" stood at my shoulder and I was framed in the doorway, looking back over the way we had come.

Wheeee-crash! A smashing explosion. A shell had dropped right in front of the shed and exploded in the air. Johnson was knocked over by the concussion. I was driven back against "Old Bill" so that we both fell. We scrambled up. The smoke and fumes were stifling. I looked at Jones. "That was too close," I said.

He never answered. He was still seated as he had had been, his chin in his hands, but blood was pouring from a hole in his temple; he had been instantly killed. There was a cry just behind me. I turned in time to see Mills tumbling into the arms of his brother. He was ghastly white. "I'm hit," he said and tried to hold out his arm. His wrist was almost severed and I also saw that he had a dreadful wound in his stomach. His brother, who had been transferred to be with him, lowered him to the floor but the boy was dead before we could do a thing.

The brother would not believe it. He sobbed and fumbled with field dressings and begged us to get a stretcher bearer. I was sure that Mills was dead but I could not stand the pleading, and I ran across the field to a stretcher bearer of another platoon. I told him what had happened and he refused to go back with me. "You'll get hit by some of them shells," he said, "and you can't do anything for a dead man."

I ran back again. When I started out from Jemappes I had had for the first time a sickening sense of fear. All the long endless months of fighting

I had been spared the feeling, so clinging to my thoughts of Steve and depending on his touch that I was never greatly worried. Now it was different. I felt that I had glimpsed safety and had been snatched back again; and I was now more determined than ever to carry on.

The brother was still trying to get the others to help him when I reached the shed. "Old Bill" had tried in vain to soothe him. I told him that the stretcher bearer could not come and that we would have to get on with the fighting as machine guns were firing fiercely. Then I thought of a test I had seen applied and took my steel mirror from my pocket. "If there's a breath on this he's still alive," I said. "If there isn't, he's dead. Watch."

I held it over Mill's nostrils and there was not a trace of breath. The brother got up, sobbed again, and followed us out and over the field. We had narrow escapes as the shells were falling fast and then we had reached the first houses. We entered the cellar of the nearest and found it filled with frightened Belgians. Men and women and children were crowded in the narrow space and near the door a young fellow sat with a girl on his knee. An old man caught my arm and pointed at them. "They're just married," he said. "Just married."

I tore away from him. Just married! I hated them. Jones, seated on that barrel, stiff in death, almost within sight of home, was all I could think of. We made a wild dash across the road. Snipers and machine guns shot too late. On the other side we found that we could work through gardens. Sambro and Kennedy were there and told me that the officer had been caught by the machine gun and had gone back wounded. A sergeant called us to keep low, that the Germans were hiding in the houses and that there was to be no further advance until dark.

For a time we stayed in a cellar and then I saw a man from thirteen platoon with rifle grenades in his belt. I waved to him to come and gave him my rifle in exchange for his. Then I went into the gardens and worked forward. A Belgian beckoned to me from a cellar door and whispered in his fright, saying that one of the machine gun posts that had been holding us up was just ahead and near a house, but he begged me not to peer from his doors or windows as the Germans would kill him afterwards.

I went on, and saw the bomber following at a distance. Sambro was out in the garden to the left as a sort of outpost, and Kennedy was with him. I squirmed under a gate and got to a corner of wall that protected me. Rising, bareheaded, I got a glimpse of two Germans in a yard near the street.

They had their machine gun there. I set the rifle as carefully as I had in the old crater line at Vimy, and fired. It was a perfect aim and I saw the boots of one German, as his legs were on the cobble, beating, drumming on the stones; then he quieted. I sent another grenade in the same direction, at an angle that allowed a higher burst, and then ran along the wall, keeping stooped, until I was near an open space. I hoped to be able to get a look into the street from there and see if I had cleared the way. Instead, I almost bumped into a German who had evidently been reconnoitering the gardens. He was watching the other way as he hurried and never saw me.

I stared at the windows and brick walls of the house beside me but saw no faces and worked forward on the path the German had used. Just ahead, by a post and tree, a machine gun was mounted, and the Hun who passed me was standing there with his back to me, talking to two gunners. In a moment I had my rifle adjusted and for the second time that afternoon made a beautiful aim. The grenade exploded just at the height of their heads and two of the Germans were killed. The third man staggered and then dodged from view; the machine gun was knocked to the road stones.

I had no more grenades and did not know how far I had come. Going back to a cellar I found it full of Belgians, all talking together and preparing for the night. It was getting dusk. The sergeant in charge of our platoon came and told me that we would have to get out and get moving. I simply looked at him, never telling him of what had happened or where I had been. When he had gone I went out and found Sambro and Kennedy, and the three of us located an officer in a bigger house that was nicely furnished. He made a slight flurry and pretense of getting ready for action, but was alone and too drunk to talk straight, so we slipped away and went on. Suddenly, as we were near a bridge, we saw a dark group of figures in kilts. Hurrying over we found the captain leading a party he had gathered; we were glad to join it.

We reached the big station of Mons and were greeted by a spray of bullets that hummed and sang down the wide way, the last salute of fleeing gunners, then shortly we were on our own, in sections, scouting up the streets and lanes. We were in Mons.

CHAPTER XII

And We Go On

Sambro and Kennedy and I kept together. We went down a side street where we saw Belgians peering from their doorways, and asked them where the Germans were. They pointed in different directions and shrugged their shoulders. A woman brought us hot coffee, and another brought wine. We heard shouting and saw a soldier who called that he had seen two Huns but they had escaped him. A dignified Belgian in a frock coat and top hat guided us to a building and into its cellar. It had been a German billet and many tumbled beds were there; the enemy, however, had flown out one of the windows.

We went on up the street. Women and children cried welcomes as we passed and a group of them corralled Sambro and Kennedy. I went on alone, then at last entered a home to accept more coffee, for I was utterly weary. I had seen "Old Bill" with the Mills brother, trying to console him, for the fellow was half-crazed by grief and swearing vengeance on the first "brass hats" he saw, blaming them for the order to fight again.

The old lady who gave me coffee suddenly jabbered something and pointed excitedly. I looked out the window. A German soldier was escaping out of a house further up the street. He was unarmed and was watching some officers who were coming toward him, probably meaning to surrender to them. He had to pass a big gate to get outside the yard and as he did a burly Belgian rose from where he had been waiting and struck with a sledge, crashing the German's head like an eggshell. No one rebuked him or went near the body.

When I left the house I went to the Square where many of our boys were resting. The new men were talking loudly and a photographer was there taking pictures. I left and went away back to the little building where Jones and Mills were lying. A sergeant was there, with others helping to get the bodies from the shed. "Know them?" he asked me.

"I was with them when they were killed," I answered curtly.

"Phew!" he said. "Close enough. Well, considering everything, we got off light. And now she's ended. They're going to give these boys a bang-up funeral and ..."

"What good'll that do?" I snarled. Something seethed within me.

The sergeant looked at me. "The best thing you can do," he said, "is to get some liquor and find a bed somewhere. The brass hats are coming into town as soon as it's safe and there'll be all kinds of ceremony and all that."

"I'd like to shoot every blasted one of them," I grated, and left him.

I walked on and on, thinking of Jones, his kissing the little girl, drinking that mocking toast ... had he known? Away on the outskirts an old man hailed me from a little cottage and I went in. He and his wife could not speak English and they were very deaf, but they wanted to do something for me. I told them I was very tired and they offered me a bed. I had a good wash and then promised I would go back to them if possible, after I had seen the orders of the day.

Down on the Square I met Tommy. It was the first time I had seen him since the previous morning. "Where have you been?" I blurted.

He looked at me oddly, and flushed. "I'll tell you the straight truth, Bill," he said. "I steered clear of you. Did you ever stop to think about all the fellows who've been killed alongside you? Every time it's the other chap who gets it. I've thought about it and this time I wasn't taking any chances."

We looked at each other a moment, then grinned in a confused way, and I went on. "They want to watch that Mills don't plug some of them gilded guys," he called after me. "He's in the humour to do it."

Everywhere there was wild celebration. The new men were drinking and laughing and shouting with the Belgians. Officers were posing in the public places. The older hands were conspicuous by their absence. Mostly they had found places to sleep and were sleeping, indifferent to everything. Other soldiers were crowding into the city, riotous, loquacious, wine-mettled fellows, and were shouting things about the Kaiser and the German navy. "Nothing ahead but home now, Jock," one shouted at me, and I wanted to hit him.

An inexplicable bitterness had seized me, gripped me. I hurried away from them, walked the streets until I found my way back to the little cottage. There I went into the room the old Belgians had given me, kicked off my boots and sat on the bed, thinking, thinking. I was needing sleep more than anything else, and yet I did not lie down. My mind was a turmoil of visions, vivid pictures. I was back again on the Ridge that first winter, with Mickey and Melville and MacMillan, shooting rifle grenades, seeing Burke sitting in the mud, trying to form fours in a rain of gas shells to please a small-brained major. I crawled again on my first patrols and felt the muddy ooze under my knees, wet grass and weeds against my face, saw red-eyed rats creeping away from nameless things among the slimy craters. The pictures would not fade nor remain definite. They swung to a long line of snaky trenches with chalk parapets, to old ruins, shell-battered villages, gaunt ribs of shattered roofs, the sunlight catching bits of glass that remained whole. What sensations! Thrills! Horrors! Chills! Dreads!

I saw undergrounds, dugouts, tunnels, stinking, rat-ridden places; an existence among mud and rusting wire; mud and rain, mud and sodden sandbags, mud and mire, always mud ... war! Brick dust and ashes and broken timbers, and twisted iron and gateways into houses that were not there; gaping cellars, bedding and toys and clocks and cradles in a chaos of destruction; a lone crucifix at a crossroads where all else was ruin. War! A plot of white crosses sandwiched among heaps of rubble, and a sign board saying "Dangerous Corner." War! Hollow, reverberating sounds, the steady, measured tramp of marching feet, the dazzling floating whiteness of a flare, twisted long-barbed black wire, gray sandbagged trench walls, a desolation that seemed increased, that seemed peopled with grisly spectres when the Very lights became fewer just before dawn. War – I hated it, despised it, loathed it – and yet felt I was a part of it.

I saw Mickey's white face close up to mine, felt him in my arms. "And we – go – on." What a hopeless, gasping surrender his had been! And Melville going steadily forward, set, composed, ready, Ira beside him; Sparky's sudden tremors, the questioning in his staring eyes; Eddie coming and saying "good bye"; Siddall in that old foul Somme trench, murmuring, "Stay close beside me, Bill – till I go – to sleep." I could see ...

"Kamerad!"

I sprang to my feet. A closet door I had not noticed was suddenly ajar. I jumped to it, flung it open. There, blinking in the lamp light, cringing, white-faced, stood a German!

He was a young fellow, and his eyes held the fright of a hurt animal. "Kamerad!" he said again, in a whisper.

Still I did not speak. All that day I had burned with rage and bitterness. Why did they stay and shoot till they had killed Jones? Why did they keep on fighting if they had decided to stop? The German, watching my face, huddled, gasped "Kamerad," and offered me his red and gray cloth cap. "Souvenir – Kamerad." I motioned him to put it on again.

All at once there were ribald shouts in the street, the sound of many feet on the cobbles, a rollicking song.

I'm out to catch a Hun, a Hun,
I'm out to get the son of a gun;
And when I do I'll bet he'll rue
The day he left the Rhineland.

The German, listening, whimpered with fear and stood watching me, dry-lipped, wide-eyed, terror-stricken.

"Kamerad?" he whimpered. I shook my head, motioned him to be still. No use to put him out on the street for that crazed bunch of celebrators. Even the Belgians would kill him. I made him sit down beside me on the bed and we waited. He lost some of his fright. I did not like the stale smell of his dirty gray uniform or admire the cut of his bulging trousers, but his face was clean and boyish and he might have looked well in a kilt.

Finally the town grew quiet, the long day of rejoicing had taken its toll. I got up and looked into the closet where the German had hidden; probably he had ducked in there during a mad flight and had not been heard by the old couple. The place was partly filled with old clothing. I searched among it and found a long blue coat and a limp cloth cap, and handed them to him.

The German's eyes lightened. He understood, and slipped the coat over his tunic. It fitted well and he put on the cloth cap. The change was effective. He appeared a young Belgian and would never draw a second glance. It was only a short distance to the open and beyond that the outposts would be relaxed, scattered, easy to avoid.

I opened the door of my room and saw that the old man and his wife had retired. Outside, the way seemed clear. The German stepped out hastily, then hesitated, turned and held out his hand. I gripped it with a warm pressure.

"Kamerad," he said with a soft accent.

"Good luck to you," I answered, and he was gone.

When I fell asleep it was to dream so wildly that I woke a dozen times, sweating, starting up, talking with Jones. In the morning the old lady came with hot coffee. I got up and went to the barracks where the sergeant-major met me. "You," he said, "are orderly sergeant. Get busy and round up the men. A lot of them are absent."

Many of the fellows had had too much liquor, but some of the officers were no better, and it was night before all was in order. We were in good quarters with plenty of room. The big soup boilers in the kitchen were still filled with the dinner the Germans had forsaken. Tommy came and said there were enough brass hats to load a box car coming to the funeral the next day, and that there had been grand speeches in the Square and grand posings of the beribboned staff heroes. Mills, he said, had regained control of himself.

The Belgians made a fine service for the dead, a room in the City Hall being decorated for them. The divisional padre conducted the funeral. I did not go near it, and I felt sure that Jones would understand my feelings. One striking feature I did witness. A group of the veterans of 1870 attended the service, old men in faded uniforms, with decorations on their breasts. And we go on – how such things made one remember!

The R.S.M. was very strict. As I watched a band of officers wend their way into the gayly-lighted city places for a night of hilarity he came and gave me gruff orders that all the "other ranks" were to be tucked in their beds by nine-thirty. I said nothing to him, but back in the barracks I helped the boys arrange a plank out one window to the top of the wall surrounding the big building. They could go out on it and down to the ground by means of a short ladder, and could come in by the same means. We hid both plank and ladder in the daytime. Each night I reported my company "all present and correct sir," and heard the other orderly sergeants telling of eight, ten, even more, "absent, sir." They would be crimed for having a good time, for daring to wish for pleasures that were arrayed for men no better than they who happened to be wearing a Sam Browne.

Each evening, when I had finished reporting, I went out myself. I had my room with the old couple and I slept there every night, in a clean, sweet bed, and each morning had hot coffee and fried eggs and chips.

Always the old lady got me out in time to reach the gate before reveille, and no sentry ever reported my going in.

Tommy was silent, brooding, sombre; he did not even quell the new-comers who shouted around his bunk at night. As for myself, I was no better. A seething unrest swelled and burned within me so that I could scarcely bend myself to discipline or give civil answers to those in authority. The Belgians wanted to talk to me, to point out houses where the Kaiser and Hindenburg and Ludendorff had lodged, to tell me of the time in '14 when the Boche had come, Von Kluck's army, and how our Dragoon Guards had routed the Uhlans. I listened at times, but mostly I could not. I tramped the streets, going all around the city and far out on the roads into the country. War – war – war. My head was filled with memories, with all the poignant scenes I had witnessed. I was soured, morose, cynical, and could not rest. Gradually Tommy and I found solace in each other's company. He seemed dreadfully changed. "Bill," he said, "While it lasted I didn't want to get mine. I sweat buckets when I was in it those last few weeks, but now I wish – oh how I wish – that I was under one of them white crosses. I don't want to go back and leave the boys."

He was sincere. All the oldtimers were talking morosely. They were sardonic, bitter, caustic, needed careful handling. And the brass hats rose to the occasion. Drill and shino stuff was pushed to the fore. We must jump to it, snap into it, be "smart" soldiers. Now was the time to show our stuff. I heard terrible suggestions, bloody ones, cruel ones, and was thankful that my leave came through – at last. Leave! It seemed an irony now. I tried to locate my pack, all our things that we had left in billet as we went to attack Mons. Only the pack remained. All my treasured war souvenirs were gone. Those camp followers, the transport men, and batmen, and cooks, had stolen everything. Tommy's was the same, emptied of everything. Probably there is to-day in some part of Canada a home decorated by a Luger, an Iron Cross, a German officer's cap and gloves, all taken by the gallant fighter who brushed mules in French stables and shivered when the bombing planes were over.

Leave! Bitterness welled within me and was increased by all the petty final delays of getting my warrant. I could not go to see the old man by the waterfall, I was not fit to meet him. Nottinghamshire looked changed and peaceful, but I could not rest. I left abruptly when I saw fat, contented German prisoners loafing about farm stables. On the boat from Boulogne there had been some of our lads who had escaped from the Hun lines, gaunt skeletons, with sores that made one's flesh creep, living dead men who would never again know the blessing of good health. Up in Glasgow the crowds were after Ramsay MacDonald, and machine guns and barbed wire barricades were about, so I went back to London. There I seemed to be always meeting officers and I tried to forget myself in the extremes of "Zigzag," "The Better 'Ole," "Seven Days Leave," "Going up," "Yes, Uncle," and kindred plays. When it was time to go back to France I thought I was glad.

On the boat an officer spoke to me. It was the lad we had found under the tank at Cambrai – already on leave. I had been once since the fall of '16!

He was eager to talk and asked questions that would have enraged Tommy, but I really liked the man. He was his natural self and had simply followed the flow of circumstances, as he always would. Then a gunner chap came and spoke to me, a clean-looking, wistful-eyed fellow.

"Do you know, Jock," he said, "that I'm going back with three hundred dollars in my pocket, simply because I couldn't spend it."

"Why not?" I asked.

"I don't drink," he said, "and I don't gamble, and my chum was killed at Cambrai. I'd like to see this country but I'm one of those queer ducks who won't travel alone."

A few hours later he and I were on our way to explore France. We went away down south, through sunny little towns and lovely sea shore places, where the war had not reached. We visited American encampments, and were treated royally, being fed real steak and onions and potatoes, dinners we never saw in our battalion. The Yanks we were with were fine fellows, and denounced their army bitterly, saying that the "dagoes" and "bo-hunks" were in the majority, and ruined it. When we left them we were convinced that the real American of British descent is as good a man as any on earth.

On and on, back to the war zone, on trains, lorries and barges, in barracks, hotels and theatres, with French and Welsh and New Zealanders. Back on the Somme for a last look on those terrible fields. It filled me with a chill I did not lose for days, for it was evening when we reached that desolate part where not even a blade of grass was growing. It was motionless, a stark sea of tragedy, where not even a bird sang or a hearth smoke broke the sky line.

Lille, Tournai, Namur, and Charleroi, and then we went to Ypres, out again over that awful, death-ridden ground where shaky duckboards still survived among obscene slimy places more horrible than words could paint. The fearful stench of death was there, hovering, clinging, and along the old used ways there were stiff legs sticking from the mire, and bloated bodies of mules not entirely sunken in the muck. Old stubs like jagged spikes still toothed the skyline. It was a cesspool of human desolation, shaking into abominable rottenness, a succession of stagnant, dis-coloured, water-logged shell holes, cankering the dead crust of a vast unhallowed graveyard. Standing there in the twilight one could *feel* the damp odours, and with them a mysterious eddying clamminess. Relax the will ever so little and one heard long-drawn, shuddering sighs, saw broken forms twisting in agony, visioned once more hell's hurricane over that most-tortured scene that man has trod.

I reached the battalion at Genval, fourteen days over my leave, and reported. The sergeant-major looked at the captain, then back at me, and gave me the orders for next day. I was to carry on as orderly sergeant. That reception broke my defiant bitterness, and I found billet in a lovely home that had been refused the officers. In that town we had our Christmas din-ner, my third in France, and then we moved back across the border.

All the fool drilling had been discarded and we just did enough to keep in good physical shape. There had been a rebellion at Mons that made the brass hats realize they were facing serious problems, and orders had changed overnight. I was asked to take a third stripe, and refused, then bitter again, I paraded and asked to be allowed to revert to the ranks.

The captain granted it, but I wondered just how he judged my peculiar attitude. He had always treated me fairly though I know my conduct was trying at times. I felt, however, that he did not know anything about myself or Tommy, that he had never been aware of our work on patrols or in the trenches, knew that he did not have opportunity. We did not mix freely with the men and I had little in common with sergeants, and so it was a shock when I was given the ribbon for the Military Medal. More surprising was the award:

Operations at Mons, 10/11th November, 1918.
For courage and devotion to duty.

This N.C.O. was in command of a section during the attack on Mons
on the night of November 10/11th. When the advance was held up by
two enemy machine gun posts he worked his way forward, and by
bringing heavy rifle grenade fire on the posts forced them to withdraw. He showed great gallantry and initiative throughout.

I had not seen the captain until I joined his party just before we crossed
over to the station, and yet there was proof that he had seen and known
what others did not, and it made me wonder just how many other things
there were of which he had not made mention.

Another leave was offered, the final battalion leave, and I was given a
chance to go again. I went to see the old man by the crooning water. It was
evening when I got there, and the little cottage was closed. I went to the
"Black Boar" and was welcomed with a sincerity that warmed me. The old
man? Did I not know? He had died in November, yes, the day before the
Armistice was signed.

It was a chilly night in February but I went to the place by the waterfall
where I had first met Phyllis, and stood there a long time, how long I do
not know, and all at once I saw her, and Steve with her, close together. They
were indistinct save for their faces, and it was as if they were lighted by a
glow. I was startled, voiceless, and their eyes held me. They were full of pity.

"Why?" I tried to shout my question, but choked – and they were gone.
And then the night was cold and very dark.

We were billeted at Bramshott Camp. I was more bitter than before, and
would not attend parades or stay with the company. Tommy and I roamed
around like strangers in a wild country. One day he took a little Testament
from his pocket.

"My mother gave me this when I left home," he said, "and told me to
read something in it every time I went into the fighting. I did, and after a
while I got to thinking that it was a charm that kept me safe, and I always
read in it before every trip outside the bags. Now it's all over and I read it
just the same, but it's got me thinking that there's nothing right. Back
home they'll be waiting with all that hero stuff, and we-won-the-war stuff,
and telling you that right was bound to win. I don't want to hear it. The
first Germans in the war were brutes, I think, but the last crowd were just

like we are, and their papers and preachers told them the same twaddle ours told us. Which one was right? Was either of them right? I've got so that I don't believe anything, and I'll have to go back and pretend I do because I could never make my mother understand that the Germans aren't horned devils, and that the British weren't haloed champions of Christianity. I wish I was with Mickey."

He was terribly in earnest. Tommy was utterly weary of everything, and I could understand him. There always had seemed to me a peace deeper than sunsets in that world of little white crosses, a peace that couldn't be taken away. When the gunner and I left the Salient we stood near Sanctuary Wood and I was impressed by the very atmosphere of that region. It seemed as if something tremendous, solemn, inviolable, was over all, an invisible and yet an invulnerable keeper. Even the wind seemed comforting those sleeping amid that stiff, stark horror, and chilling us outsiders. Down near one of the make-shift shelters to which the Belgian fugitives were returning I saw an old woman gathering wood for her fire. She stopped in her prowl and gazed over the gray sweep of the Salient – then hastily made the sign of the cross.

We went to one of the big entertainment huts and after the regular concert was over they prepared to hold some sort of religious service. Tommy promptly rose to leave and a padre tried to stop him.

"No," said Tommy, "I don't want to hear any more twaddle. I've had to go on church parades, but this isn't compulsory, and once I'm out of this rig no man will ever make me listen to your stuff."

The padre tried to argue. "We're going to teach a real gospel now," he said. "The war's over and we're going to, first of all, prove to the people what a horrible crime it is."

"Don't do that," cried Tommy. "You'll lose the few you've still got if you turn hypocrite. The war hasn't changed. If it's wrong now it was wrong in '14, and what did you shout then?"

The padre's eyes flooded full. He could not talk.

Next morning Tommy was feverish, then he was taken to the hospital. I inquired and found that he had flu. He grew worse and after enduring all kinds of snobbery from officials I finally reached his ward. They made me wear a sort of mask and sprayed some disinfectant about. Poor Tommy. I hated going in to him looking like some grotesque monster, but he had seen others. He did not talk at first, did not seem to understand who l was, then, all at once, he knew. His eyes lighted, almost sparkled. His fingers pulled at the sheets. He wanted to sit up.

"Bill," he said, and his voice was only a husky whisper. "I'm – going – to the Boys."

"Nonsense, Tommy," I said sharply. "Don't talk that way, old man. Buck up. You'll be all right in a few days."

And I laid my hand on his, stroked it, pressed it. Inwardly, I felt as if cold talons had squeezed my heart.

He sank back, his eyes still smiling into mine, happy, satisfied, and I knew he would not live. He did not want to. As long as I have memory I'll not forget Tommy's look as he watched me go from his ward. It was almost as if he pitied me, were sorry that I could not share his joy. I tore the mask from my head and flung it aside, and went from the hospital without hearing a word anyone said to me.

Next night Tommy joined "the Boys."

We got on the boat at Liverpool. My brother was there in hospital and he came to see me just as we embarked. While talking to him I missed my pick of a hammock. The "Adriatic" was a clean-looking vessel and I wandered slowly to the first deck. A white-painted cabin had no name on the door. I seized a chalk and wrote "Occupied," and went in. All the way over no one came to me or molested me.

There were a number of nurses and passengers on board and the ambitious Sam Browners got some of the men lined up and tried to make them do monkey tricks, but the older heads left us alone. Kennedy and Sambro and I talked hours on end. At other times we stood silent, moody, cynical, watching the water, indifferent to everything. Several of the lady passengers were loud in their talk and we heard them exclaiming as they saw the "real kilties: they're famous, you know, for their bayonet fighting." And they eyed us as if we were wolves, on chains, being exhibited.

One of the boys saw an officer among the admiring fair sex, showing them his trophies. He had a German Luger and helmet, and a Prussian sword. He had come to us a few weeks before the finish of the war and we could imagine the lurid stories he was telling.

Sambro and I looked at each other. We had no souvenirs of any kind. "What are you taking home?" I asked him. "That book I had said that the Crusaders took back to France the Damask rose, the mulberry tree, black rats and venereal diseases."

His face hardened, but he said nothing. Then he pointed to a fellow seated in the sunshine, a soldier who had lost a leg and who handled his crutches awkwardly.

"I'll let them take a leg off me or an arm, any old time," he said, "if they'll take the pictures of the war out of my mind."

All the next day I thought of what he said. I'd seen men twisting and writhing in their sleep after big battles, tortured by visions that held them on a rack, by screams and shouts and the sounds of fighting that still echoed in their ears, and I knew that years would not entirely remove such remembrances. Those images of war would be with us as long as memory remained, needing but a slight impetus to make many nights an ordeal of dread, haunting us like scuttling winged ghouls, obliterating the finer, saner susceptibilities. It would be harder for us than any others in the competition of life, for all our constructive thinking would be marred by overshadowing visions and phantoms. Some grisly trench corner would leap at us in uncertain moments and drag us back to bitter dreams of the futility of war, hideous nightmares leading from the stark savagery of Giger's killing to the strategy of gilded staffs that ended in the filling of more graves.

At night I stayed on deck for hours. It was clear and calm and the stars were wonderful. I watched them, studied them. Back in boyhood days they had been to me the greatest marvel of all creation, and it was my fantasy that they sprinkled the "roof" of our world. Many and many a night when relaxed on outpost duty I had turned on my back for the moment and rested my eyes on the great star-lit spaces overhead until I felt lifted away from all the foul and cruel existence that we knew. Stars in the sky, twinkling stars! What a sense of the infinite they endow! It came to me as I watched them that even the war, the greatest catastrophe this world knew, was but a momentary episode, that Time and Space were limitless. And we go on. Where?

From the hour I had walked out of Tommy's ward I had not let myself think of him, I could not, dared not. It had seemed to me a tragic thing that he had had to die after going unscathed through all he had endured, but now I wondered … And, more startling than any thought, there came to me the conviction that he had known, had sensed his end. During those last days we had been together he had grown kinder, more patient, different. He had omitted further talk of what he would face when he got home and had reminisced continually about Mickey and the Professor and the Student. And how his eyes had lighted as he told me …

On the evening of the last night out our emotions ruled us, turned us to a riot of horseplay. We scuffled and wrestled and dragged each other about and made mock speeches. Then, gradually, we quieted, each with his own thoughts. And when all was still I went on deck and stared over the dark waters ahead.

Darkness. The rush of the ship. I felt my way again into a stifling dugout, into an atmosphere rancid with stale sweat and breathing, earth mould, and the hot grease of candles … I saw faces, cheeks resting on tunics, mud-streaked, unshaven, dirty faces, some with teeth clenched in sudden hate, some livid with pulse-stopping fear … I saw men turning on their wire bunks, quivering as if on some red-hot grill … I heard them gasp and sob and cry out in agony, and mutter as they tossed again. Then, a machine gun's note, louder, higher, sharper, crack-crack-crack as it sweeps over you in a shell hole where you hug earth … the growl of guttural voices, heavy steps, in an unseen trench just the other side of the black mass of tangled, barbed barricade beside which you cower … the long-drawn whine of a shell … its heart-gripping explosion … the terrible oppressive silence that follows, then the first low wail of the man who is down with a gaping, blood-spurting wound …

I moved about, shook myself, sniffed the salt air, tried to rid myself of my dreams, and as I stood there came a sudden chill. I grew cold as if I had entered a clammy cavern. I could not understand but went and got my greatcoat. A dim figure passed me as I returned to the deck and a voice said, "We're getting nearer home. I can feel the change."

Ah – I knew. We had left the warm current and were into the icy waters – nearer home. We had left behind the comradeship of long hours on trench post and patrols, long days under blazing suns and cruel marches on cobbled roads – the brotherhood of the line; and we were entering a cold sea, facing the dark, the unknown we could not escape.

Dark figures came and stood beside me. I had not thought that anyone save myself would come on deck, and here they were, ten, a dozen, still more, all hunched in greatcoats, silent, staring. I looked at my watch. It was three o'clock in the morning. These men could not sleep; they were come to see the first lights of Halifax. I moved quietly among them, scanning each blurred face. It was as I thought. They were all "oldtimers," the men of the trenches. We went on and on and on, and no one spoke though we touched shoulders. I tried to think of a comparison. Ah – we were like prisoners. I had seen them standing like that, without speaking, staring, thinking.

Prisoners! We were prisoners, prisoners who could never escape. I had been trying to imagine how I would express my feelings when I got home, and now I knew I never could, none of us could. We could no more make ourselves articulate than could those who would not return; we were in a world apart, prisoners, in chains that would never loosen till death freed us.

And I knew that those at home would never understand. They would be impatient, wondering why we were so dumb, unable to put our experiences into words; and there would be many of the boys who would be surly, taciturn, moody, resenting good intentions, perhaps taking to hard liquor and aimless drifting. We, of the brotherhood, could understand the soldier, but never explain him. All of us would remain a separate, definite people, as if branded by a monstrous despotism.

But I warmed as I thought of all that the brotherhood had meant, the sharing of blankets and bread and hardships, the binding of each other's wounds, the talks we had had of intimate things, of the dogged simple faith that men had shown, flashes of their inner selves that strengthened one's own soul. Perhaps, when my bitterness had passed, when I had got back to normal self, to loved ones tried by hard years of waiting, I would find that despite that horror which I could never forget I had equalizing treasure in memories I could use, like Jacob's ladder, to get high enough to see that even war itself could never be the whole of life.

The watchers stirred. I tingled. My throat tightened. Waves of emotions seized me, held me. I grew hot and cold, had queer sensations. Every man had tensed, craned forward, yet no one spoke. It was the moment for which we had lived, which we had dreamed, visioned, pictured a thousand times. It held us now so enthralled, so full of feeling that we could not find utterance. A million thrills ran through me.

Far ahead, faint, but growing brighter, we had glimpsed the first lights of *Home.*

FINIS

How *And We Go On* Became *Ghosts Have Warm Hands*

DAVID WILLIAMS

Canada was celebrating her centennial year when, in February 1967, Will Bird offered a "new" book entitled *Ghosts Have Warm Hands* to the Toronto publisher Clarke, Irwin. His cover letter portrays an author intent on cashing in on the national exuberance as he recalls the popularity of recent books on the Great War, "plus the fact that the Government is now planning to take a number of veterans to Vimy Ridge and other war areas" to mark the fiftieth anniversary of the Canadian Corps' famous victory. The new book will, he says, give "an account of my army life from enlistment to finish, trying to avoid grim routine and to feature the unusual and human interest stories." He does not mention *And We Go On*, already out of print for three decades. Editorial correspondence preserved in the William Ready Archives at McMaster University points to his intent to mislead Clarke, Irwin about the character of his earlier memoir. Bird puts *And We Go On* near the bottom of a list of fifteen books he had published to date, classifies it as a "War Adventure," and situates it late in his career, as if to make fact-checking beside the point. A page of front-end material in *Ghosts*, "By the Same Author" lists *And We Go On* as the twelfth of thirteen titles under the heading, "Fiction." Even more revealing is Bird's response to a clause in the contract stipulating that there should be "no prior publication ... of any part" of the work. While *And We Go On* makes up 60% of the text of *Ghosts*, he never mentioned this fact to his editor, admitting only to a private printing of one thousand copies of his war diaries in 1927, for which he retained copyright and on which he was now "elaborating." Ruth DonCarlos, the trade editor at Clarke, Irwin, took him at his word. So did every reviewer of *Ghosts*.

Most of these reviewers, however, knew all about Bird's diaries. Philip Child, a University of Toronto English professor who read the manuscript for Clarke, Irwin, noted that Bird had "made good use of these [diaries] fifty years afterward to refresh the memory, so that in reading the book, I had the feeling that the days and incidents were unfolding before me – not in 1967, but in 1916 and 1917." Yet Child, whose novel *God's Sparrows* (1937) ranks among the best Canadian fiction of the Great War, seems oddly unaware of his friend Bird's 1930 memoir. Roy MacSkimming, the in-house reader of the manuscript, who informed me, "I just wanted to per-suade Clarke, Irwin to publish it and thus let me get my hands on it" as its editor, also foregrounded the diaries in his report to the board: "Bird has built his story out of diaries he kept from the time of his enlistment in 1916 until after the Armistice. As a result he is able to describe his daily experience of war in fascinating detail. On finishing his ms. you feel as though you've been through the war yourself." The CBC program *Maritime Magazine* (25 June 1968) likewise noted that the "book is built on the foundation of diaries he kept at the time, and this solidly factual basis gives it much of its strength." The novelist Kildare Dobbes wrote in the Toronto *Daily Star* (10 Sept 1968) that it was the diaries that allowed Bird to create such a remarkable "portrait of men at war," though Dobbes sounded surprised that Bird had just now completed "his memoirs, believe it or not, of World War One." And Hugh Laming, the *Globe and Mail* reviewer (3 Aug 1968), wondered why Bird was dredging up bitter memories so long after the fact, arguing that it was "hard to understand a man whose mind remains fixed on the hates and grudges he felt 50 years ago, seeing only the mud, blood and cowardice of an admittedly grim war." The question, then, is not why reviewers knew about the diaries but not *And We Go On*, but why Bird tried to blot the earlier work from the record.

A partial answer appears in an early review of *And We Go On*, published in July 1931 in *Saturday Night*. In contrast to glowing notices of Bird's work in the daily press of 1930, A. (Arthur) Raymond Mullens wrote about *And We Go On* – which he mis-titled *And So We Go On* – in slighting terms, mislabelling it a "war novel" (as Bird himself would claim, falsely, in correspondence with Clarke, Irwin), and comparing it unfavourably to Robert Graves' *Goodbye to All That*. The British-born reviewer (and old Brightonian) praised Graves for having treated "even the most tragic events cynically not to say humorously," while mocking Bird as "a mystic" who had "seen and heard things that are not likely to be encountered again until the Day of Judgment." Mullens, who had waited until 6 August 1918 to enlist, in Montreal, made no mention of his own war record. Nor did he hint at his creative rivalry with Bird: in May 1930, Mullens had published a military-sounding story, a social satire called "Generalissimo" in *Maclean's*. It followed two stories by Bird in the April issues, including one entitled "Old Soldier." Dismissing the style of *And We Go On* as "sometimes stilted, sometimes astonishingly naïve," Mullens nonetheless admits that the Maritimer has "written a book which I am sure will delight the average returned man beyond measure." His grudging prediction of the old soldier's popularity was confirmed later that year when *Maclean's* took the unprecedented step of sending Bird on that extended European tour to write *Thirteen Years After*.

The "Judgment Day" review appears to have continued to rankle deeply when, thirty-five years later, Bird set out to revise his lost masterpiece in ways that, despite its new title, would spare him the embarrassment of being called a "mystic." He stripped it of its ghostly appearances by a factor of seven or eight, leaving a reference to them in the title in order to keep faith with his dead brother, and replaced this material with stories of the foibles of authority and the ignorance of the public. Ironically, in view of Mullens' 1931 review, MacSkimming's report on *Ghosts* described it as "autobiography written in the stark, unadorned, anecdotal style of Robert Graves' First War classic, *Goodbye To All That*," while recalling the "strong revival of interest lately in World War I" and its link with "the 50th anniversary of Vimy Ridge" that had been "covered intensively on television." Like Child, who claimed he had never "read a fuller account of the daily life of the frontliners, whether in trench life, on raids, in battle, or 'on rest,'" Bird's future editor favoured the worm's-eye view of the infantryman over Graves' lofty view of a privileged British officer. Clarke, Irwin seized on these literary and social comparisons, claiming in their "Publication Data," under the rubric "Competition," that "other books describe the war from the relatively comfortable point of view of an officer – even Robert Graves, who wrote the classic *Goodbye to All That* was a lieutenant." The reviewer for the Toronto *Telegram* (27 July 1968), however, made an unfavourable comparison to Graves, noting that Bird, was a young man with the solid, Victorian attitudes of a certain kind of Maritimer of the period. He neither smoked, drank nor swore. Eggs and chips, not champagne, sustained him in the estaminets. As his book relates, he, like Sassoon and Graves and Sitwell, saw lives prodigally wasted, met stupid or cowardly officers and existed, month after stinking month, among the mud-holes, the swollen unburied corpses, the gas attacks, the shellfire and machine gun scything of the Western Front, 1917–18. Yet – and this is what makes the book so extraordinary – Mr. Bird never ceased to see all this through the eyes of a Henty hero, a Robert Service character, a "fine clear-eyed upstanding Canadian lad," to borrow his own sort of language.

Bird must have felt that he was back where he had begun, still pigeonholed as a poor-man's Robert Graves, still the artless "naïf." At least, since he had cut Steve's apparitions in the text to two, no one was likely to call him a "mystic"! No matter if his title still flaunted its "ghosts," the story was now far more ironical than mystical.

Other reviewers sounded more like MacSkimming in his letter to the author (17 Jan 1968), where he introduced himself as Bird's editor and assured him that "the contrast of humour and horror in your account is superbly achieved." In this, they likely took their cue from the jacket copy:

In spite of its tragic subject, *Ghosts Have Warm Hands* contains much fine humour and much evidence of warm friendships made under fire. Throughout the war Mr. Bird never allowed despair to destroy either his sense of compassion or his sense of humour. For the men in the line, he writes, laugher was better than medicine – it kept them human.

Nonetheless, Kildare Dobbes found this humour posed a difficulty, in that Bird "retains a typical Maritimer's sense of humor," meaning that, "The sophisticated reader may smile" at such adolescent pranks as sprinkling cheese on a sleeping soldier who fears rats more than bombs; at the end of the day, such pranks are still low comedy. For the *Telegram*'s reviewer, worse than the lack of refinement were "the attitudes, the prejudices, the code of behaviour and the literary style of a certain type of man (a type which is uniquely Canadian)" – which is to say Anglo-Canadian, anti-Catholic, anti-French, and anti-foreigner. Bird, in other words, was no Shakespeare in his blending of comedy and tragedy. While he might have had a greater affinity with Sophocles or Euripides, some reviewers saw the admixture of comedy to a classical vision of tragedy as a serious flaw.

Given the ultimate mysteries of fate and death that inform *And We Go On*, the revised version of 1968 can seem as if Bird were painting over the portrait of the Mona Lisa with the face of Phyllis Diller. Almost, but not quite, for Bird doesn't just mock the class-consciousness of Georgian Britain or Victorian Canada but also appeals to growing anti-war senti-ment and a broader culture of American individualism. Both form a visi-ble subtext in *Ghosts* and in his correspondence with editors. For example, Bird did not reply to Clarke, Irwin for eight weeks after their offer of a contract because he was waiting on an offer from a New York publisher. Ruth DonCarlos wrote to him on 24 October 1967, "It was very good news to learn from you over the telephone today that Doubleday are returning the manuscript of GHOSTS HAVE WARM HANDS to you and that you will then return it to us after making the minor changes we recommended in my letter of September 1st." In a subsequent letter on 6 November, she added, "I can't tell you how pleased we are to have the manuscript back in our hands once more. We felt that it was our discovery and would have been very disappointed to have it snatched from under our noses by a postal misadventure. Thank you for recalling it." A mere ten days before the Tet Offensive began on 30 January 1968, convincing Americans that the war in Vietnam would not be a walkover and rousing vehement anti-war sentiments on both sides of the border, Bird claimed in a letter to MacSkimming, "Doubleday wrote me it would go well across the border. They were very disappointed not to get the manuscript." Two days later, MacSkimming replied, "I'm afraid Doubleday in the States won't be tak-ing GHOSTS; I don't know whether it was their Canadian or American branch that advised you it would go well there, but their New York office regrets they can't use it at the moment." Bird had gravely misjudged his potential audience; his decision to change the "we" narrative of *And We Go On* into the "I"-story of *Ghosts*, with himself cast as an anti-war, anti-establishment hero, was evidently a failed gambit.

In her letter of acceptance, DonCarlos had proposed that Bird write a prologue informing the reader "of the campaigns you were in and some-

thing of your personal background before enlisting. We feel that a prologue such as this would set the stage nicely for your story, which begins
somewhat abruptly." Bird agreed and added an epilogue as well, further
marking his change of direction to a more cynical and satirical account.
Most of the officers of *Ghosts* turn out to be the familiar asses of 1960s
Great War historiography, the literary descendants of Alan Clark's *The
Donkeys* (1961), which had helped to popularize the myth of British fighters as "lions led by donkeys."[1] This myth, which completely ignores the
stunning success of British military planners in the Last Hundred Days,
due in part (but only in part) to the tactical genius of Canadian Corps
commander Sir Arthur Currie, has come under attack in the last quarter
century from a new generation of British historians led by Brian Bond
and others (Williams, "Film," 165–6).

Of course, the myth was already implicit in the title *Generals Die in Bed*
(1930), which has latterly obscured the fact that more British generals died
at the Battle of Loos (1915) than in the whole of the Second World War.
Predictably, the controversy over Harrison's book was most fierce in
Canada, leading Bird's quondam commander in the 7th Brigade and
future friend Lt-General Archibald Macdonell to rage, "I hope to live long
enough to have the opportunity of (in good trench language) shoving my
fist into that s – of a b – Harrison's tummy until his guts hang out his
mouth!!!" (qtd. in Vance, *Death* 194). Arthur Currie, who was not likely to
allow an American enlistee to dishonour the memory of his comrades
Major-General Malcolm Mercer, killed in action at Mt. Sorrel in June 1916,
or Major-General Louis Lipsett, killed on front-line reconnaissance in
September 1918, wrote back to Macdonell, "I have never read, nor do I
hope ever to read, a meaner, nastier and more foul book" (ibid.).

Indeed, the myth of staff incompetence would be contested in Canada
until it entered the popular imagination in the 1960s, largely through Joan
Littlewood's stage musical *Oh, What a Lovely War!* (1963). Roy MacSkim-

---

1 Although Capt. P.A. Thompson had used the phrase after the war to criti-
cize the general staff, his sub-title is more critical of the German High Command. See *Lions led by donkeys showing how victory in the great war was
achieved by those who made the fewest mistakes* (London: T.W. Laurie, 1927).
Who, then, were the "donkeys"?

ming, Bird's editor, was quick to recognize this feature of Bird's memoir as a strong selling point: "His first experience of stupid, bullying officers at training camp in Nova Scotia put him squarely on the side of the enlisted man." Catalogue copy did much the same thing: "In 1916 at Aldershott Camp in Nova Scotia, Will Bird was selected as officer material. But the arrogant bungling of some of his officers made him determined to resist all offers of promotion." In "Publication Data," this became the ultimate marketing strategy: "The last chapters bitterly describe how the victorious soldiers were treated by their officers after the Armistice. In fact instances of official bungling and mistreatment of the men run throughout the story." Even the reviewer for *The Canadian Military Journal*, Lt-Cdr. D.H. Mackay, had to admit, "No officer, sergeant-major or sergeant is spared who lets the men down or bullies them," although he added, of necessity, "nor is loyalty, or support or praise ever omitted from those who led, supported and looked after their men. Needless to say failures were often due to being political appointments, a dastardly thing to do when the lives of others depend on their leadership."

Other reviewers hailed the presence of this myth of "lions led by donkeys" in *Ghosts*. Writing in the Toronto *Daily Star*, Kildare Dobbes had no doubt that Bird's readers would be "familiar with the scenes he describes," including "the brutally stupid generals who refused to go near the battlefield for fear of losing their nerve." While Dobbes judged Bird to be "an artless writer," he added: "[T]his is why his story rings true. It is the account of what one man did and suffered in some of the bloodiest and most senseless fighting in history." What "one man did and suffered" was on this view to bear witness to the criminal stupidity of the "donkeys." Tellingly, every illustration for Dobbes' thesis is drawn from material that he had no idea had been added to *Ghosts*. For example, Bird's "donkey" in the new prologue is the despotic Major Fordley who failed to follow his own written orders, proving that "there was no justice whatever in the army." The actions of this ass made Bird all the more "determined to buck every Simms and Fordley I met, to outwit all their type if possible." In the new epilogue, he continues, in scenes set after the war, to rail against the major as the avatar of staff incompetence: "How different things might have been, had there been no Simms or Fordley at the beginning, I will never know." The only redeeming feature of the war as he now sees it is the camaraderie of old veterans at the Legions where Bird was invited to speak after the popular success of *And We Go On* and *Thirteen Years After*.

The final anecdote in the epilogue to *Ghosts* is an adaptation of the one used to end *Thirteen Years After*. Telling of an isolated group of soldiers in Belgium at the end of the war, Bird adds the new detail of "a dapper British officer" who "adjusted his monocle and read a copy of the all-important cease-fire message" to his men "in grave and impressive tone [sic]. After he had finished there was a heavy silence, then an old Cockney stepped forward and saluted. 'Beg pardon, sir,' he said, 'but 'oo's won?'" Kildare Dobbes was surely right; *Ghosts* was on the whole completely in tune with the 1960s mantra that no one ever wins a war, that no war is a good war, and that Bird's war had led to nothing but more war. Call it a Damascene conversion, if you will, but it seems to be "an irrevocable insult," as the younger Bird had predicted, "to those gallant men who lie in French or Belgian graves." *Ghosts,* it turns out, is less about the Great War and the sentiments it had generated than about anti-war sentiments of the 1960s.

Though Dobbes concluded that *Ghosts* "is an honest and always interesting document, a genuine voice from the ranks of death," he added that it was "[c]arelessly written," and "can hardly be judged a 'good book.'" Nor was Dobbes out of line to say that, "One has no impulse to compare it with, say, Robert Graves' *Goodbye to All That* or Siegfried Sassoon's *Memoirs of an Infantry Officer*. Such books are records of an intellectual response to war." His only mistake – for which he could not be held responsible – was to assume that the narrative persona of "a simple and unreflecting farm boy" in *Ghosts* was the one that also appears in *And We Go On*, a book which actually does invite comparison with the work of Graves and Sassoon as "an intellectual response to war." If she had been writing about *And We Go On* rather than *Ghosts*, I would fully endorse Margaret MacIntyre's judgement in *The Bluenose Magazine* of Fall 1977 that, "For me, it beats that all-time classic 'All Quiet on the Western Front.'"

In her doctoral thesis, Monique Dumontet shows that the most damaging loss in *Ghosts* is the removal of the broad spectrum of voices heard throughout *And We Go On*, from that of Tommy (who largely disappears in the later version), to the Professor and the Student (who are entirely excised from *Ghosts*), to others who debate the war's justice, the ethics of killing, the fate of the human soul, and even the value of beauty.[2] The absence of a Socratic symposium in *Ghosts* greatly lessens the weight of the narrative and makes it a far less important work. And the lack of dialogue and the preponderance of monologue in *Ghosts* lend weight to Hugh Laming's question, "Did he never speak of poetry and music or was he deafened by the roar of guns?" As the reader has seen, Bird speaks often and eloquently of such things in the original version of his memoir. Perhaps the best assessment will be made by readers who compare *Ghosts* with *Go On* and then judge for themselves.

ACKNOWLEDGMENT

The author is grateful to the University of Manitoba for travel funding to examine the Clarke, Irwin fonds in the William Ready Archives at McMaster University in Hamilton.

2 Those wanting further guidance may wish to explore the textual comparisons on offer in Dr. Dumontet's "Appendix" to her dissertation, "'Lest We Forget': Canadian Combatant Narratives of The Great War," which can be found online at http://hdl.handle.net/1993/4246

Works Cited

Barker, Pat. *The Eye in the Door.* 1993. New York: Dutton, 1994.

— *Regeneration.* 1991. New York: Plume, 1993.

Bird, Will R. *The Communication Trench.* Amherst, NS: self-published, 1933.

— *Ghosts Have Warm Hands.* Toronto & Vancouver: Clarke, Irwin Co., 1968.

— *Private Timothy Fergus Clancy.* 1930. Nepean, ON: CEF Books, 2008.

— *Thirteen Years After: The Story of the Old Front Revisited.* Toronto: Maclean's Publishing Co., 1932.

Bond, Brian. *The Unquiet Western Front: Britain's Role in Literature and History.* Cambridge: Cambridge University Press, 2002.

Child, Philip. *God's Sparrows.* 1937. Toronto: New Canadian Library, 1978.

Clark, Alan. *The Donkeys.* London: Hutchison, 1961.

Conan Doyle, Sir Arthur. *The History of Spiritualism.* 1926. New York: Arno Press, 1975.

Davies, Robertson. *Fifth Business.* 1970. New York: Penguin, 1977.

Eksteins, Modris. "*All Quiet on the Western Front* and the Fate of a War." *Journal of Contemporary History* 15.2 (1980): 345–66.

Findley, Timothy. *The Wars.* 1977. Toronto: Penguin Canada, 1996.

Fussell, Paul. *The Great War and Modern Memory.* New York & London: Oxford University Press, 1975.

Graves, Robert. *Goodbye to All That.* 1929. 2nd ed. London: Penguin, 1960.

Harrison, Charles Yale. *Generals Die in Bed.* 1930. Toronto: Annick Press, 2007.

Jünger, Ernst. *In Stahlgewittern.* 1920. *The Storm of Steel.* Trans. Michael Hofmann. London: Penguin, 2004.

Khayyám, Omar. *The Rubaiyat.* Trans. Owen Fitzgerald. Edition unknown. First published 1859.

Noyes, Alfred. *The Loom of Years.* London: Grant Richards, 1902.

Owen, Harold. *Journey from Obscurity, Wilfred Owen, 1893 – 1918. Memoirs of the Owen Family.* London & New York: Oxford University Press, 1963–65.

Owen, Wilfred. *The Poems of Wilfred Owen.* Ed. Edmund Blunden. London: Chatto & Windus, 1931.

Remarque, Erich Maria. *Im Westen nichts Neues.* 1928. *All Quiet on the Western Front.* 1929. Trans. A. W. Wheen. New York: Ballantine Books, 1982.

Sassoon, Siegfried. *Diaries 1915–1918.* Ed. Rupert Hart-Davis. London: Faber & Faber: 1983.

– *Memoirs of an Infantry Officer.* London: Faber & Faber, 1930.

– *Sherston's Progress.* London: Faber & Faber, 1936.

Scott, F.R. *The Great War as I Saw It.* 1922. 2nd ed. Vancouver: Clark & Stuart Ltd., 1934.

Vance, Jonathan. *Death So Noble: Memory, Meaning, and the First World War.* Vancouver: UBC Press, 1997.

– "The Soldier as Novelist: Literature, History, and the Great War." *Canadian Literature* 179 (Winter 2003): 22–37.

Williams, David. "Film and the Mechanization of Time in the Myth of the Great War Canon." *English Studies in Canada* 41.2–3 (June/September 2015): 165–90.

– "Spectres of Time: Seeing Ghosts in Will Bird's Memoirs and Abel Gance's *J'accuse*." *Canadian Literature* 219 (Winter 2013): 113–30.

Winter, Jay. *Sites of Memory, Sites of Mourning: The Great War in European Cultural History.* Cambridge: Cambridge University Press, 1995.